THE CUOMO

A NEW AMERICAN FORMULA FOR A STRONG ECONOMY

Foreword by
James D. Robinson III

LEWIS B. KADEN,
CHAIRMAN OF THE COMMISSION

LEE SMITH, DIRECTOR
OF THE COMMISSION AND EDITOR OF THE REPORT

A TOUCHSTONE BOOK

COMMISSION
REPORT

*By the Cuomo Commission
on Trade and Competitiveness*

Introduction by

MARIO M. CUOMO
GOVERNOR OF NEW YORK STATE

Published by Simon & Schuster Inc.
New York   London   Toronto   Sydney   Tokyo

Touchstone

Simon & Schuster Building
Rockefeller Center
1230 Avenue of the Americas
New York, New York 10020

Designed by Irving Perkins Associates
Manufactured in the United States of America

10 9 8 7 6 5 4 3 2 1

10 9 8 7 6 5 4 3 2 1 Pbk.

Library of Congress Cataloging in Publication Data
Cuomo Commission on Trade and Competitiveness (N.Y.)
    The Cuomo Commission report.

    A Touchstone Book
    Bibliography: p.
    Includes index.
    1. United States—Economic conditions—1981– . 2. United States—
Economic policy—1981– . 3. Competition, International. I. Smith, Lee
(Lee Orr) II. New York (State). Governor (1983– : Cuomo) III. Title.
HC106.8.C86   1988   338.973   88-15648
ISBN 0-671-66963-X
ISBN 0-671-66964-8 Pbk.

CONTENTS

Contents

Contents

LIST OF CHARTS

Charts

PREFACE

THIS report represents the culmination of the work of the Commission on Trade and Competitiveness appointed by New York Governor Mario M. Cuomo. The report represents the views of the Commission, though obviously not every word, phrase, or idea reflects every member's views. Several members of the Commission have chosen to write separate statements, and these are included as an appendix to the report.

THE MEMBERS OF THE COMMISSION:

Roger Altman
Vice Chairman
The Blackstone Group

John A. Georges
Chairman of the Board
Chief Executive Officer
International Paper Company

Lewis Preston
Chairman of the Board
Morgan Guaranty Trust
Company of New York

Robert Rubin
General Partner
Goldman Sachs & Company

Richard Simmons
Chairman of the Board
Chief Executive Officer
Allegheny Ludlum Corporation

Ira M. Millstein
Senior Partner
Weil Gotshal & Manges

Carol Tucker Foreman
President
Foreman and Heidepriem

Lewis B. Kaden
Partner
Davis Polk & Wardwell

Eugene Keilin
Partner
Lazard Frères & Company

Lawrence Klein
Professor of Economics
University of Pennsylvania

Robert Browne
Staff Director
House Banking Subcommittee
on International Development
Institutions and Finance

Michael Piore
Mitsui Professor of
Contemporary Technology
Massachusetts Institute
of Technology

Irving Bluestone
University Professor of Labor
Studies
Wayne State University

Edward J. Cleary
President
New York State AFL-CIO

Jan Pierce
Vice President
Communication Workers of
America

Jack Sheinkman
President
Amalgamated Clothing and
Textile Workers Union

Lynn Williams
President
United Steelworkers of America

Laura D'Andrea Tyson
Associate Professor of Economics
University of California, Berkeley

Clyde Prestowitz
Senior Associate
Carnegie Endowment for
International Peace

Lester Thurow
Dean
Sloan School of Management
Massachusetts Institute of
Technology

The Commission wishes to express its appreciation to Governor Cuomo for the opportunity to address these issues. The Commission owes a special debt to Lee Smith, who directed the Commission's staff and edited the report. His energy, patience, and creativity kept the diverse members of our group driving toward a consensus on policies to enhance America's economic future. To the extent this report contributes specific ideas and analysis to the debate over these important matters, Lee Smith deserves much of the credit.

Lewis B. Kaden
Chairman of the Commission
New York City
April 1988

ACKNOWLEDGMENTS

THE research and work of the Commission took place over an extended period of time and involved many people. This report is just one product by an enormously productive and creative group. Particular mention and appreciation are owed to Jeff Levin and Walter Russell Mead. Sarah Bernstein, Jerry Sanders, and Mark Green played key roles. Don Terry, Steve Quick, Ron Blackwell, and Tim Wendt made important contributions. Jon Brandt, Mark Childress, Martin Kohli, Paul Winston, and Todd Woody were essential in making the report as accurate and readable as possible. Robert Cohen, Rick McGahey, Elizabeth Engberg, Thierry Noyelle, Jack Schimmelman, Sophia Hernandez, Leslie Norton, Karen Jannicky, Gerri Goeller, Claude Reich, and Bernadine Klickner also provided valuable assistance. Thanks are also owed to our agent, Geri Thoma, and to our editor at Simon & Schuster, Carole Hall.

The preparation of the report was greatly facilitated by the support of Vincent Tese, the encouragement and advice of Al Sullivan, the input of Harold Holzer, and the extreme patience of Shelley Mayer and Aaron and Julia Smith.

Lee Smith
Director of the Commission and Editor of the Report
New York City
April 1988

FOREWORD

by James D. Robinson, III
Chairman and Chief Executive Officer
American Express Company

Several months ago, Governor Mario Cuomo gathered together a group of businessmen, labor leaders, academics, and public officials to explore New York State's and the nation's competitiveness and trade problems. The Cuomo Commission's task was to see how serious these problems were and to recommend possible solutions.

The Commission's topic of American competitiveness is clearly a timely one. How America can compete in the world economy is perhaps *the* major issue facing the U.S. today. It subsumes a host of other issues, ranging from budget deficits to trade deficits to human deficits in employment and education. It underlies basic questions about our country's economic and political future and about the quality of American life.

The Cuomo Commission counted twenty-six prior studies since 1981 on competitiveness. What is new in this report is its historical depth, the breadth of its recommendations, and the extent of consensus on prognosis and prescriptions reached by its diverse members on some highly complex issues. The Commission report is articulate and readable. It explains why lack of competitiveness is a problem for Americans, how our competitive position eroded, what is being done to restore competitiveness, and what else needs to be done.

As the Commission suggests repeatedly, the U.S. faces three choices: 1) We can do nothing, and let market forces wring out noncompetitive businesses and drive down wages and prices to low enough levels that American goods and services can compete in world markets. 2) We can react emotionally to the decline, with protectionist measures and isolationist xenophobia that will impoverish the whole world as well as ourselves. 3) Or we can act now to adopt the disciplined but difficult policies and practices that will reverse our downward course and ensure a brighter future.

In my view, the Commission has reached the right basic conclusion: while the U.S. has lost its dominant position in the world economy, it need not lose its position of leadership. The Cuomo Commission calls for a program of international and domestic reform to restore competitiveness. The principles of that program are sound, comprehensive, and appropriate. First, domestic growth and prosperity *are* linked to international growth and prosperity. Second, consumption and production *should be* more balanced between nations. Third, we *need* a national strategy for competitiveness. And fourth, cooperation between labor and management, cooperation between government and the private sector, and employee participation *are* key elements to improvement in competitiveness.

The Commission has also asked the right questions, including:

- How can the U.S. trade deficit be reduced without beggar-thy-neighbor trade policies?
- How can growth in, and U.S. exports to, Latin America be restored?
- What is the best way for the U.S. to reduce budget deficits without hurting competitiveness?
- What can be done to encourage savings and investment instead of consumption?
- Where should public resources be concentrated to revive industrial competitiveness and technological preeminence?
- What, if anything, should the government do to help industries and workers adjust to changing global demand for products?
- What changes in labor/management relations, compensation, and employment can improve productivity?

Do I agree with all the recommendations of the Commission? No. But neither do all the Commission members. The Commission sought consensus, not unanimity. From my own perspective, I share the caveats of Commission members Lewis T. Preston and Robert Rubin about the risks of too much government involvement in the economy and the need for more adherence to free market principles and to fair trade. In addition, the record for some specific remedies, such as wage, price, and salary guidelines, and coordinated management of interest and exchange rates, is not very encouraging.

One area of the Commission's report that I find particularly timely is its analysis and recommendations on Latin American growth and debt relief. As the Commission has noted, Latin America has been a major market for American goods in the past, but its ability to import those products has been impaired by the crushing burden on Latin American countries of servicing current debts. The Commission's call for the government to take a more active role in the debt crisis is on target.

Whether or not one agrees with the Commission's recommendations, they are inventive, provocative, and thoughtful, and certainly worth consideration. The Commission has cast a wide net, and brought back many valuable ideas that can help foster American competitiveness. The American people and their political leaders should give these recommendations serious reflection.

Governor Cuomo on a number of occasions has reached out to the diversity of professional talent in New York and elsewhere to examine issues of serious importance and to develop recommendations for policymakers. The Commission's report is a fine example of the benefits of this approach and of the contribution that men and women of goodwill can make when they identify key areas of mutual interest and seek meaningful alternatives where there are any points of disagreement.

Clearly, this report should stimulate discussion and debate. That's a very important result. If the U.S. is to avoid the fate of other nations that have lost their competitive position in the past, we will need more deliberations of this kind.

INTRODUCTION

The New Realism

by Mario M. Cuomo,
Governor of New York

ON October 19, 1987, Black Monday, the Dow Jones Industrial Average plummeted 508 points in a single day, making it impossible to pretend any longer that America did not face serious economic difficulties. At that moment we saw our massive trade and budget deficits in stark relief, towering above the economic landscape, symbols of a system out of balance and harbingers of hard times ahead. Around the world, investors began to show doubt as to America's ability to address its problems. Regaining the world's confidence by demonstrating an ability to master these new challenges will not be easy.

Even before the Crash, Americans were debating our nation's economic future. This debate, in which "competitiveness" became a key word, raised a series of questions: Could America compete in a world economy, and, if so, how? What should government do to help make this country more competitive and restore a balance in trade? Most important of all, what should the American people do to strengthen our economy and create more opportunity and security for themselves and their families?

It was in this context that I called together a group of experts and leaders from business, labor, and the public, to report to me and to the people of New York State on trade and competitiveness.

Their report examines these issues thoroughly and insightfully. It demonstrates the immense complexity of competitiveness, and deals with questions about the way we live and work, as well as the kind of society we wish to become. It also points out clearly the path we need to take to build an America ready to meet the challenges of the next decade and next century.

Despite this complexity and the fact the Commission's members have very diverse backgrounds, occupations, and views, the Commission achieved a high degree of consensus on a broad range of issues. Their agreement is significant, and demonstrates what Americans can do when they focus on what binds them, not on what divides them. It gives hope that we can build a new national consensus on our economic future.

Seeing Our Problems Clearly

Among the many virtues of the Commission's report is its unflinching honesty. Recognizing that we can't hope to deal with problems we refuse to acknowledge, it lays bare our failures and vulnerabilities with clinical objectivity.

The report is comprehensive, examining both the domestic and the international economy, delineating how conditions at home are intimately linked to conditions abroad. Matching the comprehensiveness of the Commission's analysis is the realistically broad scope of its recommendations. Its proposed solutions are, as they must be, both national and international in reach.

At the center of the Commission's focus is an emphasis on the importance of reducing our continuing trade deficit. Last year we set another world record in trade deficits, exceeding $170 billion. While recent monthly trade deficit figures suggest some decline, even our most unrestrained optimists do not predict anything approaching a trade balance for years to come. In the meantime, American dollars flow abroad to purchase imports, without a reciprocal inflow, and we as a nation are poorer for it.

The unhappy concomitant of our trade deficits is enormous debt. In 1985, the United States became a net debtor nation for the first time since World War One. Since then, we have descended into debt faster than any country in history and now owe more abroad than Mexico, Brazil, and Argentina combined. The need to pay back this debt will impede our economic growth, lower our living standards, and vastly complicate our international relations. Indeed, it is already having an effect. Because the United States is now a debtor nation, we are no longer able to pursue domestic policies without considering the reactions of foreign creditors or worrying about the value of our currency.

Our debt to foreign investors is only part of the problem. The Reagan Administration has added over $1 trillion to the domestic federal debt, as much debt in eight years as the nation managed to accumulate during the previous two centuries. The interest payments that debt demands make it harder to pay for essential services—for Medicare and social security, for investments in education, infrastructure, and child care. Our combined foreign and federal debt is a ball-and-chain around our economic future.

Republicans and Democrats, conservatives and liberals alike have warned about our present course. Peter G. Peterson, a Republican investment banker who served as Secretary of Commerce in the Nixon Administration, believes that economic decline threatens our position of world leadership. "It's hard to stand tall on bended knees," Peterson wrote in a devastating article in *The Atlantic* magazine last fall. The Joint Economic Committee of Congress reminded us that "no country has ever managed to be a great power and a great debtor at the same time," pointing to sixteenth-century Spain and twentieth-century Britain as examples of societies whose world power was undermined by debt.

As the Commission astutely observes, one of the most dangerous consequences of our weakened competitiveness is the threat to our standard of living. Throughout America's history, we have been a nation of opportunity where those who worked hard could reasonably expect their standard of living to rise. Today, many Americans find themselves working harder while receiving less in return for their efforts. Real wages have been falling for fifteen years, and parents today can no longer assume that their children's lives will be better than their own. Indeed, a *New York Times*/CBS News Poll in February 1988 indicated that for the first time in many years, Americans no longer have faith that America's future will be an improvement over its present or past.

The Commission is particularly effective in analyzing the historical context out of which these new concerns arise. The world today is in many respects the one the great statesmen of the 1940s set out to create when they began rebuilding after World War Two. The rise of competitors—Europe, Japan, and now parts of the Third World—is not a defeat, but rather the fulfillment of a long-term plan for global peace based on growth and prosperity. Given this, we should regard the changes America has experienced not so much as a failure, but in part, at least, as the result of our extraordinary success. Now we must learn to share the benefits of that achievement.

Perhaps the Commission's greatest service is that it provides a framework for American renewal that is both hopeful and realistic. During much of the 1970s our country was gripped by pessimism and anxiety. In 1984 the Reagan Administration won reelection on what now seems clear was a message of unfounded optimism. Preaching easy and painless solutions to our pressing national problems, the Administration raised expectations it could not meet. Its failure, and the end of the "Morning in America" optimism, threatens to add to disillusionment among voters. If this comes to pass, and it surely will without strong leadership, the resulting distrust of our institutions, cynicism about politics and government, and discouragement about the future of this country may be the worst legacy of recent failures.

The Commission's report acknowledges that and makes a good case for believing that we have not come to the limits of American economic growth, and have not arrived at a point where we must sacrifice cherished national values to reach economic goals.

The report also makes clear that our ability to maintain our values and restore vitality to our economy will depend on a national willingness to do what must be done to adjust to our changing relationship with the rest of the world.

The New Interdependence

The most profound change in our time has been the emergence of a global economy. Today, America's economy is inextricably intertwined with those of other countries.

The full flowering of the global economy in the 1980s marks the end of the postwar era. The world of the late 1940s and the world of the late 1980s are vastly different. Europe and Japan, having moved from postwar devastation to stability and prosperity, are no longer our economic dependents. In the Third World, industrialization has proceeded with surprising speed. The American economy no longer looms with awesome height over its trading partners.

The reality of the global economy has rendered irrelevant our present approach to international relations. Other countries think long and hard about how government can further their economic interests, and economic interests play a critical role in the foreign policies that other countries adopt. The time has come when we, too, must have an overall foreign policy that advances our basic economic objectives, not only our political and military concerns.

America is moving from a period of its history in which our worldwide political challenges—the reconstruction of Europe and Japan as allies in the conflict with the Soviet Union—overrode our immediate concerns about our economy. Now our own economy is our primary concern, and we are forced to confront the problems of restoring economic balance, growth, and stability on an international level.

If we meet these challenges, our security interests will be easier to defend and a spirit of constructive compromise will reign in international forums. If we fail, economic rivalry among the advanced countries and rampant poverty in the developing world could create new security threats which would quickly spin beyond our control.

Since World War Two we have kept our markets open to those who closed their markets to us, tolerated chronic trade deficits, and borne disproportionate shares of the military and economic costs of the Western alliance. Now, we must insist on stricter reciprocity with our partners.

Many speak of burden sharing as if it were just a question of a reallocation of the costs of defense to our allies. Even more fundamental is the question of whether the United States can and should bear most of the cost of underwriting the world's economic system. The Commission's analysis shows clearly that the United States can no longer serve as the world's "consumer of last resort."

To survive and prosper in the years ahead we must understand the diverse ways in which nations organize their economies and conduct trade—ways markedly different from our own. This diversity has made increasingly less meaningful the old debate between "free trade" and "protectionism." Our preoccupation with the rules of trade rather than the reality of trade has not, in recent times, served us well. As the Commission's report suggests, we need to pay more attention to the way trade is actually conducted—the balancing of end results, not just an empty debate over largely artificial rules—and seek new ways to bring it into greater balance. Neither a quixotic effort to impose free trade rules on economies which will not accept them nor a self-destructive plunge into protectionism are real alternatives.

What we need is *responsible internationalism:* an effort to put America's relations with its partners on an enduring, stable basis that can be sustained over the long term. We must expect a partnership with our allies, not just a trading relationship.

The Commission has sketched out a program of reform based on responsible internationalism. It is a bold and hopeful proposal, but certainly not an impossibly naive one. The great institutions created after World War Two by the Bretton Woods agreement were founded on the concept that national interests and international cooperation are in many ways compatible. These institutions worked because they embodied the idea that mutual growth could provide that better future to which all countries aspired. Today, the nations of the world are more inextricably interdependent than ever before; global integration has reached the point where we need each other as buyers and sellers in the same worldwide marketplace. There can be no real progress unless policies accommodate to this reality.

The Individual's Role

Global interdependence is not the only important theme contained within the Commission's report. Much attention is also devoted to the importance of the individual's participation in achieving national competitiveness.

The Commission tells us that the sum of individual ambition and ingenuity is what will restore America's competitive position. They make the point (obvious, but certainly worth emphasis) that any nation's greatest resource is its people—all its people. The development of human resources is an essential part of any attempt to improve our economic condition, which, in turn, requires that we give education primacy in our hierarchy of values.

The Commission recommends that education should become a lifelong process so that American workers and industry are not left producing second-rate goods by second-rate methods. And it points out that well-trained and well-educated workers will need to be given a fuller opportunity to share in the American Dream. The kind of low-wage jobs that have characterized American employment growth in the 1980s won't do. Instead of putting the weight of our economic resources into the production of goods—our trade deficit is, after all, a deficit in goods—we have concentrated on financial wheeling and dealing that frequently diminished the opportunity for ordinary working people to contribute to national competitiveness. This must change.

The Commission is also right in emphasizing the importance of allowing workers more participation in decision making. When individuals are given the chance to participate in the decisions that govern their working lives, productivity, quality; and morale all rise. This has been demonstrated in company after company that has had the courage to break with rigid convention and make its workers partners, not parts. There is profit in participation—not only for individuals, but for whole industries and the nation as well.

A New American Formula

The United States has reached a critical point in its history. Difficult questions lie ahead: as the Commission makes clear, we cannot expect a painless transition.

But the changes we must make to become a more competitive economy do not mean that we must become a poorer, more divided society. On the contrary. As the Commission's report indicates, the adjustments and reforms that will make this country competitive are also those which open the doors of opportunity, create more good jobs, improve the quality of education, and give us more control over our lives.

The Commission calls its program of reform "A New American Formula" for a strong economy. The principles behind it are sensible and pragmatic. First, it embraces a new realism about our place in the global economy and recommends that we base our policies on the world as it is, not on what it once was or what we might wish it to be. Second, it upholds the primacy of growth and production. Unlike some who see austerity as the major avenue to restoring balance to our production and consumption, the Commission recognizes the downward economic spiral that dramatic cuts in consumption can produce. It advocates instead growth, both here and abroad, and suggests we raise our level of production, not lower our living standards. Finally, it realizes that America must be competitive to earn, not borrow, its standard of living. It is to these ends that the Commission's reforms are directed.

Among those reforms are revenue measures and spending cuts to reduce our federal budget deficit. Budget reduction is important, but so is the growing inequality of income among Americans, caused in part by changes in federal tax policy. For this reason the value-added-tax (VAT) suggested by the Commission may not be the right approach. If revenue increases are needed, they should not increase inequality, but rather make our tax system more progressive.

On the whole, the Commission's program of reform is excellent. I believe that by using this New American Formula as our guide to action, we can harness our national strengths. There is much that we have to build on, and our task is to do so in a way that fully capitalizes our potential as producers.

To produce more requires we invest more in the things that truly strengthen us—schools and laboratories, machines and factories, highways and harbors. These are the kinds of investments we can't afford not to make. Not if we want a strong America and a society that helps all of us—not just the lucky few—to succeed.

Our society is not condemned to decline. The American people possess enormous reserves of talent and ingenuity. Researchers and inventors are constantly developing new products and techniques that make our work more productive, our leisure more rewarding, and promise to extend our lives. Entrepreneurs and businesses are finding new ways to lower the costs of production and bring new products to market. Our state and local governments have forged alliances for progress with the private sector, and have put whole regions of the country on the road to rapid economic growth.

The American system that has guided our thinking for the last fifty years is based on the belief that we all rise fastest when we rise together. Poverty drags down the prosperity of the whole nation. The buying power of the average family is the measure and the force that determines the prosperity of the whole country.

This is the tradition that we must again embrace, the tradition that was largely abandoned during the last eight years.

In a sense the principle that the individual good depends on the common good has always been a part of our nation's history. It's there in the preamble to our constitution, in those magnificent three words "We the people." But it required a Civil War to affirm that truth and another century of legal and political struggle before *we* meant everyone: minorities and women and the disabled.

Fifty years ago, it took the vision and courage of Franklin Roosevelt to put into practice a program that cut across regional barriers and asserted our responsibility for one another: the cities for the sharecroppers, the advantaged for the disadvantaged, rich states for poorer ones, all of them sharing benefits and burdens for the good of all.

American society rests on a compromise between competition and cooperation, freedom and responsibility, individualism and solidarity. Without individual freedom and opportunity, society stagnates and the economy ceases to progress; the dead hand of the past keeps new generations from finding new answers to age-old human problems. Yet unbridled competition transforms society into a jungle where the benefits for a few take precedence over the needs of many.

Of course, the proper balance between competition and cooperation can be hard to strike. Sometimes as a nation we have gone too far in one direction or the other. But as conditions around us change, we need the courage and insight to let both of these values contribute to our social health and dynamism.

It's here, I believe, the new realism must begin and end; here in the ancient wisdom that says no state, no city, no neighborhood in this country can make it alone; that we can only do it together, as a people, as a nation, as a family.

In the end, the best model for society is not the economic model of the marketplace, but the social model of the family. Each member of the family has different needs and different abilities, yet each gains by contributing to common goals. Social life, like family life, is an exercise in the art of constructive compromise, in which each member gains by giving. In family life, as well as in the wider society, leadership involves creative thinking about how the group and the individual interests can complement each other to the benefit of all.

The Commission's emphasis on cooperation is, therefore, perfectly fitting. Both competition and cooperation have deep roots in the American character, and a healthy American society is one in which both qualities can be freely expressed. This report is an excellent beginning of the discussion our country needs of its economic future. I hope that the people of the state of New York, and others interested in our nation's future, will find it helpful as they seek to cooperate more efficiently and to compete more effectively.

CHAPTER ONE

Losing Ground in the Global Economy

A Nation at Risk

AMERICA has failed to adjust to the new reality of a global economy, and we are beginning to pay the price. The price of failure will not be just economic; the consequences in the next decade will be more than a slower rate of economic growth or a stagnation in living standards and opportunities. Just as any debtor is at the mercy of its creditors, if the U.S. continues to sink into debt, our foreign creditors will eventually have undue influence over our future and the policies of our elected government. And if America fails to grow—and it cannot grow without becoming more competitive in markets at home and abroad—it will be unable to sustain national security commitments and the network of alliances and institutions that has preserved America's place in the world for the last forty years. Without a growing American economy whose growth is earned, not borrowed, the world will be a poorer and more dangerous place, not only for Americans, but for all those in Europe, Japan, and the developing world who depend on our markets to keep their own economies healthy and growing.

These are the conclusions of Governor Cuomo's Commission on Trade and Competitiveness, reached after more than a year's study of the relationship between the American and the world economies.

The members of the Commission came from different walks of life and included representatives of finance, manufacturing, labor, and consumers, and experts in trade and economics. When our work began in January 1987, we did not expect to agree about all of the issues studied. Some of the disagreements were on matters of emphasis and some were more substantive. Many of us found ourselves reexamining long-held beliefs about the economy and about what life for Americans could be like in the next decade. In the course of the study we developed broad areas of agreement, and all of us came away from this process with a new sense of urgency.

By any realistic view of our prospects, it is clear that America does not have much time to make the changes that are needed. The rate of change of the global economy is too rapid to assume that other nations will put their own agendas on hold and wait for the U.S. to put its economic affairs in order. It is equally clear that the cost of not acting would be high. America and the world are at an important turning point in history, and the years to come hold challenges—and opportunities—as great as any in our history. How well we pull together to respond to these challenges, how willing we are to think in new terms, and how able we are to reform our economic institutions and practices will determine whether we prosper or decline in the years ahead.

Seven Warning Signs

As the Commission reviewed the long-term picture of America's economy we identified seven warning signs of serious economic trouble. While any one of these signs might not be dangerous by itself, together they constitute a tangible threat to our economic system and our way of life. Left untreated they will seriously weaken, even undermine, our economy in the next decade.

1. *The Trade Crisis*

For most of this century America has been a surplus nation, selling more goods abroad than we purchased—but no longer.

- The U.S. has not had a surplus in the trade of merchandise since 1975.[1] (See Chart 1.1.)

- Our trade deficit has grown steadily—from a few billion dollars per year in the 1970s to more than $156 billion in 1986 and $171 billion in 1987.[2]

- In 1987 imports reached a record 22.7 percent of all goods consumed in the U.S. (excluding oil)—up from 16.0 percent as recently as 1982, over a 40 percent increase.[3]

- The U.S. has lost 30 percent of its market share of total world exports since 1950.[4]

It is encouraging that exports have increased in 1987 in some sectors as American manufacturers are finally receiving the benefits of a lower dollar and increases in quality and productivity. But imports are still strong and the trade picture remains discouraging in industry after industry:

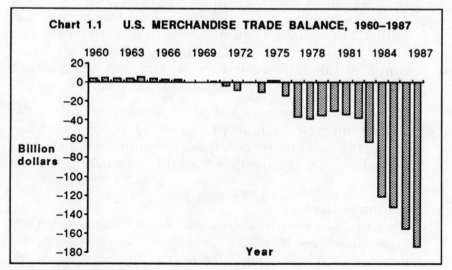

Chart 1.1   U.S. MERCHANDISE TRADE BALANCE, 1960–1987

Source: U.S. Department of Commerce, Survey of Current Business

- *Agriculture:* Traditionally one of our strongest industries, agriculture now faces tough competition abroad; 1981's $27 billion agriculture trade surplus dwindled to $7 billion in 1987.[5]

- *Automobiles:* In 1972 fewer than one of every six cars sold in the U.S. was imported; by 1986 the figure was approaching one in three, and many "American-made" cars included imported parts.[6] Our trade deficit in automobiles grew by over 1,000 percent, from $2.6 billion in 1972 to $37.3 billion by 1987.[7]

- *Consumer goods* (excluding food and automobiles): In 1976, the U.S. had a consumer goods trade deficit of slightly more than $9 billion; by 1987 it was nearly $69 billion.[8]

- *Consumer electronics:* In 1972 imports outvalued exports by $1.7 billion; by 1986 that figure had climbed to $11.7 billion.[9]

- *Oil:* American dependence on foreign oil and the price we pay for it have risen enormously in the last twenty years. U.S. oil imports have climbed from 3 million barrels a day in 1970 to more than 6.5 million in 1987. At current prices, that constitutes an annual imported oil bill of over $40 billion. Meanwhile, domestic production continues to sag. Since January 1, 1986, production has fallen about 8 percent.[10] At this rate, many experts think U.S. dependence on foreign oil will double in the next ten years.[11]

- *Capital goods:* We have lost our reputation for making the best engineered machinery in the world. In 1977, the trade surplus in machinery, construction equipment, and other capital goods was more than $25 billion; in 1987 it was $4.2 billion.[12]

2. *A Nation in Hock*

If there is one word which captures the feeling of anxiety among Americans, it is debt. Total household, corporate, and consumer debt has risen 60 percent in the past five years, rising from $4.9 trillion in 1982 to $7.9 trillion in 1987.[13] It is true that rising levels of private and public debt have helped maintain high levels of consumption and spurred growth. There are also signs that the worst years of the "debt explosion" are over, since the rate of debt growth has slowed. But once the economic expansion ends, the weight of the debt burden will surely increase and in the next recession will drag us even farther down. And under any circumstances, it will depress growth and the nation's standard of living.

A quick review shows that the nation's balance sheet is deep in the red.

- *Consumer debt:* In the third quarter of 1986, household installment credit debt reached 16.5 percent of total personal income, a postwar record. Overall individual debt at the end of 1986 equaled 66 percent of that year's income, also a record.[14]

- *Farm debt:* In 1984, the proportion of total farm debt to net farm income hit a postwar record. It continues to rise. By late 1987, some Federal Farm Credit System banks faced financial collapse, prompting the President to sign an emergency $4 billion capital bond bill to maintain solvency.[15]

- *Corporate debt:* In the 1950s and 1960s, businesses spent about $1 of every $7 of earnings to pay interest on business debt. In the 1970s this figure rose to $1 in every $3. Since 1981, corporations have been paying more than half of their earnings to service their debts. In other words they are more "leveraged," or loaded with debt, than ever before.[16] In the next recession profits will probably fall and leave corporations with even less of a cushion to pay off these debts.

- *Federal debt:* Because of increasing federal deficits (see Chart 1.2) our national debt has grown astronomically. In 1980, the national debt was less than $1 trillion. Today it is more than twice that, and by the time the next President takes office the national debt may have tripled since 1980.[17] Interest payments have become the fastest-growing line item in the federal budget (see Chart 1.3); in 1987 interest

5

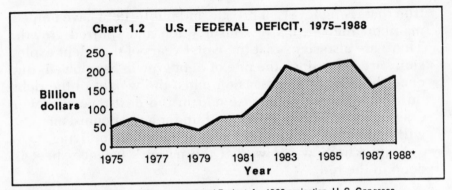

Chart 1.2   U.S. FEDERAL DEFICIT, 1975–1988

Source: for 1975-1987, Office of Management and Budget; for 1988 projection, U. S. Congress, Congressional Budget Office
* Projected

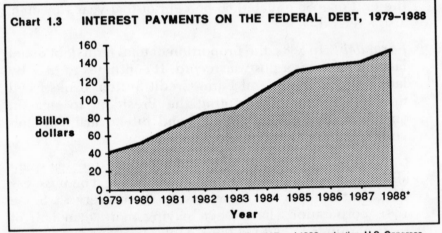

Chart 1.3   INTEREST PAYMENTS ON THE FEDERAL DEBT, 1979–1988

Source: for 1979–1986, Office of Management and Budget; for 1987 and 1988 projection, U.S. Congress, Congressional Budget Office
*Projected

on past debt was greater than the total budget deficit. In effect, the U.S. government is borrowing new money to pay interest on old debt. From 1970 to 1987, interest on the national debt grew from 7.5 percent to more than 22 percent of federal revenue.[18] The national debt is no longer something "we owe to ourselves." Foreigners hold over a quarter of a trillion dollars of federal debt. Annual interest paid to foreigners doubled since 1980 and approached $24 billion in 1987.[19] (See Chart 1.4.)

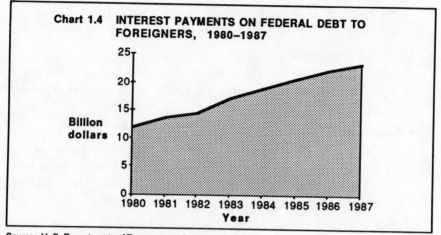

Chart 1.4 **INTEREST PAYMENTS ON FEDERAL DEBT TO FOREIGNERS, 1980–1987**

Source: U. S. Departments of Treasury and Commerce
Note: data for 1981-1983 and 1985 were interpolated.

- *Foreign debt:* Less than a decade ago, the U.S. was the world's largest creditor; today, it is the largest debtor in world history. The combination of trade and budget deficits is responsible. From 1981 to 1986, the U.S. went from $141 billion in the black to $263 billion in the red. (See Chart 1.5.) The Commerce Department has estimated that

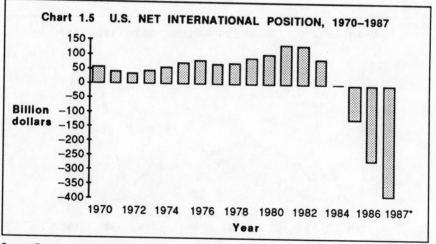

Chart 1.5 **U.S. NET INTERNATIONAL POSITION, 1970–1987**

Source: Department of Commerce
1987 estimate based on data through third quarter

7

our foreign debt will peak at about $700 billion. Congress says it could exceed $1 trillion.[20]

3. *More Risk, More Volatility*
Closely related to the increase in debt has been an increase in risk in the economy and volatility in financial markets around the world.

• Business bankruptcies have soared. In the worst years of the worst recessions since World War Two, an average of 49 businesses out of every 10,000 failed. But in 1982 that number climbed to 88 and in 1986 it reached 120 before dropping off slightly in 1987.[21] (See Chart 1.6.)

Banks failed in the 1980s at a rate not seen since the Great Depression. Between 1943 and 1981, bank failures averaged less than ten per year. In 1986, 138 banks failed, and in 1987, 184 failed, the most failures in any year since FDIC was founded. (See Chart 1.7.) Almost 1,600 banks are on the FDIC's list of troubled institutions. In the second quarter of 1987, the 13,937 insured banks in the FDIC system posted a total loss of $10.6 billion.[22]

The turmoil in the banking system has affected the health of the federal agencies that guarantee U.S. bank deposits. In 1986, auditors declared that the Federal Savings and Loan

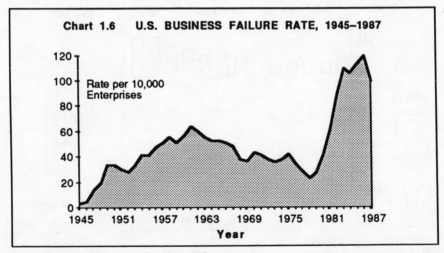

Chart 1.6   U.S. BUSINESS FAILURE RATE, 1945–1987

Rate per 10,000 Enterprises

Year

Source: *Economic Report of the President,* 1987

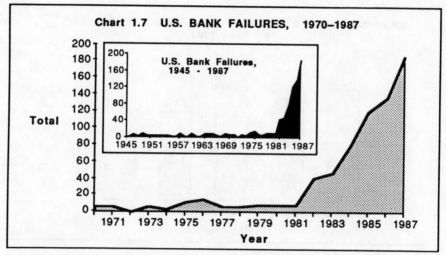

Chart 1.7 U.S. BANK FAILURES, 1970–1987

Source: U.S. Historical Statistics, Federal Deposit Insurance Corporation

Insurance Corporation (FSLIC)—the agency responsible for protecting more than $1 trillion in deposits—was insolvent. An emergency bailout avoided a crisis, but mounting thrift losses indicate that the FSLIC will be unable to rescue or close insolvent institutions without additional government assistance.[23]

- Volatility—the rate at which interest rates change—is also up from previous years. The prime rate, which once remained stable for years at a time, has been on a roller coaster in the 1980s, rising as high as 21 percent in 1981. Bond prices, which reflect interest rates, have also plunged and soared. These volatile rates vastly complicate the work of banks and corporations that need to decide on long-term investment strategies in an unpredictable environment.[24] Stock price volatility is also high; 50-point rises and falls in the Dow Jones Industrial Average have become almost commonplace.

4. *Slow Growth*
The U.S. economy is still growing, but ever more slowly. In the 1960s the annual average GNP growth rate was 3.8 percent. In the 1970s, it fell to 2.8 percent. From 1980 through 1987 it slid even further to 2.2 percent.[25] (See Chart 1.8.)

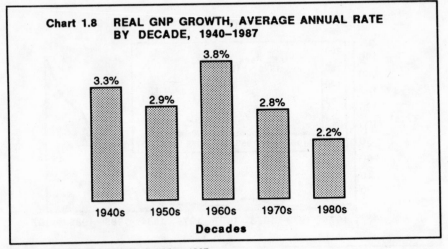

Chart 1.8   REAL GNP GROWTH, AVERAGE ANNUAL RATE
             BY DECADE, 1940–1987

Source: *Economic Report of the President,* 1987

The relative stagnation of the nation's economy can be seen in the degree to which industrial capacity is being underutilized; the lower the capacity utilization rate, the more industrial facilities are standing idle. In 1966, the capacity utilization rate was 91 percent. As of January 1, 1988, the peak for the 1980s was less than 83 percent.[26] In industries which experienced growth, such as paper and chemicals, factory use is at its limits, but uncertainty about the future has made these industries reluctant to add capacity.

Another indicator of industrial health has also declined—profitability. Since the mid-1960s, the rate of profit in U.S. manufacturing industries has headed down. (See Chart 1.9.) The profit rate in 1984 was less than half what it was in 1966.[27]

5. *A Less Innovative Economy*
Long-term trends show that our economy is losing its dynamism. Investment, productivity growth, and savings are weak; in education and innovation we have lost our lead.

• *Weak investment:* Low levels of capacity utilization have accompanied a drop in private investment. Annual average investment (as a percent of the GNP) was 34 percent less for the period 1980–1986 than it was, on average, during the three preceding decades.[28] (See Chart 1.10.)

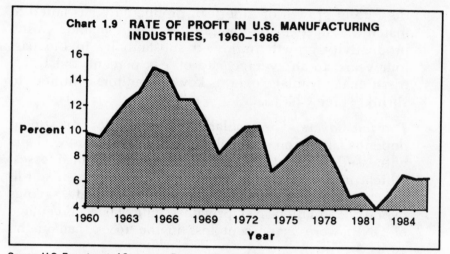

Chart 1.9 RATE OF PROFIT IN U.S. MANUFACTURING INDUSTRIES, 1960–1986

Source: U.S. Department of Commerce, Bureau of Economic Analysis

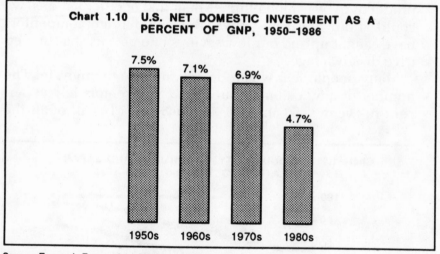

Chart 1.10 U.S. NET DOMESTIC INVESTMENT AS A PERCENT OF GNP, 1950–1986

Source: *Economic Report of the President,* 1987

- *Diminished advantage in productivity:* Are we losing our edge? Investment in plant and equipment is essential if the nation is to raise productivity, a key ingredient for improving the competitiveness of U.S. industry and stimulating incomes. Partly because investment has slowed, the rate of growth of American productivity has failed to match that of its major competitors. While manufacturing productivity growth improved substantially in the past four years, to an average rate of 4.25 percent, the U.S.'s traditional advantage over its key competitors continues to shrink.[29] (See Chart 1.11.)

- *Too few savers:* The availability of funds for investment depends largely on national savings. Here, again, we have witnessed decline. The internal savings of businesses, which previously made possible a high degree of self-financing, have been shrinking. Indeed, private savings overall have fallen. Net private savings (as a percentage of GNP) were 25 percent less in the 1980s than in the 1970s.[30]

The U.S. traditionally has had a low rate of savings compared with some of its trading partners. And as long as our productivity was much higher than that of other nations, we could afford those low rates. But now foreign competitors have caught up and our low savings rate puts us at a competitive disadvantage.

Many people fear we are losing the race to innovate. The number of new patents issued to U.S. inventors fell 39 percent between 1966 and 1983. (In 1987, nearly half of all the

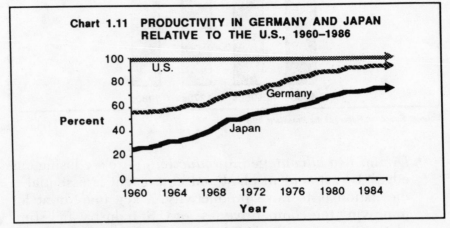

Chart 1.11 **PRODUCTIVITY IN GERMANY AND JAPAN RELATIVE TO THE U.S., 1960–1986**

Source: U.S. Department of Labor, Bureau of Labor Statistics

patents issued in the U.S. were given to residents of foreign countries, more than doubling their share over the last twenty years. Japanese inventors received more than one-third as many U.S. patents as did residents of the U.S.[31]) Since the 1970s the U.S. has increasingly lagged behind its allies in civilian R&D. Currently, Japan spends 47 percent and Germany 32 percent more (as a percentage of GNP) than the U.S. on civilian R&D.[32]

We are also losing the race to educate. Nearly forty percent of German college students graduate with degrees in science or engineering.[33] Less than 10 percent of U.S. graduates earn degrees in these fields.[34] Fewer American citizens received science and engineering Ph.D.s in 1985 than in 1970.[35] While our system of higher education remains the best in the world, American primary and secondary education has fallen behind our competitors.

6. *Increasing Exposure to Tough Foreign Competition*
More American industries than ever are exposed to foreign competition. Today the effect of that competition can be seen across our nation's landscape.

- In New England and the Southeast, the textile industry competed successfully in world markets throughout the 1960s. But as textile technology was disseminated abroad, producers from low-wage countries seized their opportunity, and the growth rate of textile imports exploded. Between 1980 and 1984 imports grew at an average annual rate of 18 percent.[36] Since 1981 nearly 100,000 U.S. textile jobs have been lost.[37] The industry has now rebounded because of its high productivity and continued restrictions on imports. Some observers believe it is likely to hold its own if current conditions prevail, but could begin to decline again if imports start to increase.

- In Pennsylvania, West Virginia, and Ohio, shuttered steel plants are a common sight. Imported steel, which in the 1950s was less than 2 percent of the American market, now constitutes around 20 percent. U.S. steel firms lost nearly $12 billion between 1982 and 1986.[38] About half those who were steelworkers in 1981—over 200,000—are no longer employed in steel.[39] The steel industry has recovered somewhat in the last two years and is now competitive in some markets, but it could easily go into decline once more if imports increase or the pace of improvement declines.

- Detroit has lost its position as the auto capital of the world. In 1960, American automakers produced more than 75 percent of the world's automobiles. Today the U.S. produces less than 25 percent of the world's autos.[40] In 1986, the auto industry employed 140,000 fewer workers than it did in 1978.[41]

- In Iowa and the rest of the farm belt, agriculture suffers from tough foreign competition. The Green Revolution made more of the Third World self-sufficient for its food, a worthwhile goal by any standard. But this has reduced U.S. exports and placed the nation in direct competition with farmers around the world scrambling for shares of the shrinking export market. Since 1982 the number of American farms has dropped by nearly 10 percent.[42]

- In California's Silicon Valley, the high-technology companies told themselves for years that "it can't happen here" and heralded themselves as America's manufacturing future. But in the mid-1980s, the semiconductor industry lost $2 billion, and laid off nearly 25,000 employees.[43] In the last two years, conditions for semiconductor manufacturers have improved somewhat, but are still difficult. Not surprisingly, manufacturers have come to the forefront of the battle for reform of U.S. trade laws.

7. *The End of a Rising Standard of Living for Many Americans*
One of the key features of life in postwar America, a rising standard of living for most people, has virtually disappeared. Real income levels for many Americans have declined since the early 1970s, not coincidentally just at the time the U.S. began importing more goods than it exported.

Hourly income for production workers, as measured by real spendable earnings, rose 56 percent from 1948 to 1972.

The long upward trend in wages has stopped (see Chart 1.12.); real hourly wages have stagnated since 1973.[44]

Between January 1981 and January 1986, more than 13 million Americans lost their jobs. One-third of those workers have remained unemployed or have given up and left the work force. Almost half those who did find new jobs earn less than they did before.[45]

While it is true that the U.S. economy created millions of new jobs in the 1980s, many of the new jobs are very different from the jobs that were lost. As the National Association of Manufacturers has pointed out, "While there has been a great deal of political emphasis on the gross number of jobs created in a dynamic U.S. economy, it appears that there has been a permanent loss of jobs in manufacturing due to the impact of trade."[46]

This Commission's study of the trade deficit's impact on employment in New York State confirms NAM's view. We found that between 1980 and 1986 over half of New York's manufacturing job loss was related to trade. New York's export industries declined because they lost customers abroad, and import competition hurt other New York manufacturers. Because these industries were found, by our study, to have

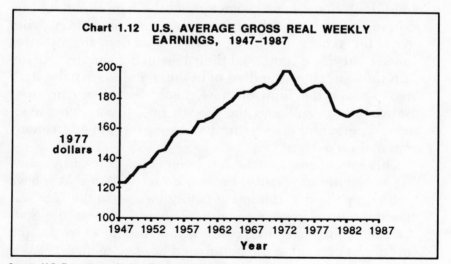

Chart 1.12 **U.S. AVERAGE GROSS REAL WEEKLY EARNINGS, 1947–1987**

1977 dollars

Year

Source: U.S. Department of Labor, Bureau of Labor Statistics

had above-average wages and growth in productivity, the job loss in these sectors has had an important impact on living standards.

The manufacturing jobs lost because of the trade deficit are being replaced by service-sector jobs which, on average, pay less. Part-time jobs are replacing full-time work. By 1986 almost one in five workers was working part-time.[47] Not surprisingly, the growth of part-time work has meant lower take-home pay.

Perhaps the best way to understand these changes is to think about the situation of working families today. Between 1973 and 1983, the real income of the average 30-year-old male fell by 23 percent.[48] To take up the slack, the number of working married women with children increased more than 50 percent from 1969 to 1985.[49] Many of these women took jobs not just because they wanted to—they had to. And their wages continue to lag behind those of men.[50]

These changes in the workplace made life more difficult for many families. By 1986, almost one out of seven Americans was living below the poverty line. The number of children in poverty has been on the rise—today, more than one out of five children live in poverty.[51]

The decline in real incomes contributed to a rise in household debt. Some have characterized the household debt increase as evidence of a consumer "spending binge." But given the squeeze on income, the rise in debt suggests that households have increased their borrowing simply to maintain their previous standard of living. Families may be starting to reach the limit on how much debt they can carry. Between 1951 and 1973 the growth rate of borrowing averaged 3 percent; between 1974 and 1984 it dropped to an average of 1.8 percent.[52]

This loss of real income has been accompanied by growing economic inequality. From the end of World War Two until 1973, the distribution of family income in the U.S. was moving toward greater equality. This is no longer the case. As good jobs have disappeared, the income share for the middle 60 percent of the population has declined.[53]

A Census Bureau study of the middle class illustrates this

reversal. Between 1970 and 1985 the number of American families with incomes between $15,000 and $35,000 (as measured in 1985 dollars) fell by approximately 10 percent.[54] As reported by the Federal Reserve in 1984, 55 percent of American families had accumulated no net worth at all.[55]

Things are not so discouraging for everyone, of course. Many Americans have prospered. Between 1973 and 1984 the number of families increased by 14 percent but the number with incomes greater than $75,000 (in 1984 dollars) rose more than 33 percent.[56]

The outlook for our economy suggests a future with a stagnant or falling standard of living for many and a rising standard for some. If allowed to continue, this trend will destroy one of America's greatest strengths—an economy which produced a rising standard of living, and increasingly offered equal opportunity to all.

Competition: The Heart of the Problem

The Commission thinks these seven warning signs, taken together, lead to a single conclusion: the nation is not keeping pace with changes in the world economy and has a serious competitiveness problem.

The trade deficit is perhaps the most outstanding manifestation of the American loss of competitiveness. The enormous and persistent gap between the value of American goods sold abroad and foreign goods bought at home shows the U.S. is not holding its own in the global marketplace.

Americans should be concerned about the trade deficit for a number of reasons. First, the money Americans spend on foreign goods contributes to the loss of jobs for the millions of Americans who could have made those goods at home. Second, it leads to a decline in profits for domestic industries, which in turn lessens their ability to invest and create new jobs. Third, it allows the economic stimulus provided by federal deficit spending to "leak" to other countries. By one measure, 63 percent of the $1.1 trillion in federal budget deficits accumulated in the last six years ended up stimulating foreign economies.[57] And because trade deficits mean less growth from government spending, bigger deficits are needed to spur the domestic economy. In short, the trade deficit gives other nations the benefit of our tax dollars and purchasing power and leaves us with growing debts.

Another reason to be concerned about the trade deficit is that it causes the wealth of America, our assets, to fall into foreign hands. Dollars—which are claims on American wealth—are being accumulated by other countries every time Americans buy foreign products without selling an equivalent amount overseas. Some of this money comes back to us when foreigners buy bonds to finance the U.S. federal budget deficit. Some is used for loans to American business. In both cases interest must be paid to foreign creditors. At the same time, much of this money has been invested in American stocks and in direct investment, including real estate. Foreign ownership of American assets is an ever-growing lien on America's future prosperity, because foreign owners and creditors will require a share of the annual earnings and output of our economy. Even if the growth of real GNP continues at the pace of the last seven years, these transfers, made up of profits, earnings, and interest payments on debt, will cut into growth and make U.S. living standards lower than they should be for years to come.

In 1987 the interest payments to foreign bondholders on the federal deficit alone were $23.5 billion.[58] In five years total payments made to foreign investors could exceed $75 billion per year. This loss of funds will depress our living standards. By one calculation every $40 billion in annual interest payments sent abroad results in a 1 percent reduction in living standards at home. Seventy-five billion per year in payments would result in almost a two percent drop in living standards. By comparison, the 1981–82 recession caused a 2.5 percent decline.[59]

There are those who still try to minimize our competitiveness problem. They speak with optimism when the trade deficit shrinks in a given month, or when U.S. exports rise. But these trends have not been consistent; imports continue to outpace exports. The fact is that even if the annual deficit does begin to come down, our debt to foreign interests will continue to grow, and will not stop growing, until we balance our trade. Reducing the trade deficit by several billion dollars on a monthly basis is one thing, and regaining our competitive position and creditor status in the world economy is quite another—and by any estimate is years away. Democrats and Republicans alike now recognize that this process of increasing debt cannot continue indefinitely, and if we want to avoid pawning our economic future, competitiveness must become a national priority.

Can America Compete?

While it is a positive sign that "competitiveness" has entered our national political vocabulary, a certain ambiguity still surrounds the word. How we define this idea is important, because the definition determines what we will do to achieve it.

The definition that was used by the President's Commission on Industrial Competitiveness is the one this Commission accepts:

"Competitiveness is the degree to which a nation can, under free and fair market conditions, produce goods and services that meet the test of international markets while simultaneously maintaining or expanding the real incomes of its citizens."[60]

The President's Commission also declared that "Competitiveness is not an end in itself; it is a means to an end. Competitiveness means a high standard of living and the growing wealth that allows us to attain other vital national goals . . ."[61]

We cannot compete by simply cutting costs. Indeed, becoming competitive requires us to spend considerably more on education, for example, and on civilian research and development.

As the Cuomo Commission studied competitiveness and trade we learned that competitiveness is not one issue, but many. Every industry, every factory and office, has unique strengths and unique problems. There are no panaceas for our competitiveness problems, nor any single solution that will work in every environment.

Economists draw a distinction between microeconomics, the study of individual firms and small-scale phenomena, and macroeconomics, the study of national and international factors. We found that competitiveness is in many respects a microeconomic issue: how efficiently does this factory produce this product; why are goods made here of better quality than goods made there?

Too often, the discussion of competitiveness is confined to macroeconomic factors—exchange rates, interest rates, and fiscal policy. These are important, but a nation's competitiveness results from the interplay of macroeconomic and microeconomic factors. For example, the U.S. balance of trade worsened in the early 1980s when the policies of the Administration and their interaction with the policies of the Federal Reserve pushed the dollar to a high level against other currencies. Imports became cheap for American consumers, while American exports were expensive in foreign markets. It seemed obvious, from a macroeconomic point of view, that if raising the value of the dollar created a trade deficit, lowering that value should eliminate the deficit.

But pushing the dollar back down after 1985 did not eliminate the trade deficit. Faced with import competition in the early 1980s, many firms made microeconomic decisions to shut down factories, defer investments in new capacity, or to transfer production to cheaper sites in developing countries. Imported goods had won a significant share of the American market, and it turned out to be easier to let them in than to push them back out. Even those economists who anticipated a lag between the time when the dollar started to fall and the time when improvements in trade began to appear have been disappointed at how long it has taken to see change, and disappointed as well that the change has shown up mostly as increased exports rather than decreased imports. The devaluation of the dollar has done very little to eliminate the deficit which the high-value dollar had created.

In the last analysis, what matters is production. Macroeconomic factors influence the costs and the methods of production, but the real work of an economy takes place on the factory floor and at the office desk. Many observers argue that America's productivity has grown more slowly than that of other nations because we have paid too little attention to the fundamentals. We are like a football team that spends all its time on razzle-dazzle plays and fancy maneuvers while it neglects the daily practice of blocking and tackling on which everything else depends.

The Commission decided to take a "back to basics" approach to competitiveness issues. We wanted a practical, results-oriented report, and this meant a concentrated study of key industries had to be the foundation of our work. We selected five industries that enabled us to study different aspects of the competitiveness question: apparel, steel, telecommunications, financial services, and food processing. These industries include basic manufacturing, agriculture-related business, "information" industries and high-tech industries. All of these industries have experienced significant challenges from international competition and will face even tougher conditions in the years ahead. Among the lessons we learned, described in Chapter 6, is that each of these industries needs to adjust to a more competitive environment, yet the situation in each case is unique. We also saw very clearly that no single macroeconomic policy, such as a lower value of the dollar, will miraculously solve all the problems in these industries. At the same time, without the proper government policies, particularly as they relate to trade relations and overall growth, no industry, no matter how strong, can go it alone in the world economy.

Leadership at the national level is essential for each of these industries and, we are sure, for many others. It has been a national mistake not to have developed strategies for enhancing the competitiveness of critical industries. While economic debate in other countries centers around practical ways to overcome specific economic problems, Americans too often engage in sterile arguments over whether government should do anything at all to safeguard our economic future. Countries presently winning competitive battles with producers based in the U.S. are clearly not hamstrung by partnerships with their governments; the Commission believes that America must return to the idea of a positive government able to forge public policies that can strengthen our economy.

This should not be confused with national economic planning, with the federal government controlling the direction of the national economy. Central planning would only worsen our problems; government decrees should not replace individual enterprise and the role of the market in allocating capital. At the same time, we reject the belief that government has no legitimate role in the economy.

The absence of national leadership today is particularly striking from a historical viewpoint. Looking back we can see that our prosperity over the last fifty years has been secured by skillful action on the part of the federal government. Obviously government has not done it alone. Millions of individuals and companies working together in the private sector have been the engine of the economy. But on the domestic front, a variety of government initiatives helped America grow and stabilized our economy. And it was creative government leadership which laid the foundations for the international economic system that brought stability and peace after World War Two.

The Commission believes that new initiatives to renew the international order can reestablish a climate for growth and enhance American economic competitiveness while an emphasis on the economic fundamentals at home can make us a more efficient and productive society. We need what might be called a "New American Formula," an approach which incorporates a new realism about the global economy in which America exists and which is directed toward production—production that can sustain a high standard of living.

We are optimists. We went out of our way to gather the irrefutable bad news for this study in order to rid ourselves of comfortable illusions and to see the truth plainly. So we now have worked our way to a clear sight of America's problems, and we do not want to underestimate them. America has no problems it cannot solve—that is the good news. None of the nation's problems will solve themselves—that is the bad news.

Back to the Basics

America does not suffer from a shortage of competitiveness studies; this Commission began its work with a study of twenty-four major studies of competitiveness prepared since 1981. But the problems will not be solved by committees of experts meeting and debating among themselves. They can only be addressed by millions of American citizens educating themselves about the causes of our current difficulties and dedicating themselves to helping the nation overcome them.

The time has come for a wide-ranging public debate concerning our increasingly serious economic problems. Instead of a series of typical government reports setting forth the results of our trade and industrial studies, the Commission thought it necessary to do more. To put our ideas and recommendations before a wider public, the results of our work have been put in book form, written in laymen's language for—we hope—a wide audience, not just the experts.

Most of all, the Commission wanted to broaden the public debate to encompass the full range of issues. A narrow focus on individual monthly trade statistics or quarterly GNP results can detract attention from long-term trends that have been building for decades, and that will continue to affect us for decades to come. We have therefore taken the long view in this report, looking beyond the immediate issues of 1988, and attempting to put the debate over our national future in the proper historical perspective. The report has also focused on the issue of how people produce, how work is organized, and what can be done to increase the contribution every American can make.

To understand our choices, the kind of life Americans can expect in the next decade and the possible consequences for good and for ill of the choices we must make, we need to go back to the past, to 1945, and renew our understanding of how today's world came about. Only then can we see how programs and policies developed back then need to be reformed to meet our national interests today. Finally, only by understanding how life for Americans has changed in the last forty years can we understand how to change it for the next forty.

CHAPTER TWO

Made in the U.S.A.: America Rebuilds the Postwar World

From War to Recovery

IN 1945, millions were haunted by the horror of the war just past and the fear of what further catastrophe the future might bring. None were more preoccupied with the shape of the future than those who were charged with steering the world back toward normalcy and peace.

Economically, World War Two was a great boost to America. The U.S. entered the war still suffering the aftereffects of the Great Depression, and emerged in 1945 with an industrial capacity greater than that of any nation in history. Our revitalized steel, manufacturing, and transportation industries, untouched by war, were eminently prepared to meet a surge in global demand.

But in the places where the war was actually fought, World War Two left another kind of legacy. Nations had sustained enormous numbers of casualties, with disproportionate losses among young men of military age. The wounded and disabled required huge welfare payments to stay alive—one-fourth of the German budget in the early 1950s went for such payments. Schools were closed throughout much of Europe;[1] hospitals were bombed-out shells or lacked the personnel and equipment to meet even the basic medical needs of a war-weakened population.

The war had destroyed housing everywhere in Europe. In

some German cities, including Berlin, Hamburg, and Bremen, one-half or more of the housing lay in ruins. In the Soviet Union an estimated 25 million people were homeless.[2] Water mains, gas lines, telephone lines, sewers, and the rest of the complicated infrastructure of modern industrial cities had been destroyed. The avenues of many European cities were little more than paths twisting through masses of rubble. In Frankfurt, weeds grew in the streets.

Throughout the war zones civilian life was shattered. An entire generation had come of age knowing nothing but war. In China, Japan, and Europe, people had grown up without the skills and attitudes needed for normal civilian life. Young veterans returned from the fronts knowing too much about death and too little about farming and manufacturing.

The physical and moral devastation of war was staggering in extent and complexity. This is difficult for some of us to grasp forty years later. War had destroyed not only houses, bridges, roads and factories; there was equal, and in some cases more severe, damage to the invisible network that keeps an economy functioning. Commercial relations had broken down across the continent. Europe's productive capacity had been ruthlessly distorted toward the needs of war. In the postwar chaos it was often not possible even for undamaged facilities to resume old relationships with suppliers and customers; in many cases it was unclear who actually owned a particular facility. With Germany utterly prostrate, its government disbanded, its citizens unable to send or receive mail, the Germans were removed for all practical purposes as customers or suppliers. Across Eastern Europe, the Red Army was uprooting the prewar social system and replacing it with new, Soviet-controlled institutions with which it was increasingly difficult for Western managers to deal.

It was hard to procure raw materials, and even harder to find machinery or parts. Railways were destroyed, bridges bombed, harbors blocked. In 1946 there was only one passable bridge over the Rhine, and one over the Elbe. The French ports of La Rochelle, Calais, Boulogne, Dunkirk, and Toulon were virtually unusable. Much of Holland was flooded with salt water; canal systems everywhere had been closed or diverted.[3] A flourishing black market in every imaginable product from ball bearings to synthetic fibers vastly complicated the task of restoring production.

The sole source for most goods was the U.S., the only major country to have escaped the war's devastation. Machines and agricultural products that once had come from Germany now came from the U.S. In the first six months of 1947, the U.S. accounted for one-third of all exports worldwide, and Europe's trade deficit with the U.S. had grown 700 percent in the decade following 1937.[4]

Europe's merchant fleet also lay in ruins. In the six years of war, merchant ships had been confiscated, scuttled, and fired upon by all sides. Even those who wanted to import raw materials and consumer goods from abroad found no way to transport them. A letter written by a German woman to thank an English friend for the gift of a CARE package, which contained, among other things, a lemon, shows how normal trade had broken down:

> We had a long debate as to what to do with the lemon. Pete, my little brother, did not know what it was as he had never seen one. Here people would go crazy if they saw a lemon or some nuts or even a single unrationed apple or plum. Last time I ate a hazel nut was in 1939, last time I had a banana in 1938. My last orange I had in 1942. . . .[5]

Japan's merchant fleet, which provided transportation among the home islands as well as for international trade, had been an early casualty of the war. Impoverished Europeans and Japanese needed dollars or gold not only to purchase American goods, but to hire the ships to bring the goods across the sea.

The devastation was so overwhelming, the problems of reconstruction so difficult, that it was not certain for several years that the world would recover. Food rationing in Britain actually became more severe *after* the war. The crippling winter weather of February 1947 almost brought the British economy to a halt. The railway system collapsed; coal could not be shipped from mines to factories, so factories closed, and power was cut off to residential districts. In the spring of 1947, industrial production in the British and American zones of Germany was only one-third what it had been in 1938.[6] Real wages in Belgium and France were falling in 1947, adding to political instability and leading to a wave of strikes that threatened to strangle their economies.

There were fears of a postwar recession. After every war in modern times, a deep recession had followed a short-lived boom. Everyone remembered vividly how the Great Depression had put the world on the road back to war. The link between economic prosperity and world peace had been dramatically demonstrated; economic chaos gave militaristic forces in Germany and Japan the chance to take power, and even in the middle of a life-and-death struggle, American leaders were determined that the future world economic system would provide even former enemies the full opportunity to prosper.

Establishing International Order

In 1945, despite America's industrial might, the victorious Allies faced a situation much less promising than the one facing those who negotiated the Treaty of Versailles in 1918.

America's leaders were well aware of reconstruction's importance. The failure of the Allies to construct an enduring peace after World War One haunted every American leader in 1945. President Roosevelt and the congressional leadership resolved that the U.S. would do its part to avoid the mistakes of the past.

They also believed that it was in America's interest to establish democratic governments in the former enemy nations after the war, and to give these democracies the prosperity they needed to succeed. As Roosevelt said to Congress in 1944, "People who are hungry and out of a job are the stuff of which dictatorships are made."[7] In the communiqué that became known as the Atlantic Charter, Roosevelt and Churchill defined the war aims of the U.S. and Great Britain. Two of the eight points were devoted to economic objectives:

[T]hey will endeavor, with due respect for their existing obligations, to further the enjoyment by all States, great or small, victor or vanquished, of access, on equal terms, to the trade and to the raw materials of the world which are needed for their economic prosperity;
[T]hey desire to bring about the fullest collaboration between all nations in the economic field with the object of securing for all, improved labor standards, economic advancement, and social security. . . .[8]

Long before the shooting stopped, British and American representatives met to determine the economic structure of the postwar world. While the British and Americans disagreed sharply on many issues—Britain wanted to preserve its privileges and special trading relations throughout its world empire, and America wanted that empire dismantled—they agreed on the critical points. From their deliberations came the first great economic agreement of the postwar world, the Bretton Woods agreement, hammered out at a meeting in Bretton Woods, New Hampshire. In subsequent years, as the magnitude of reconstruction became more clear, Bretton Woods would be modified and new agreements reached to expand and strengthen international cooperation. Bretton Woods and its associated initiatives (including the Marshall Plan, the International Monetary Fund, and the General Agreement on Trade and Tariffs, or GATT) formed the foundation for the great postwar expansion in Europe, America, and Japan.

The first principle of this international system was growth. The Allies hoped to avoid a return to the conditions of the 1930s —high unemployment and slow or stagnant growth. Besides preventing a depression, growth was regarded as the key to long-term balanced trade. "If active employment and ample purchasing power can be sustained in major centers of world trade," wrote John Maynard Keynes, "the problem of surpluses and unwanted exports will largely disappear."[9]

The Americans and the British believed that recovery depended on the ability of European countries to purchase capital goods from America. Since Europe was without the dollars or gold to buy goods, the U.S. would have to supply the money. Just as national governments used deficit spending to stimulate their domestic economies, the U.S. would spend the dollars necessary to stimulate the international economy.

The second principle of the postwar world, then, was that the U.S. would underwrite the growth of the world's economy. Only the U.S. had the productive capacity and the financial reserves for such a role. This role was in both the short- and long-term interests of the U.S. In the short term, American manufacturers had to adjust to the loss of the demand for their products represented by U.S. wartime spending. While the pent-up desire for consumer goods unavailable during the war could replace some of this demand, without export markets U.S. manufacturers would have to cut back on their production, plunging the country into recession.

Over the longer term, it was in America's interest to promote the recovery of Europe and Japan for security reasons. As the wartime alliance with the Soviet Union chilled, the U.S. focused on a new alliance that would include the noncommunist victors and vanquished of World War Two. By the late 1940s, the U.S. was promoting limited rearmament in Germany and Japan; the willingness and ability of these countries to bear such a burden was obviously dependent on their economic health.

Another concept guiding the makers of the postwar world was the principle of multilateralism. The International Monetary Fund (IMF) and the International Bank for Reconstruction and Development (better known as the World Bank) would not be operated by any one nation. Instead, these international financial agencies would have a large membership with many interests represented.

On a broader basis, the U.S. encouraged the political and economic integration of Western Europe. Even before the war, the levels of productivity and industrial output in the U.S. had been a source of wonder in Europe. Both European and American observers agreed that the reasons for America's rapid development included the size of the U.S. market, which created economies of scale in production, and the benefit of a continent-wide market. Goods produced in Yugoslavia had to cross half a dozen international frontiers before reaching a consumer in the Netherlands, while goods from California could be sold and consumed in New York without any customs duties or delays. Many Americans and some Europeans wanted to transplant the American system to the other side of the Atlantic.

The U.S. was also determined to lower the barriers to international trade that existed before the war. Much to the chagrin of the British, the U.S. used its economic muscle to move the world down the road to universal free trade in the 1940s and 1950s. The British were forced to modify their system of "imperial preference" and to lower tariff barriers between their empire and the rest of the world. America supported movements for independence among countries in what would soon come to be called the Third World, and sometimes imposed sanctions on European countries that recognized too slowly the independence of their former colonies.

The system for international commerce we put in place after World War Two was based on the concept of open markets and the process of multilateral negotiations to reduce trade barriers. After the 1930s, when discrimination and retaliation in trade policy deepened and prolonged the Great Depression, an International Trade Organization (ITO) was proposed to promote free and stable trade among nations. The ITO would have been a supranational organization with jurisdiction over global trade in its entirety—imports, exports, adjustments, labor markets, and differing economic practices and standards among countries. Proposed in the same period as the World Bank and the IMF, the ITO was rejected by Congress. Congress felt that world trade was not yet interdependent enough to justify the creation of a powerful international agency to deal with trade issues. Instead it settled for the less ambitious GATT system.

GATT was originally intended to be an interim measure to reduce tariffs while waiting for the creation of the ITO; once the ITO was dead, GATT was all we had left, and, by default, it became the principal international forum for negotiations over trade.

Before the GATT system was developed, trade between the nations took place under bilateral agreements; given the large number of nations involved and the huge number of products traded internationally, this gradually led to a system that was both chaotic and inefficient. Under GATT's "most favored nation" system, nations extended to many countries the treatment afforded to "the most favored nation" in any bilateral agreement. The result was to substitute a multilateral and global network for bilateral agreements so that world trade became simpler, more free, and more equal.

The Postwar World at Work

Much to the surprise of the skeptics, the postwar arrangements worked brilliantly and the world recovered more quickly than most believed possible. Though the Soviet Union forced the division of Europe into communist and noncommunist zones and interrupted long-standing relationships, Western Europe not only repaired the damage of war, but went on to enjoy a generation of rapid growth. From 1949 to 1963, industrial production tripled in Austria, Italy, Germany, and Greece, and doubled in Denmark, Finland, France, the Netherlands and Norway. Even the output of anemic Britain increased by 50 percent.[10] Unemployment fell to levels below those of the best years between the world wars, while national incomes rose faster than in any time in history. Phenomenal growth rates were posted in the 1950s and 1960s. Japan regularly grew more than 10 percent per year, while rates of 7 percent were common in Western Europe.

By the late 1950s the misery and anxiety of the early postwar years had faded, and a new sense of confidence about the future pervaded the advanced market economies. In the 1960s, the postwar institutions and policies worked so well that we forgot they were there, and forgot that our prosperity was the result not of chance, but of steps taken long before.

The postwar order, which seemed so permanent in the good years of the 1950s and 1960s, could not go on forever. The strains emerged first in the 1950s and early 1960s as a dollar problem. A decade of pumping dollars into the European and Japanese economies had worked too well; these economies were now flush with dollars, and absorbing more dollars all the time, not only from the rapid growth of their exports to the U.S., but from private loans and the huge expenses associated with maintaining American bases in Europe. Besides earning dollars from exports, Japan profited enormously from American spending on the Korean War.

In those days, foreign holders of dollars could still demand redemption of their paper currency in gold at $35 an ounce. (Americans were forbidden to own gold currency by a Depression-era law until the 1970s.) In the first years after the war, Europeans wanted America's products—our food and capital goods—more than they wanted our gold. But in the 1960s European nations had accumulated more dollars than they needed to buy American goods. Many Europeans inside and outside government came to feel that the dollar was overvalued, and they preferred to redeem their paper money for gold. Charles de Gaulle, the French war hero who became president of France in 1958, saw the French dollar surplus as an opportunity to clip the pinfeathers of the American eagle. The French treasury began presenting claims on the U.S. Treasury for payment in gold.

On the American side, President Kennedy treated the dollar problem—and the balance of payments deficit it represented—as a matter of serious concern. As Arthur Schlesinger wrote in his history of the Kennedy Administration:

> Kennedy used to tell his advisers . . . that the two things which scared him the most were nuclear war and the payments deficit. Once he half-humorously derided the notion that nuclear weapons were essential to international strength. "What really matters," he said, "is the strength of the currency." [11]

In the 1960s alone, the enormous gold reserves of the U.S. were reduced by over 25 percent, to redeem dollars presented by foreign governments. The number of "Eurodollars"—dollars in the hands of Europeans—grew, as did pressure on the dollar. This led, in the 1970s, to dramatic changes in the world's financial system; the U.S. was forced off a fixed exchange rate and the gold standard. A system of floating exchange rates among the world's leading currencies was adopted and continues today.

The changing balance in trade was a major part of the dollar problem. As the 1960s progressed, the European countries and Japan greatly expanded their exports.

Value of Exports [12]
(Billions of Dollars)

	1960	1965	% change
U.S.	20.4	27.2	32%
West Germany	11.4	17.8	56%
Britain	10.6	13.7	29%
France	6.9	10.1	46%
Japan	4.1	8.5	107%
Canada	5.6	8.1	45%
Italy	3.6	7.2	100%
Holland	4.0	6.4	60%
Sweden	2.6	4.0	54%

In 1960 the U.S. produced 29 percent of the total exports among these countries; by 1965 that share was down to less than 26 percent, and the percentage would continue to decline for the next twenty years. (See Chart 2.1.) While the U.S. economy continued to grow at a healthy rate, the growth of other countries was altering the structure of the world economy.

The effect of their export growth was gradually to reduce the U.S. trade surplus in goods. But this was the part of the nation's balance sheet, or current account, which made up for our spending overseas and our increasing appetite for imports. Consequently our overall balance of payments started to deteriorate.

The challenge to U.S. economic superiority was in some ways the result of differences between the American economy and the economies of the other advanced industrial democracies. In Europe and Japan after the war, governments had little choice but to play a decisive economic role. Food rationing continued for many years in some countries, while shortages of fuel and raw materials forced others to institute plans and ra-

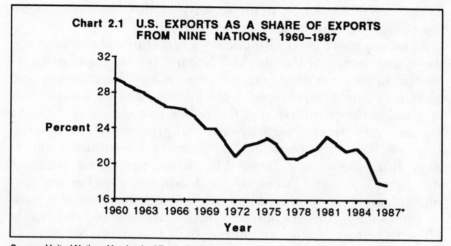

Chart 2.1   U.S. EXPORTS AS A SHARE OF EXPORTS FROM NINE NATIONS, 1960–1987

Source: *United Nations Yearbook of Trade Statistics*

Note: *The nine nations are the U.S., West Germany, United Kingdom, France, Japan, Canada, Italy, Holland, and Sweden. Data for 1961, 1962, 1964, 1966, and 1971 were not available, and so figures graphed are interpolated.*

1987 is an estimate based on six months of data.

tioning in their industrial sectors. Most important, the initial dollar shortage limited the availability of key imports, and government was the only agency capable of deciding whether scarce dollars should pay for wheat to raise the bread ration or for imported machinery and fuel.

Europe and Japan concentrated their economic efforts on reducing their dependence on American imports while increasing their dollar earnings through exports to the U.S. This required directing their resources toward goods for export. In 1945, for example, only 2 percent of Britain's factories were producing goods for export.[13] Strict controls limited the ability of British citizens and firms to acquire American dollars for personal consumption, and every incentive was given to firms willing to produce goods for export to the American market.

Virtually every country had its plans for rebuilding its industry and penetrating the lucrative American market. The Volkswagen, the transistor radio, the Datsuns, and a host of other products that appeared in the U.S. represented the fruits of their strategies. Policies that favored investment in new and efficient technologies resulted in handsome annual productiv-

35

ity gains—more than 5 percent per year in Germany through the 1950s, with similar gains elsewhere.

Although there were difficulties and failures along the way, the governments of Europe and Japan were spectacularly successful in orchestrating national recoveries. The recovery and growth of Europe and Japan were a triumph of economic strategy and of the partnership of the public and private sectors. As we saw in Chapter 1, year by year and product by product, the U.S. was losing its economic supremacy to determined competitors. But this success changed the world's economic balance. America's economic dominance immediately after the war was recognized by its leaders as an unusual situation, and the postwar plan for reconstruction and development was a deliberate effort to bring the world economy back to a stable balance. As balance returned, there was less and less need for the U.S. to bear the full responsibility for keeping the world economy growing.

But America and its allies did not respond to the altered international environment by fundamentally reforming the aging international economic system. Unfortunately, the same qualities of statesmanship that went into creating the postwar order were not available for the task of replacing it with more equitable arrangements. Instead, a series of patchwork, quick-fix solutions were adopted; with the passage of time, these solutions have become more expensive and less effective.

"The characteristic danger of great nations is that they may at last fail from not comprehending the great institutions which they have created," Walter Bagehot warned his contemporaries in nineteenth-century Britain.[14] In the 1970s and 1980s, America has suffered the consequences of failing to tailor institutions to the changes created by the institutions themselves.

The Gathering Storm

YEARS OF UPHEAVAL
In the years since 1968, the strains in the world economy have grown more apparent and the postwar system has worked less

well. A study for the OECD showed that from the mid 1970s to the early 1980s, unemployment doubled in the advanced countries, and growth rates were cut in half.[15] (See Chart 2.2.)

August 15, 1971, was the boundary between the early postwar period of rapid growth and the later period of faltering international economic performance. On that date, President Nixon ended the keystone of the Bretton Woods agreement—fixed exchange rates and the commitment of the U.S. to redeem dollars for gold at $35 an ounce.

In the weeks that followed, the world's bankers and finance officials tried to set up a substitute system, but could reach no agreement. Floating exchange rates and the abandonment of the gold standard, originally presented as a temporary measure, became permanent. Since 1971 the dollar has continued to fluctuate against leading European and Asian currencies, rising as high as 350 yen to the dollar and falling as low as 120. (See Chart 2.3.)

The end of Bretton Woods and the depreciation of the dollar signaled the beginning of the 1970s, an era many people still remember for its most frightening feature—the inflation that doubled consumer prices in ten years.

The surging inflation of the 1970s was due in part to the drop

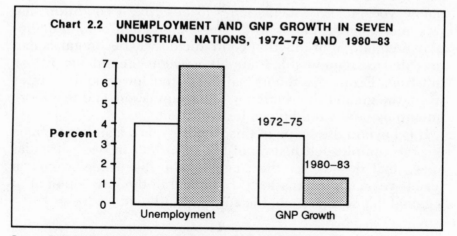

Chart 2.2 **UNEMPLOYMENT AND GNP GROWTH IN SEVEN INDUSTRIAL NATIONS, 1972–75 AND 1980–83**

Source: Organization for Economic Cooperation and Development

Note: The seven nations are the U.S., United Kingdom, Japan, West Germany, France, Italy and Canada.

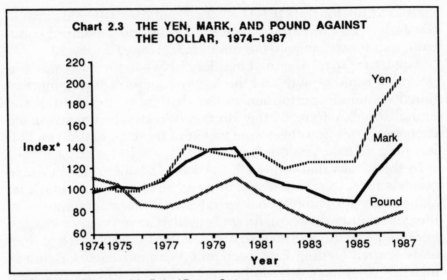

Chart 2.3 THE YEN, MARK, AND POUND AGAINST THE DOLLAR, 1974–1987

Source: Board of Governors of the Federal Reserve System
*1974-1976=100

in the value of the dollar. For example, OPEC's wave of price increases in 1973–1974 was an attempt to preserve the value of its oil holdings because they were calculated in dollars.

Worse, skyrocketing inflation was only one symptom of economic poor health of the 1970s. A new word entered the economic vocabulary, "stagflation," to describe a condition that was once thought impossible. The combination of high unemployment and high inflation contradicted what economists had regarded as an inevitable trade-off between unemployment and inflation. Economic theory said that the lower jobless rates went, the greater the tendency to have inflation, and that more unemployment would mean less inflation.

It is beyond the scope of this Commission's mandate to trace out the complicated history of the 1970s, but in two particular areas, that decade set the stage for the disturbing events of recent years. In international trade and in the development of a global financial system, the 1970s are still with us today.

THE INTERNATIONAL TRADING SYSTEM
The 1970s saw sweeping changes in the way the world trades. In the First World (i.e., the major Western industrialized na-

tions, including Japan) new levels of competition were reached. For the first time in their competition with the U.S., Europe and Japan began to win.

To be sure, they had economic troubles of their own in the 1970s, but they were also reaping the rewards of their previous policies. In Europe, the 1970s were a time of greater integration. From its fragile beginnings at the time of the Marshall Plan, growing cooperation among the Western European nations was the dominant factor of the European landscape. The European Economic Community, better known as the Common Market, helped manufacturers and banks within it enjoy the advantages once reserved for American producers: a huge internal market and a large pool of skilled labor.

The U.S., of course, had taken the lead in encouraging the establishment of the Common Market. One of the conditions of the Marshall Plan had been the formation of a joint European agency to receive and administer the aid. In the negotiations that led to the GATT system, the U.S. left room for regional customs unions like the Common Market, even though American goods would trade at a disadvantage within such a zone. The American negotiators knew that a Common Market would be a formidable competitor, but that was the price of a peaceful and healthy Western Europe.

By the 1970s the process of European integration had progressed to the point that Europe had become an aggressive competitor in many fields. Government-sponsored consortia had embarked on ambitious programs for technological development; different countries combined their resources to challenge American industries. In civil aviation, an Anglo-French joint effort created the Concorde, while a wider consortium developed and marketed—with government help—the Airbus, a passenger jet which carved out a niche for itself in what had once been a completely American industry. The Common Market's agricultural program was an expensive economic disaster for the European countries, but even there European producers made inroads into American markets.

In Japan, the 1970s saw the maturation of the export-led strategy for recovery that was founded in the darkest days of the 1940s. After a decade of exporting cheap plastic goods and textiles, the Japanese developed strong shipbuilding, steel, electronics, optics, and automobile industries. From scratch, Japan built industries whose products were as good as any in the world—or better.

In many other advanced countries as well, long-term national strategies came to fruition in the 1960s and 1970s. By contrast, American political, business, and labor leaders took our strength for granted. Leaders of other advanced countries had a more practical understanding of the public and private sectors, the needs of their economies, and the interdependence of their industries.

These leaders shared with their industries a strong sense of the crucial relationship between labor and management. In West Germany and Japan, labor and management formed particularly close ties; when government was included as a third member of the partnership, these industries built strength and flexibility which served them well in the turbulent 1970s and 1980s. Although unemployment rose and growth slowed throughout the advanced countries, the Common Market and Japan competed with the U.S. at an increasing advantage.

Our competitors also understood, in a practical way, the relationship between technology and industrial development. While America sent many of its brightest young people into careers in law and finance, our competitors never lost sight of the primacy of production. Sustained attention to production meant that our foreign competitors began to narrow the productivity gap. Their workers were becoming as productive as American workers. (See Chart 1.11.)

At the same time, the developing world experienced a decade of revolutionary industrial development. No longer were Third World countries to be regarded chiefly as sources for raw materials like minerals and oil, or agricultural commodities like rubber and cotton. Between them, these changes in First and Third World conditions changed the economic environment for the U.S.

The consequences of the trade strategies pursued by certain Third World countries were first felt in the 1970s. Over time, the newly industrializing countries (NICs) initiated new strategies for production. Just as Japan had moved up the economic ladder from simple manufacturing to higher value-added goods in the 1960s, new competitors were able to do the same in the 1970s.

Easy access to foreign technology and capital, low wages, and a variety of tax, credit, regulatory, exchange-rate, and import restrictions combined with well-educated hardworking populations helped the NICs develop their industry. Often these countries were encouraged to seek export-led growth by the U.S. government as well as by U.S.-based multinational corporations. "Export processing zones" (EPZs) played an important role in this strategy. The local host government would designate a certain area as an export processing zone and lay out the infrastructure (harbor access, ground and air transportation links, reliable power service, etc.) for an industrial district. Companies locating in these zones enjoyed special treatment under tax laws and were excused from certain labor rights requirements, antipollution controls, and other regulations. Not surprisingly, EPZs boomed. The first was established near Shannon Airport in Ireland in 1967; by the end of the 1970s there were more than eighty such zones in Third World countries.[16]

Rapid growth through exports and mounting trade surpluses have followed, but export-led growth strategies had major flaws. When only a handful of countries pursued these policies, the side effects were limited, but as more and more countries jumped on the export-led growth bandwagon, the limits of this approach became more apparent. While it is true their high growth strategies encourage investment and therefore demand for capital goods, countries following the Japanese model essentially seem to expect a free ride in the world economy: they depend on the willingness of others to absorb the increased output that comes with higher productivity and rising capacity. This is particularly true when they shelter their own markets from imports. In effect, this strategy assumes other countries will take responsibility for growth in world demand. This was the role shouldered by the U.S. after World War Two, but the U.S. does not have an unlimited ability to absorb foreign goods.

In many cases, the developing nations defended their competitive edge by holding wage increases below the level of productivity growth. This exacted an increasing toll in the form of social unrest and political instability which threatened to undermine the very production on which these countries were coming to depend.

Production moved from the U.S. to Korea, Taiwan, Hong Kong, and the other NICs, while the growth of purchasing power slowed in the U.S. and the production of foreign goods for the American market accelerated.

By the early 1980s, the world was more dependent on American demand and American willingness to accept asymmetrical trading relationships than ever before. Europe, Japan, and the Third World all saw the U.S. market as their best hope for growth. Without U.S. commitment to a role as the "consumer of last resort," every country in the noncommunist world faced serious economic problems. Yet the U.S. was less and less capable of playing this role without suffering serious internal problems. Developments of the 1970s set the stage for our international trade deficit and the liquidation of our position as a net creditor in the 1980s.

THE SLIPPERY SLOPE OF GLOBAL FINANCE

As production was becoming globalized in the 1970s, so was finance. The emergence of global financial markets and the new mobility of capital dramatically altered the nature of the world economy. Capital flows began to dwarf trade flows. The financial markets became continuous round-the-clock worldwide exchanges. The world had traveled a long way from the early postwar period, and the institutions developed then looked increasingly inadequate in light of the vastly expanded scope of world finance.

Two forces drove the development of the new global financial markets. The vast expansion of the Eurodollar market in the 1960s created new opportunities for international banking, and the economic consequences of the end of Bretton Woods made international banking critical to the economic health of many companies and countries.

The years of economic miracles in Europe and Japan were marked by strict controls on the flow of capital across national boundaries. European borrowers flocked to New York capital markets because only the U.S. offered the opportunity to borrow large numbers of dollars in a relatively free atmosphere. But even the U.S. maintained capital controls in the 1960s.[17]

The Eurodollar market, based on the excess dollars that began to accumulate in Europe in the 1950s, helped bring about the revolution in banking. Eurodollar banking began in a small way in the mid-1950s as Swiss and British banks looked for ways to use their dollar balances profitably.[18] The market grew slowly at first, then explosively in the 1960s.

The most important feature of the Eurodollar market was that it was not controlled by any national authority. American banks were strictly regulated at the start of the 1970s. This dated to the horrifying experience of 1933, when a national banking crisis forced every bank in the U.S. to close, and competition among banks was severely restricted. Both the interest rates that banks could charge and the rates that they could pay were regulated by the government. Another set of regulations limited the terms banks could offer to most foreign borrowers and lenders.

Eurodollars, however, were free from these restrictions. They had escaped the supervision of the FDIC and the Federal Reserve. Banks could charge and offer any interest rate they liked on the Eurodollar market, and in the competition for business, both borrowers and savers could get better rates.

This freedom from supervision became extremely important during the inflation of the 1970s. Inflation helps borrowers and hurts lenders. With American interest rates on savings accounts limited by law to 4 and 5 percent, and inflation running at 6 percent or more, those who kept their money in American commercial banks lost value each year. The unregulated Eurodollar markets in Europe offered an important opportunity to those who wanted more realistic interest rates on their savings, especially before the Federal Reserve imposed reserve requirements on Eurodollar accounts. Borrowers, too, appreciated the flexibility of the Eurodollar market. Eurodollar rates might be high, but money could be found by those who needed to borrow.

The end of the fixed exchange rates of the Bretton Woods system also played a role in the growth of international financial markets. Companies with significant international business were uncomfortable with the risks to their profits associated with floating currency rates. A 10 percent rise or fall in the dollar could wipe out a whole year's profits overnight. Companies learned to hedge their currency risks by buying and selling futures contracts in foreign currencies.

Business in the international financial markets boomed—from a few hundred million dollars a year in the 1950s to $25 billion and then $75 billion a day in the 1980s. (Exact figures are impossible to get in this unregulated market.)[19] American banks hurried to participate in this market, establishing offshore offices where they could deal in Eurodollars without the uncomfortable restrictions that dogged them at home.

The inflation of the 1970s had another consequence: OPEC's price increases forced the financial system to cope with huge new flows of dollars. The OPEC countries accumulated enormous hoards of surplus dollars; they wanted to invest these surpluses in safe, profitable, interest-bearing accounts. International banks were the only agencies capable of handling investments on such a scale, and OPEC was only too happy to see them take the risks.

Providentially—or so it seemed to many at the time—the increase in the price of oil that created these hoards of petrodollars created a demand for huge loans. Developing countries needed to import fuel to run their industries; what was more natural than for these countries to borrow the surplus dollars of the exporters to finance their imports? The developing countries, even those with oil revenues such as Mexico, also realized they needed to accelerate their industrial development. To make these investments—including investments in oil exploration that might reduce their import bills—these countries turned, of course, to the banks.

Bank vaults were sloshing with petrodollars to lend; governments, including the American government, were concerned that the developing countries have access to capital. The result, of course, was the massive lending to Third World countries that now amounts to more than $1.1 trillion.[20]

By 1980, the outline of the Third World debt crisis was beginning to emerge. In the coming years, the Third World debt would have a long-term effect on the world's economy and banking system. Some of the largest and supposedly shrewdest banks in the world had made enormous loans to countries which could not meet their obligations on schedule. For the first time since World War Two, the prospect of a global financial crisis became a real factor in the day-to-day thinking of bankers and regulators.

Globalization of production and of finance: both developments held out great promise for the future of the world, but both raised new serious problems. In the 1980s it would be up to the U.S. to provide leadership for a troubled and increasingly unstable world economy, but the U.S. was no longer the self-confident colossus of earlier years. During the 1980s, America would roll up trillions in deficits and debts—without addressing the growing problems of a world economic system that was seriously out of balance.

CHAPTER THREE

Debt, Deficits, and the Dollar: The End of the Postwar Era

Standing Tall on Borrowed Money

"ARE you better off than you were four years ago?" asked the Republican candidate in 1980. The American people answered clearly. With one of the most dramatic election victories in history, the Reagan Administration enjoyed a majority in the Senate while a coalition of conservative Democrats and Republicans formed behind the Administration's program in the House.

There was a widespread feeling in the country that the U.S. had taken a wrong turn in the 1970s. The defeat in Indochina, the OPEC shocks, the years of inflation, and the rise in unemployment created what was called a national malaise. Americans of both parties believed that the time had come for sweeping changes, and they were willing to give the new Administration their support as it grappled with these problems.

Perhaps the most striking single symptom of the ailing economic system was the rapid inflation of the late 1970s and early 1980s. After years of relative stability, prices rose at an accelerating rate all through the 1970s. The fight against inflation began with Carter's appointment of Paul Volcker to the Federal Reserve, and it continued under the new Administration. Interest rates soared, cutting off economic activity and plunging the country into the most severe economic contraction since World War Two. By 1982, American unemployment reached 12.8 percent, its highest level since the Depression. The inflation fighters had overshot their target, and the medicine was hurting the patient. In the years that followed, instead of inflation, the economy faced deflation as falling prices in what *Business Week* called the "Deflation Belt" threatened to ruin farmers, small businessmen, banks, and ordinary citizens who had gone deeply into debt during the years of inflation.[1]

In the face of these developments—and after the 1982 election results—the Administration made an about-face. It embarked on an expansionary program based on deficits of an unprecedented size.[2] (See Chart 3.1.)

The immediate results were spectacular. After falling 2 percent in 1982, real GNP grew at a 3.6 percent rate in 1983 and a soaring 6.4 percent rate in 1984.[3] It seemed at the time that the ads about "Morning in America" were justified. The U.S. was rapidly growing while the rest of the world stagnated or, in the case of some Third World economies, shrank. Unemployment rose to record levels in Europe, passing 20 percent of the work force in Spain, reaching the teens in Britain and France.[4] Administraton officials and economists lectured the Europeans and anyone else who would listen about the superior virtues of our economic policies.

In the jubilation over the resumption of rapid growth in the

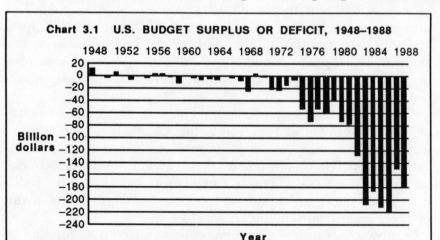

Chart 3.1 U.S. BUDGET SURPLUS OR DEFICIT, 1948–1988

Source: Office of Management and Budget; for 1988 projection, U. S. Congress, Congressional Budget Office

U.S., however, many overlooked what would soon become the most serious economic problem in the U.S.: the sudden collapse of the balance of trade.

The Great Binge, 1983–1987

While the budget deficits have received the greatest publicity in the 1980s, the trade deficits may prove more important in the long run. The U.S. balance of trade had been worsening for many years, but the deterioration accelerated in 1981, and six years later the U.S. would routinely run quarterly deficits that were larger than the trade deficit for all of 1981.[5] (See Chart 1.1.)

These huge balance of trade deficits did not come from nowhere. One factor at work was the rise in the value of the dollar. High interest rates attracted investors from all over the world to the U.S., eager to buy the IOUs of the U.S. Treasury. Everyone wanted his investments in dollars, so the dollar's value rose rapidly against other currencies of our leading trading partners.

In fact, the rush of investors to dollars forced European governments to keep their interest rates uncomfortably high to prevent a collapse of their currencies. These rates helped keep their growth rates slow, and the difference between the sluggish European economies and the dynamic American one only made the dollar-denominated investments more attractive still.

The high dollar helped spark a boom in the financial sector of the economy, but the results for American manufacturers were very different. As the dollar rose, American goods became more expensive in foreign markets, and imported goods became cheaper here. This was, however, only a part of the problem. Our goods had stopped being competitive in many markets even when the dollar was low.

Our own loss of competitiveness was caused by a number of homegrown factors, including loss of the technological edge historically held by American firms, declining growth in productivity, sluggish levels of investment and falling rates of profitability, and an increasingly unqualified labor force. They added up, in too many cases, to products whose quality and cost left too much to be desired.

An additional factor at work that helped turn the trade deficit into a trade disaster was the "go it alone" or unilateral nature of the American decision to stimulate growth in 1982. Ever since World War Two, American governments had made their decisions about whether to stimulate our economy or to rein it in based on purely domestic considerations. Our economic might was such that other countries had to adjust their policies to ours. But in 1983 this was no longer true. The U.S. stepped on the accelerator, but our principal trading partners still had their foot on the brakes because of high interest rates and policies to fight inflation.

The uneven rates of growth in the First World were not the only cause for concern. The collapse of demand in much of the Third World hurt our efforts. Falling oil prices cut OPEC's ability to buy foreign goods, while the combination of falling commodity prices and the rising costs of debt forced Latin America to cut back its consumption of imports while it stepped up its exports.

The interplay of these factors had a revolutionary effect on world trade and on the position of the U.S. The federal deficit stimulated demands for goods and services of all kinds in the U.S., and much of this new demand was met by foreign goods. The trade deficits of the 1980s were unimaginable by any earlier standard. In the 1970s we were still net creditors to the rest of the world. Even though we were buying more imports than we were selling exports, and therefore were in a trade deficit, we made enough money from interest on loans, profits on foreign operations, and other services to more than cover the deficit in trade. But in the 1980s, the enormous deficit completely overwhelmed these payments and pulled the U.S. into debt. No country had ever run such a sustained deficit in peacetime; no country had ever run through its accumulated assets to finance current consumption at such a rate. A creditor nation since 1914, and the world's largest creditor for most of that time, the U.S. was suddenly by 1986 a debtor. The U.S., and the world, will feel the consequences of this historic change for years, perhaps decades, to come, and nowhere will those consequences be more evident than in our trading system.

If the 1970s were the decade in which Bretton Woods collapsed, the 1980s were the decade in which the international trading system, in particular GATT, reached the end of its tether. The problems of the two systems are similar: Bretton Woods came apart because the U.S. could not go on forever being the world's banker, supplying dollars for economic liquidity and growth, and our trading system faltered because the U.S. could not go on forever being the world's consumer, buying huge amounts of goods from every region of the world, accumulating enormous, ultimately unsustainable deficits with both the First World and the Third.

The Debt Disaster and the Third World

The American balance of trade with the non-OPEC countries of the Third World deteriorated sharply in the 1980s. The following chart shows how imports declined through the 1980s in some of our best markets in this hemisphere.[6] (See Chart 3.2.) In fact, as the figures below show, Latin America's imports fell 33 percent during the 1980s.

Latin America's Imports, 1980–1986
(Billions of Dollars)

1980	1981	1982	1983	1984	1985	1986
115	121	93	70	72	73	79

These rapid and substantial changes in Latin America's balance of trade (see Chart 3.3)[7] did not happen by accident. They were caused by the emergence of a debt disaster for the Third World.

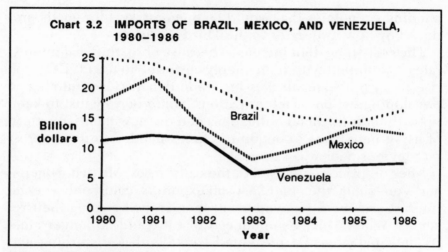

Chart 3.2 IMPORTS OF BRAZIL, MEXICO, AND VENEZUELA, 1980–1986

Source: International Monetary Fund

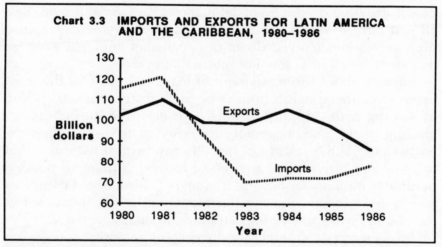

Chart 3.3 IMPORTS AND EXPORTS FOR LATIN AMERICA AND THE CARIBBEAN, 1980–1986

Source: International Monetary Fund

The quadrupling of oil prices in the mid-1970s led many Western banks to recycle billions of "petrodollars" as loans to the Third World. Developing nations were encouraged to borrow heavily to build up their export-oriented industries and infrastructure. Both lenders and borrowers assumed that the United States and other industrial countries would have expanding economies that would be open markets for goods produced by new industries in the Third World.

The cost of the debt increased because of soaring real interest rates. Combined with high energy costs due to the OPEC price rise in 1979, the result was big trade deficits for a number of developing nations. Debtor nations had to borrow just to keep up with their financial obligations and the now familiar pattern of using new loans to obtain the funds needed to pay interest on previous ones was started.

After oil prices collapsed in the early 1980s, Mexico, Nigeria, and Venezuela, the chief LDC oil exporters, could only service interest and meet repayments of their loans by using their reserves. When Mexico announced that it could no longer meet its debt payments, it presented banks with a disturbing and unexpected turn of events. Governments and the banks had always assumed that debts could be serviced indefinitely by new borrowing on the financial markets. In 1985 and 1986, Brazil and Peru reduced or suspended interest payments because their economies slowed down or because of domestic policies that sustained a high level of internal demand.

Concern about the repayment of loans led many of the most exposed financial institutions to begin to restrict their recycling of lending to developing nations. This occurred during the beginning of the U.S. economic recovery in 1983–84, when exports to the U.S. picked up, but other industrial nations failed to grow and provide the real boost in overall demand needed by debtor nations. Consequently, many Third World countries had to make extraordinary adjustments in their economies. But the chasm between earnings and indebtedness persisted.

Once the crisis emerged and stringent austerity plans were implemented by developing nations, the economies of these nations experienced another shock: the massive shift of capital into foreign banks. This "flight capital" reduced the funds that were available for investment locally, created pressures on local currencies, and raised inflation rates to double- or triple-digit levels. These factors contributed to the stagnation of developing nations' economies, making it more difficult for these nations to repay their debt.

The way debtor countries pay foreign debts is to earn the

money by running trade surpluses. Latin America cut imports to the bone and put its energies behind increased exporting to pay off its foreign debts. This policy, which the U.S. helped persuade the Latin American countries to adopt, was supposed to ease the financial crisis by putting Third World debt on a stable basis. Not only did the policy fail to achieve this goal, it had an unforeseen side effect: austerity programs in Latin America contributed to the slowdown in world growth, which in turn decreased demand for Latin America's products on world markets.

Output, real wages, consumption, and investment demand to some degree all fell in Latin America. Per capita output in 1986 was almost 8 percent lower than in 1980, the last year before the crisis. Unemployment grew at an annual average rate of 6.3 percent in the first five years of the crisis, and where real wages didn't decline, their rate of growth slowed. In Mexico real wages fell 5 percent between 1979 and 1984.[8] Private consumption stagnated in Mexico. In Brazil it fell from a healthy 9.1 percent average annual growth in the fifteen years from 1965 to 1980 to an anemic 2.2 percent. In Argentina, private consumption actually fell at an annual rate of 1.2 percent from 1980 to 1985.[9] (See Chart 3.4.)

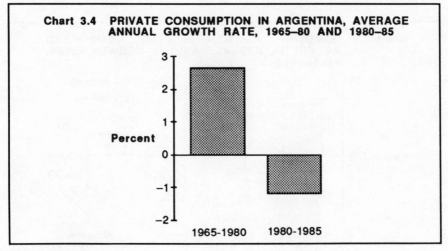

Chart 3.4 PRIVATE CONSUMPTION IN ARGENTINA, AVERAGE ANNUAL GROWTH RATE, 1965–80 AND 1980–85

Source: World Bank

Private investment was even worse hit. Medium size and large enterprises stopped growing throughout Latin America, and in three leading Latin countries—Mexico, Brazil, and Argentina—private investment declined: 9.1 percent per year in Mexico, 5.5 percent in Brazil, and 13.8 percent in Argentina.[10] (See Chart 3.5.)

Latin America's troubles were a major factor in our trade deficit. In 1985 we imported $8.8 billion more from Latin America than we did in 1981.[11] (See Chart 3.6.) Our exports to Latin America, meanwhile, fell by more than $11.1 billion, 55 percent of the total fall in our exports. Almost one-quarter of the total drop in our exports came from import cutbacks in just one country: Mexico.[12] (See Chart 3.7.) Not surprisingly, the result was a painful and prolonged worsening in the U.S. balance of trade with the region.

The costs of this situation stand out even more clearly if we contrast it with what would have happened if Latin America's imports had been able to keep growing through the 1980s at the same rate they achieved in the 1970s. Our exports to Latin America doubled between 1976 and 1981.[13] (See Chart 3.8.) If Latin America's growth had not stopped in 1981, and if the U.S. maintained its market share of exports to those countries, our balance of trade would be $66 billion more favorable than it is. (See Chart 3.9.)

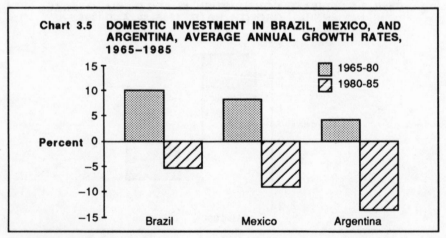

Chart 3.5 DOMESTIC INVESTMENT IN BRAZIL, MEXICO, AND ARGENTINA, AVERAGE ANNUAL GROWTH RATES, 1965–1985

1965-80
1980-85

Percent

Brazil   Mexico   Argentina

Source: World Bank

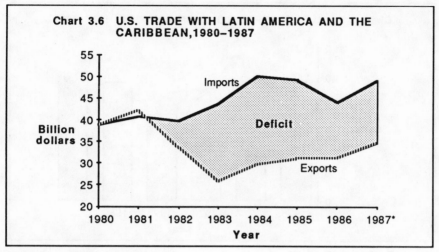

Chart 3.6 U.S. TRADE WITH LATIN AMERICA AND THE CARIBBEAN, 1980–1987

Source: International Monetary Fund

1987 estimate based on 11 months of data

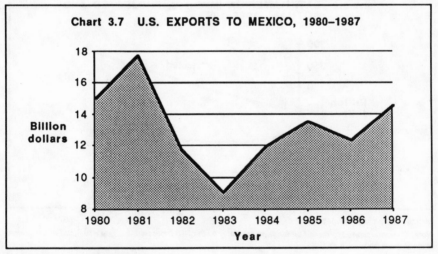

Chart 3.7 U.S. EXPORTS TO MEXICO, 1980–1987

Source: International Monetary Fund

From 1980 to 1985, American-made goods actually gained market share in Latin America. But because the market shrank, our total exports fell while our market share increased. We were actually more competitive in Latin American markets in 1985 than we were in 1980, but Latin America's poverty meant

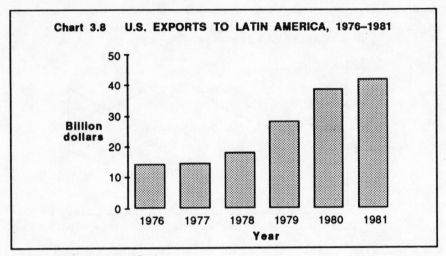

Chart 3.8   U.S. EXPORTS TO LATIN AMERICA, 1976–1981

Source: International Monetary Fund

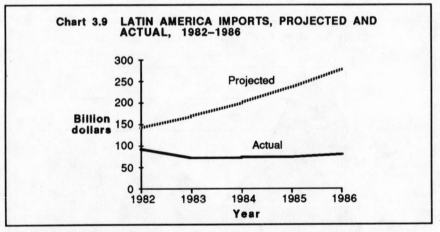

Chart 3.9   LATIN AMERICA IMPORTS, PROJECTED AND ACTUAL, 1982–1986

Source: International Monetary Fund

Note: The projections are based on average annual growth of 18.3 percent, the rate at which Latin America imports grew from 1976 to 1981.

that we were not able to reap the rewards of the competitive gains we achieved.

The lesson is clear: when Latin America prospers, we prosper, and when it suffers, we do too. Cooperation among the countries that share this hemisphere is in everybody's interest.

Oil on Our Trade Waters

OPEC's role in the 1970s was clear. By jacking up oil prices, OPEC piled up huge surpluses and contributed to inflationary pressures around the world. On the positive side, OPEC became an important market, and consumer goods, capital goods, and construction teams poured into the OPEC countries from all over the world. Saudi Arabia and its allies adopted ambitious expansion programs to build up new industries for the days when the oil would be gone. At the peak, in 1982, OPEC imports reached $153 billion. But then the price of oil began to decline and OPEC had to cut back on its imports as the value of its exports fell.[14] (See Chart 3.10.)

Between OPEC and Latin America, demand for imports in the developing world fell $100 billion in four years. The result was not simply to decrease the market for American goods. The markets for the NICs, Japan, and Europe also shrank, and there was only one economy large enough to take up the slack. All over the world, exporters turned their attention from the Third World to the U.S.; we had become the only important expanding export market in the world, and the world's most sophisti-

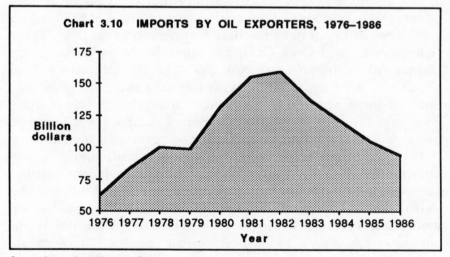

Chart 3.10   IMPORTS BY OIL EXPORTERS, 1976–1986

Source: International Monetary Fund

cated business executives made the U.S. their primary target for increased sales.

Attack of the Exports

The export surge from Latin America was only part of a world-wide surge in exports to the U.S. Many of these exports came from developing countries, many of which had little or no manufacturing capacity twenty years ago. The "Four Tigers" of East Asia—Korea, Taiwan, Singapore, and Hong Kong—got most of the publicity, but industrialization was becoming a broad phenomenon, and countries like Thailand, Malaysia, Bangladesh, and Pakistan were beginning to figure in U.S. trade statistics.

In dealing with these countries, we must be careful to note more carefully than we have done until now that competition among countries is a convenient but not quite accurate short-hand expression for a somewhat more complicated phenomenon. In many cases, "foreign" competition turns out to be competition from American-owned and American-operated companies operating in other countries.

The global nature of many leading American companies also affects the export side of our trade picture. Some of the leading producers in Japan have familiar American names: IBM, Texas Instruments, and Coca-Cola, for example. In 1985, American companies in Japan produced and sold $80 billion worth of goods (see Chart 3.11)—but with the exception of the profits, none of these showed up as American exports.[15] (In the same way, cars produced by Japanese-owned companies at factories in the U.S. do not show up as Japanese exports to America.)

The role of multinational corporations is particularly important in the Third World. There, multinationals are leading sources for new technology and investments, and without the multinational corporations the globalization of production would not yet have come very far. The rise in the dollar encouraged the move to base American production overseas.

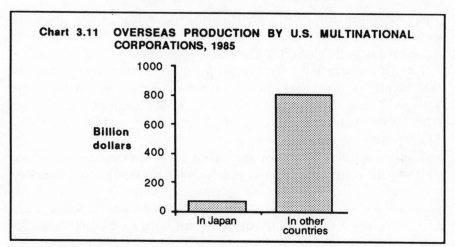

Chart 3.11   OVERSEAS PRODUCTION BY U.S. MULTINATIONAL CORPORATIONS, 1985

Source: U. S. Department of Commerce

Today the rise of the yen is encouraging Japan's multinationals in the same direction.

The use of labels like "Third World" can be confusing, giving us the illusion that all Third World countries are alike. In fact, there are more than a hundred countries in the Third World, and each one is unique. There are also major differences among smaller Third World groupings—like the so-called NICs, the "newly industrializing countries" of East Asia. The four NICs include Hong Kong, a British colony scheduled to return to Chinese jurisdiction in 1997; Singapore, an independent city state off the coast of Malaysia; South Korea; and Taiwan.

The NICs more than doubled their share of world exports, thanks in large part to their ability to penetrate the American market. By the 1980s, Americans were buying 37 percent of the exports from the "Four Tigers," while American goods make up only 17 percent of their total imports. In 1970, our imports from and exports to the Four Tigers were in balance, but by

1987 we were importing $35 billion more from them than we exported to them, and they accounted for more than 20 percent of our total trade deficit.[16] (See Chart 3.12.)

Exports to the U.S. accounted for a significant percentage of the rapid growth that these countries experienced between 1981 and 1985. Twenty-six percent of Korea's growth came from trade with America, 62 percent of Taiwan's, and 66 percent of Singapore's. [17] (See Chart 3.13.)

This was good news for the NICs, but not quite so good for the world economy. When production moves from advanced

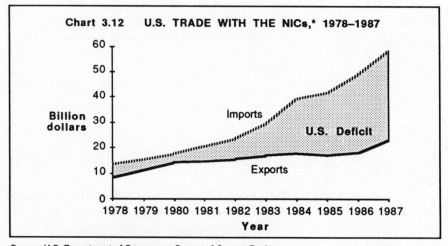

Chart 3.12   U.S. TRADE WITH THE NICs,* 1978–1987

Source: U.S. Department of Commerce, *Survey of Current Business*
*Hong Kong, Singapore, South Korea, and Taiwan

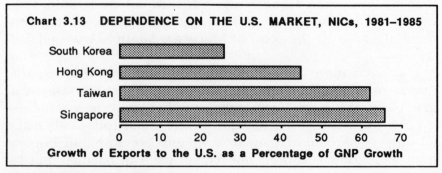

Chart 3.13   DEPENDENCE ON THE U.S. MARKET, NICs, 1981–1985

Source: National Association of Manufacturers

countries that pay high wages to low-wage countries, demand does not rise as fast as production. A Korean car factory whose employees commute to work on bicycles illustrates the problem: the number of new cars is rising faster than the number of people who can buy them.

The Import Invasion

Among the major markets of the world, the U.S. was the only one to import more goods in 1985 than it did in 1980. In a decade in which most countries were increasing their exports and holding down imports, we followed the opposite course: our exports fell and our imports rose. This development was particularly troubling because the price of oil, the single most important product in our import basket, fell by 50 percent from its peak during that time. From 1980 to 1985, our imports rose 41 percent and our exports fell 3 percent. By contrast, Japan's exports rose 35 percent and its imports fell 8 percent.[18] (See Chart 3.14.)

The single largest beneficiary of the American import boom was Japan. While our exports to Japan grew slowly, Japanese exports to us more than doubled in the five years after 1982.[19] (See Chart 3.15.)

U.S. Merchandise Trade with Japan, 1982–1987[20]
(Billions of Dollars)

Year	Exports	Imports	Balances
1982	$ 20.7	$ 37.7	– $ 17.0
1983	21.8	42.8	– 21.0
1984	23.2	60.2	– 37.0
1985	22.1	65.7	– 43.6
1986	26.4	80.8	– 54.4
1987	27.7	84.6	– 56.9

While Japan was the main beneficiary, it was far from the only one. Other nations also posted substantial increases in their exports to the American market. Almost 50 percent of West

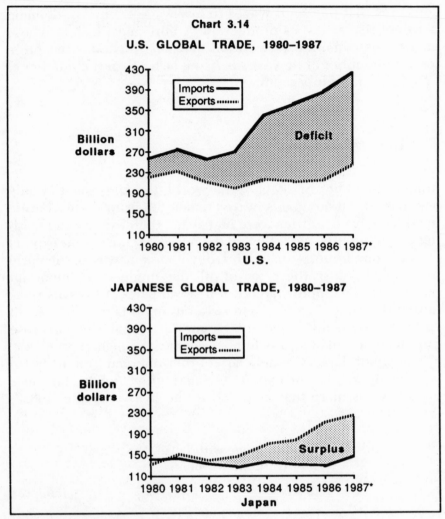

Chart 3.14

U.S. GLOBAL TRADE, 1980–1987

Billion dollars

Imports —— Exports ········

Deficit

1980 1981 1982 1983 1984 1985 1986 1987*

U.S.

JAPANESE GLOBAL TRADE, 1980–1987

Billion dollars

Imports —— Exports ········

Surplus

1980 1981 1982 1983 1984 1985 1986 1987*

Japan

Source: International Monetary Fund
*Note: 1987 estimate based on 11 months of data

Germany's growth and more than one-third of Italy's was due to their increasing exports to the American market.[21]

This is the most devastating deterioration in a nation's peacetime balance of trade in modern times, particularly since the imports were financed largely by debt. These were the years in

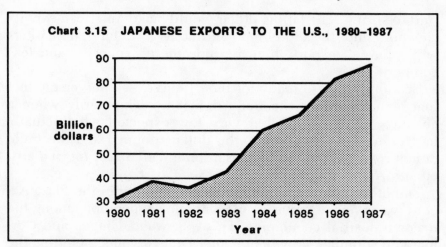

Chart 3.15 JAPANESE EXPORTS TO THE U.S., 1980–1987

Source: International Monetary Fund

which America liquidated its net creditor status and became a debtor nation.

The Morning After in America

After three years of rapid growth in the trade deficit the Administration went back to the drawing board to develop a new economic strategy. In the third stage of the Administration's economic policy, improving the balance of trade became an official goal of national policy. Ironically after five years of proclaiming the value of free exchange rates in a free currency market, the Administration began a plan to lower the value of the dollar.

The turning point came in September 1985 when the U.S. met with the other leading industrial nations (Japan, Germany, France, Britain, Canada, and Italy) and reached an agreement, the Plaza Accord, to bring down the value of the dollar, which had been falling since February, in an orderly way.

Conventional economic theory taught that roughly eighteen months after the dollar began to decline, the trade deficit would start to shrink. The falling dollar would make American exports cheaper, and therefore more attractive, in foreign markets while foreign exports here became more expensive and less competitive.

Economists were ready for the "J curve"—a perverse effect that actually drives the trade deficit up temporarily when a currency starts down—but very few expected what actually happened. For three years, the dollar dropped and the trade deficit rose in a pattern that a sardonic *Wall Street Journal* article referred to as an "x curve."[22] (See Chart 3.16.)

The other aspect of Administration policy after the Plaza Accord was a new emphasis on economic cooperation among the major industrial economies. The U.S. wanted Japan and Germany to stimulate growth at home. Yet everyone, including the Americans, understood that our budget and trade deficits had to come down, and somebody somewhere would have to import more and raise government spending. Otherwise, total world demand would fall and possibly cause a recession.

Cooperation proved easier to wish for than to get. In the face of our failure to moderate our budget deficits, both Germany

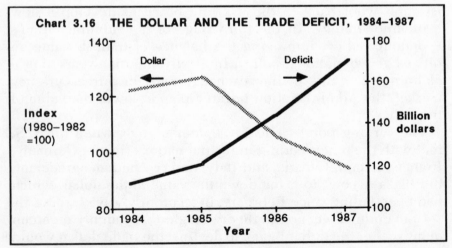

Chart 3.16   THE DOLLAR AND THE TRADE DEFICIT, 1984–1987

Source: Morgan Guaranty Trust Co., U.S. Department of Commerce

and Japan were extremely reluctant to increase theirs and stimulate their own economies, or to increase their imports from abroad. Trade surpluses seemed like a form of insurance to the Japanese; and to the Germans, inflation is still the worst of all evils, and they prefer to err, if they must, by having their economy grow too slowly than to let it gain steam and, possibly, return to an inflationary spiral.

With little to show for its policy except continuously rising deficits, the Administration's answers were starting to be challenged by Congress.

The Trade Debate

Throughout the U.S., concern over the trade deficit was gathering momentum. Congress started to stir, and many 1986 House and Senate elections featured debates over trade. The collapse of our world trading position led many to examine American trade policy more carefully, and the consequences of this reexamination began a quiet revolution in American thinking. For many years, people had taken at face value the assurances about the value of a strict adherence to a free trade program. In the early 1980s more and more Americans began to question that idea and many political leaders and policy experts started calling for the reform of trade policy, including GATT.

GATT had achieved considerable success in removing quotas and reducing tariff barriers. In seven rounds of GATT-administered multilateral negotiations, tariffs on traded goods were lowered from an average of over 40 percent to about 5 percent by 1973.[23] Uniform codes were established for subsidies, standards, government procurement, customs valuation, licensing, and antidumping. Dispute settlement procedures and review committees were put in place to examine and adjudicate trade disagreements. To this extent, GATT can be credited with having played an important role in turning the world away from the tariffs, restrictions, subsidies, and other beggar-thy-neighbor practices that were rampant in the 1930s.

But over the years, numerous factors have reduced GATT's

impact. First, GATT covers approximately 80 percent of world trade in merchandise, but trade in services, agriculture, textiles, and energy products is not included. Equally, if not more important, GATT's enlarged membership is less homogeneous than it once was and reflects a greater diversity of interests, claims, and economic strategies. The variety of economic systems and strategies at work in today's global economy make the original GATT approach to "free trade" increasingly problematic.

Approximately 75 percent of all world commerce is conducted by economic systems operating from models which do not accept the postwar ideal of "free trade."[24] (See Chart 3.17.) There are five types of economic systems operating in the contemporary world economy: 1. *rule-driven*—the U.S. and those who espouse "free trade," which accounts for about 24 percent of world trade; 2. *plan-driven*—Japan and the Asian NICs, about 13 percent of trade; 3. *mixed*—about 35 percent; 4. *developing*—17 percent; and 5. *centrally planned*—12 percent. The point is that more and more countries compete in the world marketplace holding quite different beliefs than the U.S. does about the role of government in the economy and about what is fair and unfair in the world trade system. As a result, agreement

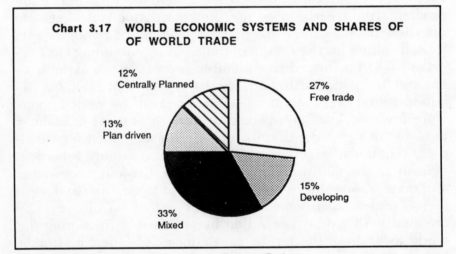

Chart 3.17   WORLD ECONOMIC SYSTEMS AND SHARES OF
OF WORLD TRADE

12%
Centrally Planned

27%
Free trade

13%
Plan driven

15%
Developing

33%
Mixed

Source: Pat Choate and Juyne Linger, *Harvard Business Review*
See footnote 24.

on principles and policies comes less easily than it once did, making negotiating rounds notoriously slow in reaching consensus. It has also led to more cases where the principle of nondiscrimination, the very centerpiece of GATT, is ignored. The multitude of voluntary export restraints, orderly market arrangements, and other market sharing measures have eroded the consistency in trade that GATT was formed to provide.

Finally, GATT's primary concentration on tariff trade barriers reduces its effectiveness. As GATT lowered tariffs internationally, many countries shifted to the use of nontariff trade barriers and practices which are difficult to define and even more difficult to negotiate away.

In the 1980s, nontariff barriers ballooned as country after country acted aggressively to promote its exports while cutting back on imports. Between 1981 and 1986, the percent of industrial country imports from other industrial countries covered by "hard-core" nontariff barriers—those barriers most likely to have significant restrictive effects, such as import prohibitions, variable levies, and voluntary export restraints—rose by nearly 25 percent. For example, the U.S. and Japan negotiated voluntary restraints on auto imports to the U.S. By 1986, 16 percent of intra-industrial-country imports were covered by "hard-core" nontariff barriers. Ores and metal products trade, which includes iron and steel, was especially hit. Nontariff barriers in this sector almost doubled between 1981 and 1986.[25]

The sheer growth of different economic sectors and countries in the share of world trade, complemented by much more sophisticated trade practices and barriers, has created new complex relationships in the world economy. Their very complexity has begun to render GATT an increasingly obsolete and ineffective forum for dealing with the significant trade disputes and issues of the 1980s.

Global Gridlock

Faced by the reluctance of the allies and a Congress flush with victory in 1986 because of the trade issue, and despite pledges to the contrary to the allies, the Administration began in 1987 to let the dollar fall even further in hopes it could induce the allies to cooperate and to stave off congressional action. As 1987 opened, despite two years of dollar depreciation, trade imbalances were still out of control, and the major countries agreed again that more cooperation was necessary. In the Louvre Accord of 1987, the finance ministers of the Big Six (U.S., West Germany, Japan, France, Canada, and the United Kingdom) announced their joint intention to "foster stability of exchange rates at current levels." They met four months later (along with Italy) for the thirteenth Summit meeting and reaffirmed the goal of macroeconomic policy cooperation. It quickly became apparent that the dollar had a course of its own, set more by the judgment of investors in the world's capital markets than by the policies of the U.S. Treasury. The dollar kept going down, and with it went the confidence of foreign investors. In 1987, private money to finance our deficit dried up and foreign central banks were forced to buy U.S. Treasury notes at a rate of almost $100 billion annually.[26]

Meanwhile, promises of macrocoordination led only slowly to policy changes. Promised German tax reductions were modest and were not even scheduled for implementation until 1988. Japan's original budget proposal for fiscal year 1987 was restrictive, not expansionary. But a supplementary spending package amounting to 6 trillion yen (about 1.8 percent of Japan's GNP) was announced just before the June Summit, and in recent months Japan has made some progress by increasing consumption at home and allowing the yen to appreciate. It took the stock market crash of October 1987 to push the U.S. to action on its budget deficit.

The small advances in cooperation, though better than nothing, were far from adequate to untangle the many binds on the world economy. Instead, the last months of 1987 brought another stunning 10 percent drop in the dollar.

The clash of economic strategies and the imbalances between the U.S. and the world, created a global gridlock.

In 1988 we find the gridlock still in place. Japan and Germany and the Third World still depend on us to absorb their exports, and we still depend on foreign lenders to finance our economy.

To all this has been added the possibility of recession in the U.S. and the anxiety caused by the Crash of 1987. In the next year the challenge will be to break the global impasse.

The Case for Reform

In the past forty years, economic integration has outgrown our international institutions. The institutions which came out of the Bretton Woods framework established at the end of World War Two—the World Bank to finance development projects around the world; the IMF to administer the financial system and to oversee balance-of-payments adjustment; the GATT to monitor trade and negotiate the reduction of tariff barriers—are clearly inadequate to the tasks imposed by today's world economy.

We have seen how this arrangement became less and less workable in the 1960s and 1970s. The failure to redistribute the burdens of economic leadership more fairly in the 1980s began to undermine the world economy and would ultimately lead to the global economic gridlock in which we now find ourselves.

The world can no longer count on one country to come to the rescue. The world economy is too large, trade and financial transactions are too active, and there are too many players for any one country to play the role formerly filled by the U.S. Global growth now depends on international economic cooperation, and that requires a clearly defined role for government. International negotiations require government participation while they are going on, and government regulations to enforce them once agreements have been reached. As international trade becomes more important within the domestic economy, international regulations must of necessity play a growing role in the national economy. It becomes vital for the government to have a clear concept of the nation's economic interests in order to defend and advance our basic interests in international negotiations.

There is no more critical task ahead than to make our international institutions relevant to the interdependent and multi-lateral world. Given the circumstances of sluggish growth and increased competition, it is unreasonable to expect the monetary and fiscal policies of individual nations to mesh without a larger framework of international cooperation. The magnitude of these challenges cannot be underestimated; their importance cannot be overstated.

For the U.S. to help achieve this new balance we must make credible proposals to other countries and have the economic power and competitive ability to make our own contribution to the establishment of a stronger partnership between the U.S. and the world economies.

CHAPTER FOUR

Toward a New International Order

Living with Interdependence

FOR forty years we have lived under the economic system developed in the aftermath of World War Two. For most of those years, the system worked well enough that we took it for granted. American producers had worldwide access to markets and raw materials, and American consumers had their choice of goods produced everywhere in the world. Our economy grew fast enough to provide most Americans with a rising standard of living and individual opportunity, and prosperity came to many parts of the world.

The 1970s and especially the 1980s have tested America's faith in an economy open to the whole world. When in this decade the trading system, including GATT, started to break down and the other multinational institutions were less than successful in advancing our interests, many Americans wanted to erect walls to world trade. The U.S. could live very well, goes the argument, behind high tariff walls. We are a large country, rich in natural resources; foreigners should realize that it is a privilege to trade with us, and they should pay for the privilege.

We sympathize with those who make these arguments; the loss of jobs and security resulting from foreign competition has had a damaging effect on many families and communities. The desire to protect ourselves from competition is an understandable response to an out-of-control trade situation.

But global interdependence is a fact and something we should embrace. The economies of the First World are connected in thousands of ways even if our political differences seem to keep us separate. The world needs the U.S., and the U.S. needs the world.

American Leadership in a World Come of Age

In the years after World War One, the U.S. withdrew from the world and put up tariff barriers against foreign goods, and foreign countries raised barriers against ours. Worse, in the absence of effective international cooperation, national rivalries blossomed. Militaristic dictatorships came to power in Germany, Italy, and Japan, and the democratic countries were unable to agree on how to handle the military threat of the Axis or the economic threat of the Depression.

After World War Two, the U.S. made a decision that we would never again withdraw from the world. Our essential national interests could best be secured by cooperative economic and military arrangements with other countries.

If the United States is to defend its interests and play a part in sustaining a healthy world economy, we will have to move in new directions in both international and domestic economic policies. This chapter contains our proposals for international policies that would help balance our economy and make us more competitive while making the world economy stronger.

The Commission believes that responsible internationalism is still the best policy for the U.S. The principles of the Atlantic Charter are still the best foundation for American policy. Every nation should enjoy the right to participate in the world economy within rules that are evenhanded and fair, and all nations have a responsibility to work together to raise living standards around the world and to promote the economic advancement of every country. These basic principles are still the right ones for us, but our policies must change. Without abandoning our commitment to cooperation and responsible engagement, our leaders must insist on fair treatment for the U.S. in international economic relations. America cannot be the only advanced country to take responsibility for allowing developing countries access to advanced markets; we cannot allow Europe and Japan more liberal trading and investment rights in our country than they allow us in theirs.

All efforts to establish unfair or discriminatory economic practices should be rejected, as should any retreat from the give-and-take of an open world economy. Because the only possible road to global prosperity lies through international economic cooperation, the United States must continue to bear a fair share of the burden of maintaining the world's economic system.

America should affirm its faith that global economic growth is both possible and desirable. The peace of the world and the health of the global economy depend on cooperation among the world's leading economies as they work together to foster growth in both the First World and the Third. No country today can, alone, be the locomotive that pulls the train of the world economy. This responsibility must be shared among all the countries of the world, each in accordance with its ability and stage of development.

This interdependence makes international cooperation more necessary now than in the past. It makes more critical the need for the U.S. to base its competitiveness strategy upon the principles of responsible internationalism.

For the United States today, responsible internationalism means that we should pursue a competitiveness strategy that includes the goal of global growth. We must not work our way out of our trade and foreign-indebtedness problems by relying strictly on selling more exports while restricting imports, as some other countries have done. This neomercantilism is ultimately a losing strategy even for those nations which practice it, because it provokes trade hostilities and thus further curtails world trade. Without global growth, one nation can "win" only at another's expense.

We should design and adopt policies of constructive competition, not policies which heighten destructive competition.

The United States should exercise trade leadership, working with other governments to formulate international guidelines that provide for balanced trade, mutual advantage, and shared prosperity.

Responsible internationalism also includes a recognition in our goals and policies that other nations embrace the notion of governmental participation in matters of industry to increase their own competitiveness and create prosperity. Rather than persist in an approach which has too often been rigid and naive, the U.S. should engage other countries as they really are, and devise a trade strategy to meet the diversity of conditions found in today's world.

All our national difficulties, of course, cannot be blamed on foreign countries. If the U.S. had pursued effective competitiveness strategies and proper macroeconomic policies over the last two decades, we would not now be facing trade problems of this magnitude.

Responsible internationalism also means being clear about where our own national interests lie, and understanding the interests of our trading partners. We can no longer count on our overwhelming economic strength to ensure that international negotiations go our way. Instead, we will have to rely on the skill of our leaders and the patience and flexibility with which they pursue America's long-term interests in international forums.

The Commission did not try to develop a complete step-by-step plan for repairing the foundations of international economic cooperation, but a consensus on basic goals and policies was reached that can move things in the right direction. Americans and others should consider carefully the following proposals, which, we believe, can help put the world economy back on the right track.

In subsequent chapters, our proposals for American domestic action are explained. In this chapter are set forth policy proposals for international reform to move toward a balanced trade regime and promote international financial stability. Below are policy recommendations that address three areas: trade reform, alleviation of Third World debt, and reform of the international financial system. While these recommendations do not amount to a complete and detailed program for international reform, they outline an approach that will advance American interests within a framework of economic cooperation.

Bringing Back Balance to Trade

We find that the traditional policy tools used by the U.S. are insufficient to bring about the redirection of trade flows of the magnitude needed. Bringing the dollar to a more realistic level against the currencies of the advanced countries was crucial, and a similar realignment must be forthcoming between the U.S. and the East Asian NICs. But devaluation cannot create a trade balance, because the problem of competitiveness goes deeper than the price of goods. And if we let the dollar keep going down we risk inflation and declining living standards in the U.S., recession abroad, and the sale of America's assets at bargain basement prices. Nor is the GATT system at all equipped to redress the trade imbalances. Although GATT is useful, it is outdated, is in need of reform, and requires supplementary measures to be effective.

The present congressional attempt to change U.S. trade policy, in the form of a comprehensive trade bill expected to pass both the House and the Senate in 1988, is in form and substance a consensus plan of action to deal with the nation's competitiveness problem and trade difficulties. It is thus an important piece of legislation which will make several essential changes in the rules and procedures under which U.S. trade policy is conducted.

The bill as it now stands—and as it will probably stand in final form—incorporates many of the proposals found in previous studies on competitiveness. These proposals include, among others: (1) amending trade law to enhance retaliation against unfair trade practices; (2) providing for greater certainty of relief if injury is due to unfair trade practices; (3) applying trade law to the export targeting practices of other countries; (4) providing a mechanism for industries seeking relief to develop an adjustment plan and a long-range competitiveness strategy; (5) providing increased support for economic adjustment; and (6) expanding the definition of unfair trade practices to include the denial of workers' basic rights.

The trade bill envisions the U.S. competing its way out of its problem by doing what other nations have done—selling more exports and buying fewer imports. But when nations frantically scramble to boost their foreign sales, increasing exports compete even more aggressively for a limited market. As we have seen, without global growth one nation can "win" only at another's expense, and even that victory is temporary if it leads to the economic destabilization of markets. This is why there must be balanced trade guided by a constant process of negotiation for mutual advantage and shared prosperity.

The trade policy debate has also been limited by the fact that the rules of conduct have become ends in themselves. American policymakers have lost sight of the end they are supposed to produce—increasing trade leading to global prosperity. Asking ourselves how to best achieve a certain set of rules called "free trade" is to pose the wrong question. The real issue is what kind of domestic trade policy and competitiveness strategy in conjunction with what set of international rules will likely produce mutual benefit and global growth.

While much of the trade debate has a "results" orientation, it at times still leaves one with the notion that others are the primary source of our problems, not our own lack of initiative. There are real foreign barriers to trade, but they would be less of an issue today if the U.S. had developed and pursued a competitiveness strategy for the last twenty years. The time has come to expand our traditional concepts of trade beyond an emphasis on rules and process to include a national strategy to compete.

The current system of world trade is neither fully free nor fully protectionist. The GATT system and the various subsidiary bilateral and regional agreements that make up the complicated network of international trade regulations form a system for managing trade on a global scale. The world trade system was designed to promote the growth of international trade in a balanced way.

As originally set up in the 1940s, GATT depended on the

Bretton Woods framework of financial institutions to help keep individual countries from running excessive surpluses or deficits in their trade. It also, as we have seen, depended on the tacit understanding that the U.S. would not assert its interests as aggressively as other countries asserted theirs.

With the Bretton Woods system in disarray, and with the end of America's willingness or ability to act as the world's consumer of last resort, we need new international policies that can achieve GATT's goal of expanding world trade in today's conditions. This set of reforms is neither pro-protectionism nor pro–free trade any more than GATT was. GATT was pro growth, and it allowed a combination of free trade policies and protectionist policies to the extent that these policies fostered global growth.

A Partnership for Growth

The imbalances that have grown up among the economies of the leading industrial democracies have reached a point where they threaten the continued performance of the world economy. The Big Three in particular—Germany, Japan, and the U.S.—have grown into an unsustainable and unstable relationship in which the U.S. borrows astronomical sums from Germany and Japan.

The United States, as the "consumer of last resort," borrows money to purchase goods made for export in other countries. Our consumption is made possible by foreign lending, and our creditors have been able to accumulate dollars from the sales of their exports, which they lend back to us to allow for further purchases. Put in the simplest terms, our borrowing has permitted our consumption to exceed our production, while among our competitors production exceeds consumption.

In 1987 this relationship entered a dangerous new phase; private investors in Germany and Japan were no longer interested in new purchases of American IOUs, and for the most part stopped investing. German and Japanese central banks were forced into the market and bought over $140 billion in

U.S. Treasury bills in 1987. It was only their efforts to stave off a dollar collapse which provided the U.S. with a continuing line of credit.[1]

The following policies can help put the world economy and trading system back on the road to balanced trade and balanced growth.

1. *A plan for long-term structural reduction of the U.S. trade and budget deficits is the first step on the road back to stability.* The American foreign debt is growing larger and more troublesome at the rate of $10 billion per month. As long as we depend on foreign investors to sustain our debt-based consumption, international cooperation for stable growth will not be possible.

These deficits must be reduced steadily over time. The world economy, not to mention the American economy, is too dependent on debt-based consumption. The economy is addicted to debt, and sudden withdrawal will lead to painful and dangerous symptoms. Later chapters discuss our specific proposals for deficit reduction and balancing our trade accounts; these tasks are difficult but not impossible, and steady progress on both fronts is essential to establishing a framework for real international cooperation.

2. *As the U.S. reduces its budget and trade deficits, Germany, Japan and other trade-surplus countries must shift over to more stimulative policies.* If we cut back on our demand for imports, and other countries do not step up their purchases, the world will quickly fall into a recession and perhaps into something worse.

Japan has already begun to increase its purchase of consumer goods and has embarked on an ambitious public works program that will help stimulate the Japanese and the global economies. Germany, unfortunately, had not taken steps of a comparable magnitude at the time this report went to press, and this failure has been criticized by many countries in addition to the U.S. The NICs, many of which have substantial trade surpluses, have done even less than Germany, keeping their markets tightly shut and holding down the purchasing power of their population by keeping wages and social benefits at a very moderate and often unrealistic level.

The U.S. should use its diplomatic and economic influence to move these countries toward more constructive policies, but we must understand that one of the most effective arguments we can have is our own good example. If other countries see the U.S. adopting sensible, sustainable economic policies, and persisting in them month by month and year by year, they will have more respect for our ideas and be more willing to follow our lead.

Leadership is something that is earned by hard work, sensible ideas, and a track record of success. If other countries are slow to follow our lead in economic policy, we must understand that we must bear some of the responsibility for this. If we want other countries to play their part in stimulating the world economy, the best way to gain their cooperation is to set an example of sober, thoughtful economic statesmanship—and at this point that means the adoption of a responsible, measured multiyear program to reduce our trade and budget deficits.

3. *Monetary policy should be coordinated for growth.* In the U.S., the Federal Reserve must help offset any reduced economic stimulus caused by changes in government fiscal policy. Moreover, monetary stimulus should come in advance of fiscal restraint because of the "lag factor" between the stimulus of an interest-rate reduction or increase in money supply and the negative impact of a tax increase or a decline in spending. Interest rates, especially the discount rate, should be within 2 to 3 percent of the inflation rate. Money supply growth, while clearly a benefit in the short run, can have an inflationary effect as a long-term policy. Therefore, the commitment to growth must not ignore the issue of inflation. (In the next chapter this issue is addressed more fully.)

Maintaining the money supply and interest rates at a level that encourages rather than retards growth will require a similar monetary policy by America's trading partners. Once a plan for U.S. deficit reduction is in place, Japan and Germany will be able to hold their interest rates in line without fear of domestic inflation and weakened currencies.

4. *Growth in living standards abroad should be emphasized in formulating trade policy.* Global economic health—and by extension the economic health of the U.S.—will require an increase in demand, and that is possible either through more investment or more consumption, both of which can potentially raise living standards. In conducting its domestic and foreign economic policy, the U.S. should support policies which lead to higher living standards in the Third World. The U.S., for example, could include the issue of rising living standards in bilateral trade negotiations.

5. *Agreements are needed to shift imports away from the U.S. to those countries which maintain large trade surpluses.* In the 1950s, when Japan was beginning to export a significant amount of products, the European countries were reluctant to accept Japanese exports, and reluctant to allow Japan to join GATT. The U.S. took the lead in backing Japanese membership in GATT—giving Japan the same rights to trade in world markets as all other countries—and urged the Europeans to open their markets to more Japanese goods.

Today, the NICs and the developing countries are where Japan was decades ago, and once again the U.S. must work to see that Europe—and Japan—accept more exports from these dynamic young economies. Currently, many developing countries have their eyes fixed almost exclusively on the American market. We should work with these countries to turn their attention to other markets, and work with the other advanced countries to ensure that they will accept more exports from the Third World.

6. *American foreign policy and our economic policy should be more closely integrated, and our economic interests should not be sacrificed for the sake of short-term political foreign policy goals.* All too often, foreign policy objectives have been pursued without serious regard for their consequences on domestic economic health. In today's world, the U.S. cannot, without debilitating effects, continue to operate in the expansive—and expensive—manner of twenty years ago. Our trade negotiations are as vital to our real national security as our

political negotiations. We must redefine foreign policy to include a greater recognition of our need to become more competitive and to restore balance in economic relationships.

7. *The U.S. government should use the American market as a bargaining chip in negotiating agreements leading to balanced trade.* Negotiation is always a process of give and take, and access to America's market—the largest and most lucrative market for business and consumer products in the world—is the most important thing that we can give or withhold. Once other countries realize that we are serious about reciprocity, then we can set up policies that all countries recognize are appropriate and fair. We can then establish bilateral and multilateral agreements which address the specific needs of those countries involved in ways that are difficult or impossible within the GATT framework.

8. *U.S. trade policy should address the problem of overcapacity through agreements that permit expanded trade and mutual growth.* World demand has not caught up with productive capacity. Many industries are characterized by overcapacity and expensive subsidies. In those cases, temporary market sharing and "countertrade" agreements are needed to orchestrate stability rather than allow destructive competition between countries with excess capacity. Both market sharing and countertrade agreements are already in use to some degree, and could be of great help in future negotiations, particularly with countries that practice industrial policy and targeting. However, agreements of this type must be negotiated on a case-by-case basis as temporary measures which are based on the individual circumstances and exceptional features of a particular industry. They must also include economic adjustment programs and other requirements of other temporary import restrictions.

The idea of shared production is to require a certain amount of domestic production in the market where sales occur. These have been used particularly in automaking by a large number of nations. Unlike quotas, market-sharing deals maintain competition, because no limit is placed on the number of items sold by the foreign manufacturer as long as some production takes place in the marketplace. Countertrade agreements stipulate that foreign goods will be purchased only on the condition that the foreign supplier distribute in his own country a similar share of goods from the purchaser's country.

9. *In those cases where import restrictions are requested, the government, to ensure the vitality of domestic industry, must require the submission of an adjustment plan and revitalization strategy.* Under the trade bill passed by the House, industries petitioning for import relief "may submit" a statement of proposed adjustment measures to the ITC and the USTR. This is not enough. A more specific and rigorous approach could look like this: the protection has a termination date set in advance; there is a plan of action by firms in the industry which includes benchmarks to insure the industry is making progress and not, for example, choosing to make excessive profits when its plan calls for increased competition to regain market share; and there is a worker-adjustment plan including retraining, relocation if necessary, and income support.

Requiring an industry to develop a strategy does not mean that government will be telling an industry what it must do. It does, however, place an appropriate responsibility on the industry for its continued well-being. Those industries which emerged strongest from protection in the past were those which made extensive plans for restructuring, such as the Harley-Davidson Company, and then carried them out. Our trade policy should also be based on a clear commitment to making tariffs and quotas temporary measures.

10. *Criteria for granting assistance should be established.*

In instances where an industry looks to the federal government for financial assistance in restructuring, the following threshold criteria should be met: (1) the industry is strategic in that it is vital to other industries and the maintenance of employment; (2) assistance is not too late to do substantive good; (3) government intervention is supported by labor and industry leaders and knowledgeable experts, and serves the public interest; (4) the restructuring program is specific and includes commitments from management and labor as to their contributions; and (5) where the industry is likely to decline no matter what, an economic adjustment program is provided.

11. *Measures should be taken to help export promotion.* U.S. export efficiency could be enhanced by making industries more export conscious and by helping industries acquire the knowledge and international support systems necessary to sell abroad. The federal government, in partnership with the states, should create an information service on world export opportunities and disseminate information on a regular basis to U.S. firms. Export financing, export insurance, and programs to help train firms in foreign marketing, all methods proven successful by the states, should be broadened and developed aggressively by the federal government.

12. *The U.S. should seek to share the technology of other countries.* Japan has required foreign firms to share technology with its firms as a price of doing business in Japan, and the U.S. should do the same. This would increase the ability of U.S. firms to get access to foreign patent information and to develop commercial products from it.

13. *The U.S. should develop a Latin American initiative.* The other nations of this hemisphere are the most important countries in the world for our long-term economic prosperity. The collapse of Latin America's purchasing power in the last seven years has been a major disaster for the U.S. and unless we help these countries recover, the consequences of the continental depression in Latin America will grow even worse for us.

Helping Latin America to grow will involve a major debt relief plan, and the elements of this plan are presented separately below. But debt relief is only part of the story. Beyond the immediate problem of debt relief lies the question of helping our neighbors resume the rapid rates of growth they enjoyed before the debt crisis hit.

The President and the Congress should work together with the leaders of Latin America to develop a comprehensive and substantial program for joint action to foster growth and new trading relations in the hemisphere. Even in a time of budget austerity, the U.S. must be prepared to make seed money available for growth in Latin and Central America.

14. *U.S. trade policy should focus on the new opportunities for trade with China.* The Chinese market is potentially the largest in the world. While per capita income is low, China is emerging as one of the world's economic giants. Rather than leaving this market to the Japanese, we should develop ways to help U.S. firms participate in China. This may mean building up a staff of experts on China in the government's trade policy agencies, particularly the U.S. Trade Representative and the Department of Commerce. We should also develop financial arrangements with the Chinese government that would facilitate the repatriation of profits, the insurance of exports, and the protection of intellectual property rights.

Overcoming Third World Debt: The Key to America's Growth

Resolution of the Third World debt crisis and the continuing problem of underdevelopment must play a central role in a strategy for balanced trade based on global growth and financial stability.

One of the lessons we learned from the 1920s and 1930s is that once international debts reach a certain size, there is no easy way to collect them. During World War One the Allies borrowed billions from the U.S. They planned to make Germany pay reparations to the Allies and assumed that they would be able to repay the U.S. with German money. But Germany could pay its debts only by exporting so many cheap goods to the Allies that their industries would be ruined.

This pyramid of debt poisoned international relations during the 1920s, and despite numerous efforts such as the Young Plan and Dawes Plan, the problem continued into the 1930s.

When World War Two began, the U.S. was determined to

avoid a repetition of the postwar squabbles over debt. The Lend-Lease program was created as an alternative to another series of Allied loans that would poison relations once the shooting stopped. The Marshall Plan aid was given as a gift, and the U.S. followed a consistent policy of opposing proposals that would saddle the defeated countries with unrealistic long-term obligations.

The World War Two approach to international financial questions worked much better than the Versailles system. While World War One left a residue of bitterness that became the seed for a second conflict, the former enemies of the 1940s became allies in later years. Moreover, the reparations agreed to after 1945 were repaid, because they were reasonable. Victims of Nazi crimes are still receiving compensation. The Marshall Plan aid created such international goodwill that the Germans established a German Marshall Fund which makes grants to American students and scholars.

The present approach to Third World debt issues threatens to return us to the policies of the 1920s. Already, desperate attempts by debtor countries to export more goods have been met by protectionism in the creditor countries. Unpayable debts supported by unsound new loans; growing bitterness and friction in international relations; unstable trading patterns based on excessive exports and constricted imports in the debtor countries and the opposite in the creditor countries— these were among the specters we tried to banish from the world after World War Two.

We are now in the impossible position of having to choose between the financial health of our banks and the prosperity of our domestic manufacturers. In the long run, this is no choice at all. Without a stable, healthy banking system, our manufacturers cannot get the credit they need to expand or to invest in new technologies. Without a healthy domestic manufacturing sector, our banks will not have reliable customers for loans.

The crisis is more complex than many Americans realize and it is difficult to recognize in most people's daily lives. But it is an important economic growth and development issue which has affected our jobs because of the reduction in our exports, our banks, and the further development of democracy in Latin America. We must come to grips with this problem for the sake of our economic future and that of the debtor nations.

The present debate over how to address this problem has been dominated by pressures to let the world financial system "muddle through." But as Paul Volcker has noted, "international money won't manage itself." Many who have been close to the action have concluded that the resolution of the debt crisis must involve a role for governments.

The stakes in the current international debt situation are high. The debt crisis has the potential to cause instability in the international financial system. Nonperforming loans weaken our banks and increase the likelihood that some major bank will fall into difficult financial straits. Over time, unless the situation improves, more write-downs of debt will be likely with consequent losses on balance sheets, reduction in bank capital, and pressures to raise additional capital in financial markets. And a major default by one or more of the largest debtor countries, the potential for which persists despite five years of crisis intervention and debt management, would add to international instability.

The debt problems will also continue to limit the growth potential of the world economy and act as a drag on overall world growth and on U.S. growth. In the 1970s, dynamic expansion in Brazil, Mexico, Argentina, Venezuela, and other developing nations was instrumental in softening the impact of the 1973–75 recession and in spurring the recovery that followed from 1975–79. During this period, exports of U.S. goods and services to Latin America more than tripled to meet the rising demand spurred by the region's rapid economic growth.

In the early 1980s, nearly half the $105 billion in potential export sales that was lost by the slowdown in world economic growth was attributable to the depression-like conditions that prevailed in the Third World.

The final concern is the unrest which is often caused by long-term economic and social problems in debtor nations. The health of these countries is being undermined. The obligations to repay the loans threaten the region's fledgling democracies.

If this trend is not arrested, social instability and political up-heaval can be expected to follow.

Since 1980, some progress on some debt issues has been made by banks, the IMF, and the debtor countries, while other issues remain troublesome. In 1987, the major U.S. banks took an important step by building up their loan-loss reserves. In 1988, a positive step forward was taken with Morgan Guaranty's new plan to reduce Mexican debt. And James Robinson of American Express has added to the debate with an extensive proposal for a new debt facility.

Much more work on the debt problem remains to be done. The developing countries need programs to create conditions favorable to growth. At the same time they need money to make new investments and finance their trade. American interests are clear—we want the debt eliminated as an obstacle to growth here and in the Third World, and we want to avoid a solution that weakens our banking system or the international financial system.

The recommendations that follow are designed to ease the debt service overhang, reverse present negative capital flow from the Third World to the First World, and increase new capital and restore credit to less-developed countries. We believe that these proposals can serve as a basis for the continuing discussions needed to solve this serious problem.

1. *An Affirmative Government Role to Improve Management of the Debt Crisis.* A solution to the international debt crisis requires new strategic thinking and new institutional mechanisms. Government should intervene more actively to develop a workable scheme for stretching out repayment of the debt, and to assure the continuation of lending for positive economic development. In seeking such arrangements, it is important for government policymakers to provide incentives for commercial banks to increase their long-term loans to developing nations, and to reduce their exposure to bad debt.

2. *A Plan for Debt Rescheduling.* A comprehensive approach must begin with the establishment of an effective international fund to purchase debt at a discount from lenders. This

arrangement would include accounting rules that facilitate the write-down of debt holding without harming the competitive standing of banks from any particular nation. The fund would establish reasonable rescheduling formulas over longer time periods at reduced interest rates on the repayment of debt.

3. *Conditionality Requirements Refocused to Reduce Capital Flight and Preserve Domestic Stability.* Budget discipline can be a good thing if it pressures government to cut unnecessary costs and become more efficient in its ability to deliver needed goods and services. But the austerity programs forced on debtor countries were often too stringent and too sudden. In the long run, they poisoned relations between the IMF and the debtor countries, and in any case there is little room for additional austerity.

What is needed now is to ensure that money that goes to debtor countries stays there and does good. Domestic capital flight—wealthy individuals within debtor countries transfering their money into foreign banks—can undo all the good accomplished by new credits.

New conditions for new loans should focus much more on ways to limit such capital flight—by making conditions more attractive for domestic investment within the debtor nations and by making it harder for capital to leave these countries except through proper channels.

4. *Long-Term Capital Plans for Financial Development.*
Slow world growth should be confronted by a coordinated plan to increase liquidity and restart economic growth in the Third World. Such a financial package could be drawn from the following combination of sources: recycled surpluses from Japan and Germany; a contribution by the U.S. drawn from reductions in domestic, primarily military, spending (otherwise, the cooperation of Japan and Germany is unlikely); absorption of Eurodollars; and a Special Drawing Rights allocation directed toward debtor nations.

Stabilizing Global Finance

Sustained global growth depends on an international financial system that is flexible and stable enough to accommodate the needs of a dynamic world economy. The violent fluctuations in exchange rates of recent years tend to destabilize trade and to encourage unhealthy currency speculation, and the globalization adds new risks at the same time that it creates new possibilities for growth. The Commission's recommendations in this area include:

1. *A commitment to stabilize the dollar will help create a stable economic environment.*   The dollar is much more than the currency of the American government. Since World War Two it has been the reserve currency of many countries—often the poorest countries, which need these reserves for essential purchases. The dollar is also the unit in which many commodities sold worldwide are priced—notably oil. The role of the dollar as a reserve currency has sometimes imposed unpleasant burdens on the U.S., but overall we benefit from having our money accepted throughout the world. To maintain the usefulness of the dollar as a reserve currency, we must keep its value stable or at least predictable.

A stable dollar is important to the American economy in many ways, because a falling, weak dollar has many unwanted consequences. For example, a falling dollar puts our banks at a disadvantage in international trade. The falling dollar makes it more expensive for the U.S. to maintain a military presence overseas, and limits the effectiveness of our foreign aid programs. It means, too, that we must sell more goods and services to foreigners to pay for our imports, and it puts American investors at a disadvantage in our own country when companies and property come up for sale. We need a stable median value for the dollar: a value not so high as to price our goods out of world markets, and not so low as to cripple us and destroy confidence.

Our current trade and budget deficits, plus the decades-long outflow of dollars to the rest of the world, have created a worrisome situation for those who hold dollars. After falling 50 percent against key foreign currencies since 1985, the dollar has depended on the commitment of the world's central banks to prevent too rapid a fall in its value. This commitment is important, but it has its limits. While central bank intervention can slow the descent of a currency, it cannot "fight the markets" for long. Worse, a decision by foreign central banks or foreign investors not to support the dollar or meet U.S. financial needs (in effect, a strike by foreign capital) would exert enormous pressure on the U.S. and the dollar. The key is to get the real economy back into balance so that the dollar has a foundation.

Reducing the trade and budget deficits will do that, and this would be the most effective means of stabilizing the dollar. But short-term programs should also be used, especially if the dollar's retreat shows signs of turning into a rout. Central banks may need additional reserves to stabilize exchange rates in the near future, and the IMF can and, if need be, should raise a fund to make this possible. Together with changes in underlying economic conditions these measures can help create more stability.

2. *Target exchange rate zones will help restore confidence and dampen speculation.* Under the Bretton Woods system, the rates of exchange among international currencies were fixed. With the exception of occasional adjustments, the values of the dollar, the yen, the franc, and the pound remained constant. The central banks of all the major countries were committed to buying and selling currencies at the fixed rate. A country whose currency appeared to be overvalued or undervalued was expected to take steps to change its internal policies to bring its currency back into line. Devaluations were rare, and usually reflected an adjustment to major long-term changes in the position of a particular country. Devaluations in this system were often traumatic events, and runs on weak currencies remained inconveniently frequent.

After the U.S. abandoned this system in 1971, world exchange rates floated. No one knew exactly what any currency would be worth tomorrow, next week, or next month. Many hoped, and some believed, that the system of floating exchange rates would be stable—that currencies would fluctuate, but within narrow ranges. Unfortunately, as time has gone on, the swings in currency values have become extreme, with currencies rising and falling 20 percent or more in a year. Often, greater profits can be made by successful currency speculation than through productive investments. Worse, many companies and banks have had to become currency speculators in self-defense. To protect themselves from currency swings, they must engage in complicated hedging strategies that have led to huge and potentially dangerous international currency markets.

An alternative to either of these systems has had considerable success in Europe. The major continental currencies have formed the EMS, the European Monetary System. Sometimes called the "snake," this is a system in which European exchange rates are permitted to fluctuate against one another, but within a relatively narrow range. The float gives bankers and governments enough flexibility to avoid repeated Bretton Woods–style currency crises, but the range is narrow enough to discourage excessive currency speculation. When a country's currency moves to the upper or lower end of its trading range, this is a signal to make policy changes that keep the currency from moving too far up or down. Adjustments in the target zone can be made periodically as circumstances change.

The U.S. should try to adopt a more formal approach to exchange rates and set up the target-zone system.

3. *An expanded role for the IMF would promote stability.* The IMF should take on a central role in monitoring the process of target-zone adjustment. This would not be an entirely new function for the agency. The IMF already has a general responsibility for surveying exchange-rate practices and for averting their manipulation, although this course has been neither vigorously pursued nor particularly effective. One way the IMF could promote monetary stability with economic growth would be to compel countries with persistent balance of payments surpluses to appreciate their currencies upward toward the target-zone goal. As it now stands, the adjustment process has a deflationary bias; the onus of adjustment is placed on deficit countries. This discourages economic growth and contributes to the slowdown of world demand.

4. *We should develop a system of international regulation for international financial markets.* The balance of the world economy depends on the stability of the world's financial system. Individual banks now operate in scores of countries around the world, and the links among these banks—borrowing and lending money to one another and making payments through one another twenty-four hours a day—mean that the financial stability of each individual country depends on the stability of the world banking system as a whole. We need rules of the road for the flow of capital and credit through the international banking system, and we need institutions with the ability and the resources to intervene at critical moments to prevent dangerous international banking crises. Just as we created domestic safeguards like the FDIC to protect our domestic banking system, we should develop, with other countries, a system to defend the world banking system against sudden and catastrophic events.

An International Bank Regulatory Office established within the IMF to administer common guidelines among all international banks would be a good start. Regulations might include reserve and full disclosure requirements by which banks would be obligated to supply relevant information to the national and international authorities charged with policing the system.

Banks in each country are subject to complex and comprehensive rules for their accounting, auditing, underwriting, and disclosure practices. Each of these national systems reflects the historical evaluation of the banking system in a particular country. The time has come to develop standardized procedures for international banks. These rules will protect borrowers, depositors, governments, and the banks themselves by making the international banking environment predictable and safe.

We have also seen an internationalization of securities markets in stocks and bonds. Here, too, we find an increasing need for consistent practices and standards, so that investors from around the world will have an equal opportunity to understand the rules of the game. The issue of securities-trading standardization cannot be separated from the issue of bank regulation, because other countries do not have anything like the Glass-

Steagall Act, which divides American banking into loan-making and securities underwriting institutions.

Some have proposed the establishment of a world central bank to act as a lender of last resort on the international scene. Such a bank might well be the logical outcome of the evolution of world banking, and we should remain open to such a possibility. But if a world central bank is created at all, it will happen toward the end of the process of global financial integration. We must resolve today's problems within the basic framework of today's institutions, while remaining open to new developments in the future.

5. *We should explore possibilities for the long-term reform of the world financial system.* Besides adopting the short-to-medium-term policies outlined above, we should explore changes in the way the world does business that can lead to stable growth over the longer run. Now that the world financial community is multipolar, with many dynamic economies existing together, we need to think about the approaches to our common objectives that depend less and less on the American economy and currency.

In recent years the world has moved uneasily toward a "multicurrency" framework in which the dollar would no longer be a unique reserve currency. The American government never intended or desired to see the dollar in this lonely position of eminence; the original Bretton Woods system relied on the pound as well as the dollar, and only Britain's dramatic economic weakness after the war ended the dual reserve system.

Originally, the dollar was the most stable currency available for use as a reserve currency, and the heavy reliance on it in international trade was justified by the economic supremacy of the U.S. Now that other countries have joined us as healthy, dynamic, and rich societies, we have a unique opportunity to develop a new and potentially more stable system of reserve currencies.

An international monetary arrangement more in keeping with real economic power today would be based on shared responsibility among four major world currencies: the dollar, the yen, the pound, and the deutsche mark. The currencies of smaller countries would rise or fall against the reserve currencies as dictated by circumstances.

Another idea for long-term study and perhaps negotiation is the increased use of the Special Drawing Rights (SDR) of the IMF as a central reserve currency. The SDR, which has been used only sparingly since it was introduced in the 1970s, should be given serious consideration as a central reserve currency. Based on an average of other currency values, the SDR is likely to be much more stable than any individual currency, and increased reliance on the SDR in international finance would reduce the destabilizing consequences of rises and drops in the value of individual national currencies.

CHAPTER FIVE

Restructuring America

PART ONE: A Choice of Strategies

THE last five years have taught us many things, including that America cannot grow alone. They have taught us that global interdependence means our long-term prosperity depends upon global growth, which in turn requires reform of the international economy.

But reform will be impossible and renewed world growth will not help us if we fail to improve our ability to compete. International reform is one half of the equation—a domestic strategy for competitiveness is the other.

We believe that America, despite serious economic problems, can meet the challenge of competitiveness and enjoy an economic renaissance in the next decade. Our optimism comes from our realism. We know America has immense national assets. We can see that some of the reforms we need to make are, already underway. And we sense the new awareness among Americans that taking the future for granted is not the way to survive in today's environment. Americans understand that the world has changed and are ready to apply the lessons of history to build a future in which our economic system is more productive and our prosperity more secure.

The Cheap Dollar and Competitiveness

What constitutes an appropriate strategy for American competitiveness? For the present Administration the solution has primarily been a macroeconomic one—i.e., they have attempted to increase U.S. competitiveness by decreasing the value of the dollar.

In Chapter 3 we described how the economic expansion of 1983 and relatively high interest rates pushed the value of the dollar up 60 percent during the first half of the 1980s. The fall of the relative cost of foreign goods and the failure of other countries to match the U.S. growth rate kept American exports low while the rapid recovery drew in imports. The result was the massive increase in the trade deficit.

In 1985 the Administration embarked on a strategy of reducing the trade deficit by lowering the value of the dollar. It hoped that this would make our goods cheaper abroad and imports more expensive, and that once the price changes went into effect, Americans would buy fewer imports and customers overseas would buy more U.S. exports. Between February 1985 and January 1988 the dollar dropped 50 percent. However, during that period the trade deficit did *not* experience a similar decline.

Many economists use the term "J curve" to explain why lowering the dollar takes time to bring down the trade deficit. These economists note that while the quantity of goods imported is less, these goods are more expensive because it takes more dollars to buy them. Therefore, the value of imports as expressed in dollars remains high until the volume of imports over exports declines *significantly*.

Buying competitiveness with a cheap dollar was supposed to take about eighteen months. But by the middle of 1987 it became clear the J curve was not working. New deficit records were being set with each month's trade figures.

One explanation often cited by American manufacturers for the failure of the lower dollar to function as predicted is that foreign exporters are cutting their profits to maintain market share. In other words, they are keeping prices steady and making less profit on their sales. Another reason often given is that the currencies of many of our competitors are tied to the dollar and appreciate little when the dollar falls—some, like Mexico, have actually seen their currency depreciate against the U.S. dollar.

All these explanations have some validity. But common sense shows that even if circumstances were reversed in each instance, there would still be obstacles to reducing the trade deficit and restoring our competitiveness. Many American industries have been so devastated in the last ten years that they have permanently lost their share of the market. And in other cases the quality of our products is not good enough to make people switch to American-made goods. The U.S. is simply not the producer it once was.

It is now clear that when the dollar was overvalued, foreign suppliers expanded their production to take advantage of opportunities in the U.S. market and were able to gain very secure shares of our market. At the same time, U.S. producers increased "outsourcing," or moving production overseas, to compensate for the currency imbalances and were left with diminished manufacturing capacity. Consequently they are now in a weak position to challenge imports even with the cheap dollar. And many U.S. producers are reluctant to expand capacity or enter new markets because they worry that today's dollar advantage is only momentary.

The Commission believes that trying to buy competitiveness with a cheap dollar will not work. Instead we have to earn it by producing goods and services that our own people and the rest of the world want. Further, dollar depreciation would be an appropriate competitiveness strategy only if competitiveness is defined as a nation's ability to maintain a numerical balance in trade. By that definition, Bangladesh and Ethiopia would be "competitive" because they have a trade balance, even though their per capita incomes are less than $200 a year. If the value of the dollar falls low enough, American goods, like Ethiopia's, cannot help but be "competitive," and the trade deficit will shrink and disappear—but so will much of the American standard of living.

As the President's Commission on Industrial Competitiveness declared in its report to the President: "Competitiveness cannot be defined as the ability of a nation to maintain a positive trade balance. The very poorest of nations are often able to do that quite well."[1]

Banking on Services

One reason for the persistence of this limited conception of competitiveness has been the lingering belief held by many that American manufacturing, the producer side of the economy, will inevitably be replaced by the service side as a normal transition to the next stage of economic development. More than one political figure has echoed President Reagan's comment: "The move from an industrial society toward a 'postindustrial' service economy has been one of the greatest changes to affect the developed world since the Industrial Revolution. The progression of an economy such as America's from agriculture to manufacturing to services is a natural change."[2]

Certainly the service sector is a vital part of the overall economy and employment in services continues to exceed manufacturing employment. But the "postindustrial service economy" can never be more than a partial economy—a partner, not a successor, of manufacturing.

The DRI Report on U.S. Manufacturing Industries concluded that "a flourishing manufacturing sector is essential to general economic growth. The demand for many of the services originates, directly or indirectly, in manufacturing activity; the production of goods is the principal component of the economic base of most communities and regions. The historical situation requires special efforts to promote the success of U.S. manufacturing industry. It would be unfounded optimism to believe that the service sector will somehow sustain the U.S.'s economic progress on its own."[3]

Basic to an American competitiveness strategy is the simple fact that some industries contribute more to the economy than others. Those with higher value added products, employment, and profitability are more important to the nation's economy than other industries. These are not the only criteria. In some cases the relationship between industries is also crucial to competitiveness. The computer industry is a prime example of an industry that has a tremendous impact on other industries. Microelectronics is another. Both have the ability to revolutionize production in other industries, creating a ripple effect of increasing productivity throughout society.

The Commission believes that America must return to an ethic that values production and a competitiveness strategy that focuses on production. As Paul Volcker, former chairman of the Federal Reserve Board, has observed, if a balance in trade is to be achieved, it "has to be accomplished almost entirely in manufactured goods."[4] Manufactured goods make up the bulk of trade and will continue to be the critical component of our trade balances.

The New American Formula

Implementing a competitiveness strategy based on production will require a national change in thinking. This is ironic because not that long ago we took pride in the fact that we were the world's preeminent industrial nation. In recent years, however, we have come to think of ourselves primarily as a nation of consumers, often forgetting that it was our success as producers that made our consumption possible.

Americans have become oriented to consumption because we created the world's first mass consumer society—the first society in history in which the majority of the population, and not just a tiny elite, enjoyed access to a wide variety of goods and services. If we have become a nation of consumers, we ought to remember that this is what we wanted—a nation in which most people enjoy access to a large and growing variety of consumer products; if we now need to modify this orientation, we must understand the forces that created this condition.

Before our economy lost its cutting edge, business and political leaders came from all over the world to learn the secrets of our success, and they left hoping to take the lessons of America to their own countries. In fact, the key to America's success is what we have called the "American Formula," a revolutionary but simple approach to development which opened new horizons in the life of the United States and, as it was exported to other countries, to the industrial democracies of Europe and Japan. The American Formula works on a basic principle: that the wealth of a modern nation depends on increasing the buying power of its citizens. Rather than slowing down economic progress, our rising standard of living accelerates our national development.

Business needs customers: this is one of the fundamental concepts behind the American Formula. Without customers, business starves; production and consumption need each other. If we reduced wages here to levels closer to those of the Third World, as some suggest we must to remain competitive, it would not just be blue- and white-collar workers who suffered. Corporations without markets for their products would go bankrupt. Banks without creditworthy borrowers could not make loans. Service providers would lack buyers of their services, and entrepreneurs would lack markets for their innovative ideas.

Rising wage levels also stimulate technological progress and higher productivity by giving management an incentive to develop new technology. Labor then demands a share of the new productivity, leading to a rising standard of living—and creating an incentive for a new round of productivity-enhancing technological progress.

The Depression taught America a bitter lesson. New technology was capable of producing millions of refrigerators, toasters, automobiles, and radios—but there were not enough customers for this cornucopia of products. Markets were glutted and profits were falling, and manufacturers began to lay off workers and shut down plants. A vicious circle developed and spun out of control. Each new layoff reduced consumer demand, and producers responded by new rounds of layoffs and plant closings.

In the 1930s, 40s, and early 50s, the foundations of the modern American system were laid. Government took a new, more positive role, with programs and policies that helped stabilize the economy. This was the other key part of the American Formula.

For example, social security provided a safety net of income for the elderly, and the Wagner Act helped working people organize for the higher wages that could keep the economy moving. The G.I. Bill made education and housing available to veterans, while federal farm programs brought a greater degree of income certainty to those engaged in agriculture. Government loan guarantees made it possible for millions of Americans to become homeowners, thus giving jobs to millions of others in the construction industry.

It seemed we were living in the best of all possible worlds, but, as it turned out, there was a catch. The extremely productive assembly-line system that gave us the ability to consume new products in great quantities, also subtly changed the American people into a nation of consumers.

The effects of the assembly-line system went far beyond the factory floor. The methods originally developed for the factory floor, called scientific management, were applied to most corporate organizations and clerical tasks. White-collar as well as blue-collar employees were performing repetitive tasks in a regimented environment. Corporations developed rigid, hierarchical methods of management; getting along and taking directions were often valued more than creative thinking and participation.

The rush to consume accelerated in our society. Many people lost sight of the link between consumption and production. Production was what you had to do on the job; consumption was what you did on your own. For millions of Americans there was not always a clear relationship between the productivity and quality of the work and the size of the paycheck. In the large, anonymous corporate organizations that grew up in the twentieth century, most workers saw little relationship between their own performance and the success or failure of their employer.

One of the lessons of the Depression was that the growth of production depends on the growth of consumption. Today, we are learning a new lesson: that consumption depends on production. In a world economy, a nation that does not produce quality goods at competitive prices will sooner or later have to cut back on its consumption.

Fortunately, our economy is in the process of outgrowing the system that led to an unbalanced pattern of consumption. New technologies coming on line—many of which are now in use by our competitors—require more work force participation. Increasingly, corporations are looking for ways to foster active employee participation in management and production at every level from the factory floor to the boardroom.

Business, labor, and government today have a common responsibility to redress the imbalance toward production. A new national consensus can make us more productive and more competitive once again.

Creating a National Consensus

A return to a producer strategy would be a key part of a new national consensus on competitiveness. That consensus would be based on a sober, tough-minded assessment of the real world in which we live and would at the same time reflect the deep concerns and needs of the majority of Americans. Such a consensus would unify the nation by bringing a clear purpose to our policies, a sense of hope, and a commitment to regain our economic strength.

A new national consensus would be comprised of four elements.

First, it would help everyone understand our place in the world. It would explain how in less than a generation the economic environment has so changed that competition now comes at us from around the world. Although we remain the world's largest economy, we can no longer dictate the terms of trade to our trading partners. Though we have lost our dominance, we need not lose our position of leadership. America can still lead the way toward cooperation and partnership at the international level.

Second, it would articulate our objectives. Today, consumption, as shown by the trade deficit, outpaces production. But if we drastically cut our consumption, we would create recession here and abroad—hardly a situation that would help us compete. Instead we must strive for a new balance built on controlling consumption while increasing our output and the competitiveness of our products.

Third, the national consensus must be clear as to the principles or methods to use in the new producer strategy. The old notions—regimented separation of workers and managers, rigid hierarchies of responsibility, adversarial labor relations between business, government, and labor—must be replaced by the principles of participation and cooperation. Increasing participation at all levels of society will greatly strengthen motivation and responsibility. Increasing cooperation will remove obstacles to efficiency and create an environment in which the spirit of innovation can flourish. As the principles of a new producer strategy, participation and cooperation can give each of us a greater stake in the success of the enterprises in which we work, and make us better able to contribute to that success.

Finally, we must appreciate the enormous strengths of our society. It would be a mistake to become disheartened by the magnitude of the challenge facing us. America has a tremendous array of national assets at its disposal. While the last few decades have brought decline in some areas, they have brought progress in others. Furthermore, many of the factors responsible for our nation's historical prosperity and past success in production are as compelling today as ever. Our new national consensus should recognize these strengths, conserve them, and build upon them.

Building on America's Strengths

America, wrote de Tocqueville, "is the noblest habitation prepared by God for man." No other nation matches our natural resources: temperate climate, fertile soil, mineral wealth, abundant waterways and harbors. And our national commitment to protect the environment proves that the American people are capable of recognizing vital national interests and acting forcefully to preserve them.

America's natural resources can still provide us with the foundation for productive strength. We remain a world leader in the production of food. In agriculture, America is the world's biggest exporter of wheat and corn, and the second-biggest exporter of rice.[5] The U.S. is also still the world's leading exporter of coal and remains a major producer of natural gas.[6] Even though our share of world oil production has diminished, we still produce one-sixth of the world's crude oil.[7] And despite setbacks, a number of U.S. manufacturing industries retain a significant share of the world market. In machinery, transportation equipment, and chemicals, the U.S. portion of the world exports is close to 20 percent or more.[8]

The size of the American market—the largest in the world—is another strength. It is our "home field advantage." In this era of rapidly changing markets, the ability to respond quickly is increased by access and proximity—and, obviously, no one has better access and proximity to America than Americans. By taking full advantage of our position in the heart of this huge market through flexible, market-responsive production, we can do much to restore our competitiveness. At the same time we can use access to our market as leverage for trade negotiations.

We can build on the strength of our open, democratic society. A nation that thrives on exchange and communication, that has always encouraged exploration and rewarded innovation, can do well in the global marketplace because it is open to change and new ideas. The large number of American scientific breakthroughs and Nobel Prize winners testifies to this spirit. Our extensive system of public universities remains a tremendous resource, providing for those with ability the chance to participate in society and expand the benefits that come when many have the opportunity to contribute.

This leads to our most important source of strength, our many hardworking people. America's greatest asset is its work force—all those who depend on their own efforts for their livelihood. That means blue-collar and white-collar workers, industrial and service workers, entrepreneurs and employees, professionals and bricklayers and farmers—everyone who needs to work for a living.

This group, over 110 million strong, is the foundation of

America's middle class. It makes up the bulk of American consumers and producers. If it falters, the nation falters.

The history of the growth of this group is intertwined with another source of national strength—positive government. The present Administration's policy of disengaging government from the economy is a departure from our traditions. At crucial moments through American history, government has actively encouraged economic development, partly to preserve and expand opportunity for the middle class.

Belief that government can play a positive economic role has deep roots in American history. The first permanent English settlement in Virginia was the result of a public-and-private-sector joint initiative, and from 1607 to the present, government has stepped in to foster economic growth in cooperation with private enterprise.

When George Washington established the First Bank of the United States, it was his intention to use government's power to stimulate the growth of trade and private business throughout the new nation.

In the "Era of Good Feeling," Americans from all parties and all parts of the country united behind government efforts to make "national improvements"—roads, bridges, and canals to promote economic development.

Even in the middle of a great civil war, Abraham Lincoln established a system of national banking, provided for joint public-private funding of the transcontinental railroads, and established the system of public land-grant colleges.

Theodore Roosevelt, Woodrow Wilson, Franklin Roosevelt, and Harry Truman all believed that government was part of the solution to the economic problems of their day, and all used their power vigorously to see that government met its economic responsibilities to the American people. Even Herbert Hoover believed that government had an important role to play; although his interventions proved too little, too late to ward off the Depression, his Reconstruction Finance Corporation broke new ground in government's participation in the economy.

Presidents Eisenhower and Kennedy, to say nothing of Johnson, Nixon, Carter, and Ford, also believed that government was part of the solution.

At crucial moments throughout American history, government has stepped in to encourage economic development, ward off depressions, and expand the economic opportunities of the middle class. Today, even in the absence of strong federal leadership, the American tradition of positive government is alive and well at the state and local levels.

State and Local Initiatives: Leading the Way

Governments at the state and local level, across the country, are participating in planning, coordinating, and promoting economic development within their borders.

State programs are typically oriented toward those industries with a strong potential for the future. Each state wants more high-quality industries, because they offer better-paying jobs and provide greater tax benefits to communities. This is an important aspect of making America more competitive.

State economic development agencies offer a panoply of services to assist industry, including information about the state's resources and services, technical support, labor recruitment and training, and location assistance. In some states, these agencies become involved in the building, leasing, and selling of industrial facilities. They nurture business by supporting commercially oriented research in state university research facilities, developing research parks, and establishing state scientific advisory councils.

Many states offer financial services such as state-chartered (but privately organized and financed) development credit organizations, as well as loan guarantees to banks to encourage lending to new businesses. In addition, states target particular communities for development through direct loans to local development corporations or by authorizing the issuance of revenue bonds by local development agencies.

State activism extends to labor issues—from recruitment and training to economic adjustment programs. In California and Delaware, business, labor, and state government have formed partnerships to create training programs, tying funding to results. In Iowa, the state is helping community colleges create training programs to meet specific companies' needs. Five states—Massachusetts, Florida, Kentucky, Minnesota, and Washington—have started "skills corporations," quasi-public publicly and privately financed organizations designed to bolster partnerships between business and educational institutions. A number of states, including New York, Ohio, Michigan, Iowa, New Jersey, Massachusetts, and Vermont, are assisting in training and employment for workers facing plant closings, easing the shock of change.[9]

States have been leaders in cooperation, establishing labor-management councils in which traditional adversaries can work together. In New York State, the Industrial Cooperation Council has initiated a number of programs. One of these is the "New York Compact," a voluntary agreement which commits labor and management to jointly develop approaches for preventing plant closings when possible, and to lessen their impact when they occur.

More than the federal government, states have recognized the demands of a global economic environment and have taken steps to meet them. About half the states maintain offices in foreign countries, promoting state products and encouraging foreign corporations to locate facilities in the state. States are working together in trade development. For example, six southern states have formed the Mid-South Trade Council to help businessmen throughout the region increase their exports.[10]

While specific program goals may differ, the overriding philosophy guiding these efforts is the same—government can improve the lives of its citizens through positive, active economic policy.

The Need for a Federal Role

As constructive as state and local economic policies are, they are not enough. National objectives require national strategies. Because of the resources and economic tools at its disposal, the federal government is the only institution capable of coordinating a competitiveness strategy for the nation. With so much economic development activity by the states and cities, the federal government does not have to start from scratch. Just as states have integrated existing agencies into comprehensive economic programs, the federal government can build on the accomplishments of the states to create a national economic program.

Anticipating that the next Administration will return to a more active approach, the National Governors Association has declared that "priority should be given to the sorting out of roles between the federal and state governments."[11] We concur. Expanding export opportunities, small-business assistance, and technology development are just a few of the areas that lend themselves to increased federal-state partnership. The federal government should also use its leadership to reduce the state-vs.-state competition in luring economic development projects.

A national competitiveness strategy should be comprehensive and long-range. The seven warning signs described in Chapter 1 constitute a strong argument against relying on short-term, ad hoc economic policies.

Some of the long-range steps we propose have been previously suggested by a broad range of experts, public officials, business and labor leaders, journalists and scientists: reforming American education, increasing investment, enhancing technological innovation, and restoring balance to the nation's fiscal policies.

Unfortunately, many of these ideas have not gone beyond the proposal stage, primarily because of lack of national leadership. If past studies of competitiveness had a common failing, it was their failure to recognize the key role the national government must play in formulating and implementing a long-range competitiveness strategy.

But the government cannot lead by edict. Restoring the American economic prowess will require teamwork and a resurgence in leadership. No team can compete effectively without a coach who can help devise a strategy that capitalizes on the team's strengths and can provide the direction to see that the strategy is carried out. A coach can coordinate the abilities of each player so that the entire team wins and prospers. It profits the team little if a few team members perform well while the team loses.

Unfortunately, instead of using government as a tool to help solve our economic problems, the current Administration has propagated the notion that "government is the problem," that government action is by definition negative, and that "market forces" should rule the day.

However much one appreciates the ideal of the market, the fact remains that this is too simplistic an approach in today's world. The history of economic growth around the world shows how "market forces" are either very influenced by or are nothing more than the economic strategies of our competitors and their governments. Take, for example, the case of Japan. With a large population but limited farmland, less coal, oil, and iron, and—forty years ago—no industry at all, Japan should have remained a producer of cheap, labor-intensive products.

But Japan and other nations, among them Korea, Taiwan, Hong Kong, and Singapore, have defied the restrictions of their resources to become industrialized economies and world class producers. This demonstrates that comparative advantage is not static, and that it can be created through a national effort. In these countries, government policies promote the development and operation of higher-value industries, and are aided in their efforts by the new mobility of technology and capital. Governments are no longer willing to leave economic outcome to chance or the effects of traditionally defined "market forces."

Our government has clung to outdated conceptions. American industry and workers have found themselves facing aggressive international competitors whose governments are down on the field with them, acting as economic "coaches," setting national economic objectives and creating policies to encourage business to meet those objectives. Our failure to do this places us at a competitive disadvantage.

Some who call for a national economic strategy favor national economic planning, with the federal government controlling the direction of the national economy. We reject this view. We do not believe that central planning would solve our problems, nor that government decrees should replace individual enterprise and the role of the market in allocating capital. At the same time, we reject the belief that government has no legitimate role in the economy.

We believe that government can form partnerships for the public good with business and labor. Business and labor are the primary factors in making the economy work, for they make the basic decisons and bear the consequences. Government's role is more limited: in the American system, government is a facilitator and a helper, not an all-powerful dictator. Neither elected nor appointed officials can or should run the American economy.

At the same time, government has several major economic responsibilities. Among the most important of these is the development of fiscal policies that promote sustainable long-term growth.

PART TWO: A Blueprint for the Future

Fiscal and Monetary Policy: Changing the Mix

To reduce the federal budget deficit will require new spending and taxing policies. But the proper combination, the right fiscal policy, is difficult to achieve, because it depends on forces not under the government's total control, namely on whether the economy is in a recession or growing and on the confidence of foreign lenders. If we have a recession or dramatic slowdown in growth, we will find reduction of the federal budget deficit more difficult and less desirable. Conversely, it is also true that a growing economy will help reduce the deficit.

Our current deficit levels are comparable to those of earlier periods in our own history and that of other countries. What is dangerous and disturbing is the sense that we lack control over fiscal policy, and that we have gotten very little in return for our accumulated deficits.

Furthermore, when spending greatly exceeds revenue on a

continuous basis, as it does now, the deficit leads to instability in our financial markets, and restricts growth and living standards. Because the U.S. budget deficit has been largely financed by capital from abroad, continued deficit financing depends on foreign confidence in the American economy. But that confidence is undercut because the U.S. has not put its fiscal house in order.

The manner and speed with which the U.S. reduces the deficit is as important as reduction itself. If the fiscal gap is narrowed too quickly and extremely, either by severe spending cuts or equally severe tax increases, the U.S. economy could plunge into recession, triggering a global recession.

The Commission believes that future fiscal policy must be based on a combination of reduced spending and increased revenue. In the following pages are some of the options we believe should be considered. We offer them without attempting to put together a specific combination. There are two ideas which have also guided our recommendations. The first is the recognition that investments to improve our competitiveness will have to be financed by cuts in spending in other programs or increased revenue. Second is the idea that spending or revenue measures are not all equal in their economic impact; they should be judged by how much they contribute to demand and to national competitiveness. Our rule should be that *every dollar must count.*

REDUCING THE DEFICIT

Our major federal expenses are for defense, agricultural subsidies, and what some people have called the "middle class entitlement" programs—social security, medical programs, and pensions. When we look for ways to cut today's federal budget, there is little else to consider. Programs specifically for the poor and unemployed have been trimmed to the point of extinction, as have those for the repair and rebuilding of the nation's infrastructure.

The first step in a structural, long-term plan for budget reduction is scrutiny of military spending. We should carefully analyze our current and projected weapons programs, and review the missions our military forces are designed to carry out, to be sure they are essential for national security. If we found, for instance, that the military budget could be held at its present level, the projected savings over five years would be in the range of $140 billion. (By contrast, the cumulative increase in defense spending authorizations between 1981 and 1987 was over half a trillion dollars—roughly equal to what the U.S., including the federal government, borrowed abroad during this same period.) [12] Actual reductions in weapons or forces as proposed by various private studies could, of course, create even greater savings. In any case, adopting a zero-based defense budget and freezing military spending at current levels is an option to be considered.

The other two major categories of federal spending, entitlements and agricultural subsidies, must also be judged on the basis of their contribution to the nation's security and their economic impact. Our ability to spend is not infinite. Entitlements which transfer income from general revenues to individuals—programs such as social security, Medicare, and civil service and military pensions—have more than doubled over the last twenty years and now constitute more than 40 percent of the federal budget. (Only about 20 percent of these are payments directed toward the poor, hence the label "middle-class entitlements.") [13]

Entitlement programs are, obviously, of important social benefit. They also help support our living standards, thus increasing demand and maintaining a healthy economy. Still, we must reduce their overall cost. A variety of measures are possible, from full taxing of social security benefits of those over a certain income to health care cost containment measures which require doctors and hospitals to limit fees and charges to all patients. Reducing certain farm subsidies, those which primarily benefit large producers, could help cut the deficit without adversely affecting supply or demand or producing devastating social consequences.

RAISING THE REVENUE

Reductions in spending must be matched by increased revenue. Here again the principle of supporting productive investment should apply. This means that nonproductive activities should be taxed at a higher rate than those which build new plants and equipment and create jobs. Taxing luxury consumption more heavily than the consumption of necessities can help meet revenue goals without reducing mass consumer demand.

Additional revenue could be raised with a prudent and progressive value-added tax (VAT), levied on goods and services at each stage of production and distribution. A VAT has the advantage of raising large amounts of money while creating incentives to save more and consume less. For example, a VAT levied at the flat rate of five percent on all goods and services, with a per capita refundable tax credit given to offset the effects of the tax on those of lower incomes, could raise $75 billion or more a year. The VAT would also help exports. Imports would pay the VAT, and for those goods produced for export the VAT would be refundable. This exception is allowable under GATT and is widely used by our competitors to boost their exports and discourage imports.

An extra tax on gasoline and diesel fuel over and above the amount now collected to finance highway construction would raise substantial new revenues. A $10-per-barrel oil import fee would add $20 to $30 billion. In addition to contributing toward the elimination of the federal deficit these taxes would also help reduce the U.S. balance of payments deficit by encouraging energy conservation and by discouraging the import of foreign oil. Here, as with VAT, ways could be and should be found to reduce the regressiveness of the tax. The issue of making the tax code more progressive is important. A VAT which increases the regressive impact of overall taxation should not be enacted. It should also be compared to proposals to raise the top rate on the income tax.

Both of these are examples of new funding sources. The Commission believes that if the American public was convinced that the new revenue would provide specific benefits and tangible results, revenue-raising measures could be enacted with the support of the electorate.

INVESTING FOR THE FUTURE
As part of a program of fiscal reform we should establish a national capital budget for investment in physical and human cap-

ital. Such a system of planning and allocation, long recognized as an elementary tool of good management in the private sector as well as in the Department of Defense and NASA, ought to be adopted for federal spending overall.

As we review federal spending, more attention needs to be given to America's physical infrastructure. A nation's infrastructure is the backbone of its economy. No nation can retain its posture as an economic leader if its spine is collapsing. We should undertake a major ten-year program to rebuild and expand America's infrastructure. Over the last two decades, net real investment in public infrastructure has dropped by 75 percent.[14] In that time, America's highways, harbors, bridges, mass transit, urban water supplies, and waste-water treatment systems have fallen into a state of disrepair. The result is that the foundation for U.S. industrial competitiveness has been severely compromised.

MAINTAINING GROWTH

Given the proper mix of revenue and spending, a growing economy is possible. But this can happen only if a tighter fiscal policy is accompanied by a more flexible monetary policy. Maintaining low interest rates while reducing the federal deficit can encourage business investment and consumer spending, as well as shore up the stock and bond markets. But it is important to reiterate that a U.S. monetary policy designed to keep interest rates down must be coordinated with other nations—specifically West Germany and Japan—in order to ensure that foreign interest rates also remain low. Attempts to reshape U.S. fiscal and monetary policies can work only in the context of international cooperation.

Given that proviso, we should adopt a flexible monetary policy, based on goals of achieving a targeted rate of real economic growth, maintaining full employment, and keeping inflation under control—not of hitting artificial money supply targets. In general, the Federal Reserve Board should adjust the supply of credit to keep interest rates slightly above the rate of inflation. Low, stable interest rates should be the goal.

An expanding economy, stimulated in part by low interest rates, may prompt new fears of inflation. Indeed, the goals of a full employment budget and inflation control tend to be contra-dictory. While some of these fears can be allayed by a budget deficit reduction, other inflation-fighting measures should be considered. The U.S. should consider doing what many other countries have done—developing forums for negotiating vol-untary wage and price restraint. If government, business, and labor representatives met annually to set voluntary targets for wage, price, and profit growth, the wage-price spiral could be slowed. Other policies such as increased energy conservation, a health care containment program to control runaway medical costs, and expansion of the housing supply in order to relieve inflationary pressures in that sector could help reduce the bot-tlenecks in the economy which produce inflation.

This overall prescription for macroeconomic policy does not eliminate the probability of sacrifice. We will not go through a substantial period of adjustment without facing alterations in the way we have lived. But sacrifice need not become a per-manent fixture in our lives. Nor does sacrifice mean an eco-nomic depression of the kind we faced fifty years ago. Through careful policy and planning, we can minimize the pain of ad-justment.

As part of that planning, we must work to see that those who have little are not made to bear the major burden of change. Fairness dictates that we cannot expect more sacrifice from the many Americans who already have lost jobs, income, and op-portunity.

Economic Adjustment: Helping Employers and Employees Deal with the Inevitable

In this era of international competition, every major industrial-ized nation must face the need to restructure its industries. In every one of these nations but ours, governments have imple-mented extensive adjustment programs for their industries in need.

Our government has handled unemployed workers in much the same way it approaches troubled domestic industries.

Workers receive income support but too little new training designed to make them employable again; industries receive some protection but are neither encouraged nor assisted to revitalize. At both the worker and industry levels, government has considered failure to compete solely as an individual failure and rarely seen it as a reflection of larger forces.

We can no longer afford to have our government remain an impartial observer. Just as the governments of our competitors have done, our government needs to work with change, not try to ignore it.

We should see economic adjustment as an ongoing process and not just something that starts when a plant closes. The consequence of international trade and the rapid industrial innovation is an ever-changing workplace. In this environment, the lack of a worker adjustment program is a source of competitive weakness. That is why a comprehensive adjustment program of the kind proposed in recent congressional trade legislation should be supported. Implicit in its inclusion in the trade bill is the recognition that an adjustment program is vital to enhancing the competitiveness of American industry.

Worker adjustment programs make sense only as part of a broader economic strategy to lower levels of unemployment and create opportunities for skilled employment. Job creation and retention are as essential as income support in economic adjustment for a variety of reasons: job transitions for workers are eased, consumer demand is maintained, unemployment costs are reduced, and greater flexibility in the workplace is made possible through increased labor-management cooperation.

State government can play a major role in economic adjustment programs, because it has a more intimate knowledge of local adjustment problems. The states should have the primary responsibility for assistance programs, even those initiated and funded at the federal level. And states should not wait for the federal government for direction, but should develop assistance strategies of their own.

The burden for economic adjustment does not rest solely with government. American management can do its part by committing itself to pursue, whenever possible, alternatives to layoffs, such as shared work programs (in which employees collect a portion of salary based on hours worked and unemployment for the time laid off), uniform reduction in hours of management and labor, elimination of overtime, corporation-wide transfers, furlough programs, early retirement incentives, and joint labor-management committees to identify ways to improve productivity, reduce costs, and create additional demand for the company's products.

Government does have a responsibility for ensuring, along with business and labor, that the rights of workers are respected during economic adjustment. These include extended health insurance, portable pensions, and a reasonable period of advance notice of plant closure. Workers will cooperate more and facilitate industrial change and more workplace flexibility if these benefits are available.

Government can also help by conforming existing programs to new goals. As part of the effort, unemployment insurance should be reformed and other income support programs for dislocated workers should be coordinated with education and retraining programs. Given that much of today's unemployment is not cyclical, as it was in the past, unemployment insurance often merely delays the loss of income that comes with long-term unemployment. Unemployment insurance could be put to better use by combining its benefits with programs that lead to new employment. At the same time, no worker participating in a program of retraining should have to go without the benefit of some income support. In light of the vast numbers of workers who are not eligible for unemployment insurance, such support ought to be part of any retraining program. Some consideration should also be given to bringing state unemployment insurance programs into greater uniformity; unlike other major industrialized nations, the U.S. lacks a single, national unemployment insurance system.

We must also do a better job of training workers for future needs. Employers are often reluctant to invest in this way because they worry that new or retrained employees will not stay with the company long enough to justify the training investment. This is why government should create incentives for businesses and labor in specific sectors to develop joint training programs. In a "training consortium," the cost would be shared; no single company would feel it was bearing the burden of training employees for its competitors. In addition, a training consortium would create a sizable, reliable labor pool from which a number of companies could draw. Because a specific industry would sponsor each program, the skill requirements of the industry would be built into the training. Companies' future needs would be met, and workers would receive training geared toward real employment. The model for this could be California's State Employment and Training Panel. By subsidizing training, California gives employers the incentive to create private-sector training in a work setting rather than solely in classrooms. Because on-the-job training (OJT) offers the greatest potential for continued employment, OJT programs should receive major support. We must also encourage training to help upgrade skills, particularly as it relates to new technology.

Toward a New View of Technology

Technology has often been characterized in a static way, as an entity or thing that is the predictable output of a well-defined series of inputs. Many people think new technology starts in a laboratory with scientists doing basic research and moves on to the industrial research facility, product development, and commercial production. According to this conception, the way to advance technology is to increase the funds for R&D, laboratory facilities, technical personnel, and so on.

We believe this notion of how new technology evolves is too narrow. Technology is not a "thing," but a dynamic process involving the application of knowledge, resources, and technique to problem solving. It is not simple or neat, nor does it happen only in one way. Technology emerges not only from the laboratory and university, but also from the manufacturing process. Often technology is born on the factory floor.

Japanese automakers, for example, employ hundreds of people whose sole task is to develop new machine tools for production. This not only leads to production innovation, but creates new tools which are sold to those making products other than automobiles. Significantly, U.S. firms have faced heavy competition in machine-tool production, both at home and abroad. The U.S. share of world machine-tool exports fell from 23 percent in 1964 to approximately 4 percent today. In the domestic market during the same period, machine-tool imports climbed from 4 percent to 47 percent.[15]

Sharing this broad view of the process of technological change are more than a few experts and business leaders who believe that a nation which curtails its manufacturing of goods ultimately loses its ability to innovate. In the name of competitiveness, many firms have chosen to move production to countries where low wages prevail. While this creates short-term advantage for individual firms, it undercuts national technology development. In many ways, U.S. trade and tax policies have encouraged this corporate migration. These policies should be replaced by others that provide incentives for domestic production.

Of course, basic scientific research and R&D are important. The point is that the laboratory *and* the workplace are crucial in developing technology. America should capitalize on both.

MAKING THE DOLLARS COUNT

U.S. technological preeminence does not depend on massive new federal expenditures. As with all things, technology is the result not simply of the amount of money spent, but of how it is spent. Making our present R&D expenditures as productive as possible, by shifting resources to targeted goals, creating new incentives, and emphasizing cooperation, can make as much of a difference as new resources.

Government, through its R&D expenditures, sets the direction of U.S. technological development. Approximately 47 percent of all U.S. expenditures on research and development are made by the federal government.[16] Because defense spending plays such a substantial role in determining the emphasis of domestic research, few would deny that the Defense Department has a considerable impact on the pursuit of new technologies, creating priorities different from those in other countries.

A study by the Berkeley Roundtable on the International Economy observed that "just as the Pentagon is contracting with American manufacturers to pursue the technological breakthroughs necessary to produce such exotic armaments as stealth bombers and laser beam defense shields, other nations' manufacturers are aggressively pursuing the same breakthroughs with commercial applications specifically in mind."[17] According to Erich Bloch, director of the National Science Foundation, "at one time, investments in defense R&D fueled advances in the civilian sector. Today this is true to a lesser extent. In fields like computers, software, biotechnology, and even semiconductors, civilian applications are ahead of defense sector applications, sometimes by many years."[18]

To remain leaders in commercial technology, we must significantly readjust the ratio between federal spending for defense R&D and spending for commercial R&D. At present, nearly three-fourths of all federally funded R&D is defense-related, preempting resources and skilled personnel.[19] We can no longer sustain funding of research simply because it falls under the rubric of "defense." As much as possible, our dollar resources need to be spent in a way that enhances the nation's commercial competitiveness.

The National Science Foundation, in conjunction with the private sector, can play a major role in this shift. The NSF, which has proved itself an effective and constructive federal agency, is presently underfunded and underutilized. With increased funding—and increased private sector participation—it could become more useful in coordinating technological development.

TECHNOLOGY IN THE WORKPLACE

Many analysts believe that the most serious U.S. technological deficiency is not in basic research but process research—U.S. industry, they say, has fallen behind in developing new ways of producing existing products.

Other governments, through incentives and funding, have emphasized producing quality goods efficiently—i.e., "targeted" innovations in process technology (the Japanese, for instance, have targeted technology that increases production flexibility but not labor displacement). The U.S. ought to do the same by assisting in the targeting of product development and process technology. Targeting could take the form of targeted tax credits or a financing facility. With the exception of a financing facility, no new government institutions are needed. Through a new partnership between the private sector and the National Science Foundation, support could be increased for the new technologies needed to make better products.

As for tax incentives, we should consider reinstituting an investment tax credit, tailored to encourage investment in new process technology and equipment. This could be part of a program of changes in the tax code to increase competitiveness. Among them would be ways to reorient capital markets toward a longer-term perspective. Without increased "patient capital," investments in technology (whose benefits may not appear in the short run) are less likely to be made. Tax incentives should be instituted for creating pools of long-term capital.

Our economic system must find better ways to diffuse technology into the commercial environment. One way would be the creation at the state and/or federal level of a manufacturing extension service to assist medium-sized and small U.S. firms. In the same way the agricultural extension service introduced American farmers to new ideas and equipment and offered technical expertise, a manufacturing extension service could help small and middle-sized firms lease and purchase advanced equipment as a major step in increasing their competitiveness. Because the greatest financial benefits of technology occur once innovations are incorporated into production, this transfer should be encouraged.

Finally, through legislation and negotiation, the federal government should strengthen protection of U.S. intellectual property rights. While it is neither possible nor desirable to completely stem the flow of technological information across international borders (we benefit as well as lose from this flow), the federal government ought to do more to help U.S. companies fight the illegal appropriation of patented products, processes, and product design. For example, legislation to strengthen intellectual property rights should permit the party whose patent has been infringed to recover damages and therefore help reduce the commercial incentive to steal ideas and innovations.

Renewing Education: A Cornerstone of Competitiveness

Education, particularly public education, has been championed in America because of its importance to a key democratic principle—increasing opportunity for the individual. But the benefits of education are not solely to the individual. Quality education produces prosperity for society as a whole.

The strength of U.S. industry rests largely on the quality of its work force. Without well-educated workers, industry suffers. The proof of this can be found in the number of major American corporations which have joined the chorus calling for educational reform.[20]

The importance to business of an educated work force is illustrated by changes in one of the nation's fastest-growing industries: financial services. Financial services firms today are eliminating many entry-level, unskilled positions; the clerical positions that remain require more judgment and analysis and increased interaction with customers and coworkers. Among upper-level personnel, there is a need for both highly specialized expertise (systems engineering, legal, actuarial, and trading expertise, etc.) and entrepreneurial skills. Middle-level personnel must now be able to deal with the broader problems involving customer relations: selling services rather than producing services. Clearly, all employees, no matter what their level, must be better educated.

But finding educated employees has proved a difficult task. In 1986, for example, a group of New York City banks pledged to fill 250 entry-level positions with high school graduates from five Brooklyn schools. But by June 1987 only about a hundred graduates had been hired; most of the graduates failed the entry-level test, the equivalent of an eighth-grade math exam.[21] Similar problems were demonstrated in the first half of 1987 when the New York Telephone Company gave its entry-level exam to 21,000 applicants. Only 16 percent passed the test.[22]

The present inadequacy of American education puts U.S. workers and businesses at a real disadvantage. Twenty percent of the entire American work force may be functionally illiterate, compared to only 1 percent of the Japanese work force.[23] Factory workers in Japan are able to perform operations—using more complex, computerized equipment—that U.S. workers cannot perform because they lack basic reading and mathematical skills. The National Assessment of Educational Progress estimates that 43 percent of Americans ages 21–25 are unable to master directions, communicate ideas, or calculate at a level sophisticated enough to perform well in high-technology occupations.[24]

Education and training are the best ways we have to help workers contribute and adapt to change. Every American should have a solid educational foundation and continuing educational opportunities throughout his or her working lifetime. Education should become a lifelong process so that American workers and industry are not left producing second-rate goods with second-rate methods.

A competitive economy demands high-quality, predictable labor markets. Mass quality labor markets can only be produced by mass quality public education. During the early twentieth century, America's system of free public education gave us the edge to surpass Europe economically. Now the situation has been reversed. To meet the economic challenges of the next century, America must match the educational systems of our competitors, beginning at the first step: primary and secondary education.

If we fail to renew primary and secondary education, we risk perpetuating and expanding America's underclass. As long as a significant portion of our population remains uneducated and unskilled, American society will pay a huge price to sustain those who lack the tools to contribute. The persistence of a large underclass puts us at a continuing competitive disadvantage with other major industrialized nations.

REBUILDING THE EDUCATION INFRASTRUCTURE

Because quality education produces a quality labor market, and because labor markets are now regional and national rather than local, the burden of education financing should not fall so heavily on localities. No discussion of improving American education can responsibly escape the issue of funding. If the benefits of education are distributed regionally and nationally, the costs should be as well. The federal government must assume the burden of financing national improvements in education. The property tax and other forms of local revenue are simply inadequate to confront a problem with national consequences.

Our nation's educational infrastructure—its facilities, its materials, and, very important, its teachers—is as vital to our national economic health as our physical infrastructure. The federal government, in the interest of national prosperity, has subsidized the construction and maintenance of such public works as highways and dams. The same consideration must be given to our educational infrastructure. America can make no better investment for the future.

Federal involvement in education should not alter state and local administrative control of schools. Nor should it inhibit the myriad educational reforms already underway. In response to a number of critical studies earlier in the 1980s, states and cities across the nation have been exploring ways to upgrade their educational systems. These efforts need federal support, but not unconditional support. Federal assistance should be predicated on the implementation of basic reforms.

Teachers are the key to educational reform. Long ago, industry recognized that to attract quality personnel wages must be competitive. Today, teachers' salaries are among the lowest for Americans with a college education. If we want to raise the quality of teachers in our schools—as well as boost the morale and performance of the good teachers already there—we must provide wages more on a par with those of other trained professionals. There is strong public support for this step: according to a 1986 Harris poll, 93 percent of the American public favored making teacher salaries competitive with other professions.[25] America's economic competitors offer their teachers better than average financial rewards and respect. We should do the same.

Along with higher pay for all teachers, additional incentives may be necessary to attract teachers in subject areas where there is a shortage. Math and science teachers are at a premium, partly because people with a background in these subjects can earn more in industry. During 1982–1983, thirteen times as many math and science teachers left teaching as entered the profession.[26] Since science and math skills are essential in the modern workplace, America cannot neglect these subjects.

QUANTITY AND QUALITY

We need a longer school year. Japanese students attend school 240 days a year, European students, on average, 220 days. In the U.S. the average school year is 180 days. There is no evidence that American students learn faster than their Japanese or European counterparts, or that Japanese or Europeans are taught less during the average school day. The Japanese school day is longer than the American one. The shorter school year clearly places American students at an educational disadvantage.

So does the lack of clear standards. The time has come to establish a standard of educational achievement, probably in the form of exit testing. A high school diploma today is no guarantee that a graduate can read or write or has a basic knowledge of science and math. Some kind of an examination should measure those basic skills. Other countries have effectively instituted such a system—France has its baccalaureate exam and Britain its A and O levels. Testing should not be limited to candidates for graduation; passing the test ought to be a prerequisite for advancing from year to year. By creating a standard to which students can and must aspire, America can produce more capable high school graduates.

And why not create incentives to increase the educational performance of school districts? Teachers in school districts where students perform better on exit tests relative to the established average for school districts of that type (e.g., suburban, inner-city, etc.) should receive a bonus. However, in no case should general federal aid to school districts be contingent upon the school's meeting a particular standard. Indeed, school districts with particular problems should be targeted.

Changing the way we teach should be part of reform. Successful businesses are the result not of individual achievement but of the achievement of many individuals working together. The importance of team effort, cooperation, and group achievement should be reinforced in the process of teaching. Schools could, in addition, examine ways to incorporate work experience into secondary education. Such a program would give students a taste of the demands of the working world and the responsibilities work carries with it. It might, too, help stem the dropout rate among students anxious to begin earning money. As part of this effort, secondary education should include a curriculum that provides students with the knowledge and skills necessary to search and apply for jobs.

Post-high-school American education also merits attention. U.S. colleges and universities are graduating fewer engineers and scientists each year, and many of these are finding employment in defense-related, rather than commercial, industries. Numerous degrees in engineering are being awarded to foreign students who take their education with them when they return to their own country. In 1985, 32 percent of U.S. science and engineering doctorates were awarded to foreign students.[27]

Currently, 6 percent of U.S. undergraduate degrees are in engineering. The figures for the USSR and West Germany are 35 percent and 37 percent, respectively.[28] Instead of concentrating on engineering and the hard sciences, U.S. students gravitate toward such fields as business administration, management, economics, and law. The number of undergraduate degrees awarded in business and management doubled between 1970 and 1982, while interest in careers in manufacturing, engineering, and education fell.[29]

Though the federal government can act to improve college education in engineering and the sciences—providing assistance to upgrade university laboratories, funding science fellowships, awarding research work to universities—it cannot directly affect the numbers of students choosing to enter these fields. But by creating an economic environment that emphasizes production and commercial innovation, government can offer students the prospect of rising opportunity in these fields. America is not languishing in technology simply because we lack trained profesionals, but because those who innovate and produce have been supported and rewarded less than professionals in other fields. Many of our best students have rejected science and engineering programs for this reason. A new orientation by government and business can change that.

A New Balance, a New Vision

Individual policies, no matter how creative, do not constitute a program. To prevent policies from becoming isolated ends with no coherence, government needs to think long-term and strategically.

In matters of foreign policy and defense, long-range strategic planning by the federal government has long been considered essential for national security. Given that in today's global competition the threats to our national security are in many ways more economic than political, the federal government's strategic thinking must move toward national economic security.

The components of a successful national economic strategy are threefold: comprehensive information on domestic and foreign economic conditions; a vision of what we want our economy to look like in the long term; and a coordinated government process that can help achieve that vision.

A nation's competitiveness will rise or fall on its ability to adapt to new conditions and take advantage of new opportunities. This requires accurate and up-to-date information. The greater the base of knowledge, the better informed strategic decisions are likely to be.

But information is only the beginning. Those giving us the greatest competition are nations with a vision of themselves in the future. Today's policies are guided by tomorrow's objectives—they know where they wish to go. Once in our history, America's government and its leaders did the same, fashioning a vision of our future that was understood and embraced by the nation as a whole. We must do so again.

Finally, we need a government process capable of taking us to the future we have envisioned. The frequently fragmented, duplicative, and uncoordinated process of economic policy-making and implementation under which we now operate is as much an obstacle to national progress as our lack of economic vision. Because the development of economic goals is a departure from present practice, new institutions unburdened by traditional assumptions may be needed to reach those goals.

By moving in a progressive direction, government can restore balance in the interests of all its citizens, a balance where the public good of many is not sacrificed for the private gain of a few. But government has a defined and limited role. It can create a fertile environment—prepare the land for planting—but it cannot do the farming. If we are to reap a harvest in which we all can share, reform of government must lead to new growth in America's private industries.

CHAPTER SIX

The Fate of American Industry

The Winds from Abroad

COMPETITION in the American market is radically different from what it was just fifteen years ago. In market after market, foreign producers have carved out ever larger shares for themselves. The evidence is all around us: automobiles from Japan, shoes from Italy and Brazil, shirts from Taiwan and Hong Kong, and VCRs from Korea.

The American consumer has grown accustomed to buying these things, and the result has been massive market penetration by foreign producers. In 1987 the combined U.S. trade deficit in six major consumer categories—passenger cars, consumer electronics, apparel, shoes, household furniture, and household appliances—amounted to more than $80 billion, or nearly 50 percent of the total trade deficit.[1] (See Chart 6.1.)

During the last two decades, American spending for consumer goods grew dramatically. But the nation did not reap the full benefit of this growth, because foreign firms' grip on the market also grew. As consumer spending expanded, purchases of foreign-made goods rose at an even greater rate.

With the decline of domestic consumer industries, Americans first consoled themselves with the continued U.S. preeminence in capital goods and high technology. But in the 1980s, the trends in these industries have been equally disturbing. Foreign companies have carved out ever larger American mar-

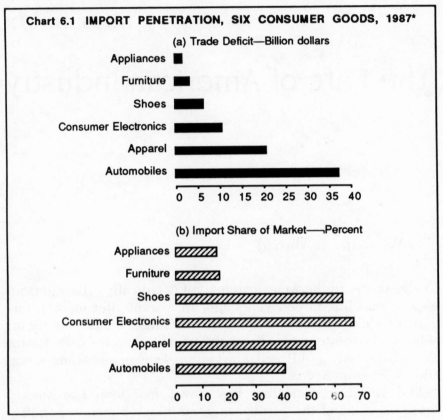

Chart 6.1 IMPORT PENETRATION, SIX CONSUMER GOODS, 1987*

(a) Trade Deficit—Billion dollars

Appliances
Furniture
Shoes
Consumer Electronics
Apparel
Automobiles

0 5 10 15 20 25 30 35 40

(b) Import Share of Market——Percent

Appliances
Furniture
Shoes
Consumer Electronics
Apparel
Automobiles

0 10 20 30 40 50 60 70

Source: Fiber and Fabric Coalition and U.S. Department of Commerce

*Note: Because 1987 data on import shares were unavailable, 1986 data were used for part (b).

ket shares in capital goods and reduced the long-standing surplus that had helped make up for the deficit in consumer goods. In this decade the trade surplus in capital goods, including high-technology goods, has dwindled away.

For a variety of basic capital goods, imports' share of U.S. consumption rose substantially in the 1980s. Between 1982 and 1987, imports' share of the U.S. market nearly doubled from 14.2 to 27.4 percent. Sizable increases in the 1980s can be found in these major sectors: [2] (See Chart 6.2.)

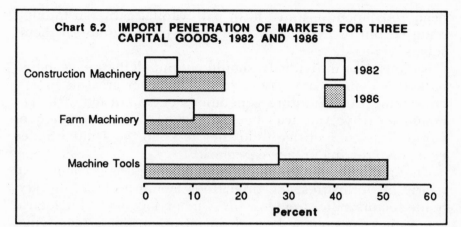

Chart 6.2 IMPORT PENETRATION OF MARKETS FOR THREE CAPITAL GOODS, 1982 AND 1986

Source: U.S. Department of Commerce

Farm machinery	78 percent (1982–86)
Construction machinery	78 percent (1982–86)
Machine tools	81 percent (1982–86)
Computers	157 percent (1982–85)
Electrical transformers	67 percent (1982–85)
Telephone equipment	200 percent (1982–85)

At this rate, foreign firms will come to dominate the U.S. market for capital goods as strongly as the market for consumer goods. In the machine-tool industry this has already occurred. In 1986, imports of machine tools accounted for more than half of the U.S. market.[3]

America will become increasingly integrated in the world economy and will compete in all fields and products. Those who argued that just a few sectors, such as high technology, would carry the load for us economically have been contradicted by events. The travails of the semiconductor industry are an example. In 1972, imports of semiconductors accounted for only 15 percent of total U.S. consumption; by 1985 that share reached 40 percent—an increase of 166 percent.[4] Nor will our service industries give us all the exports we need to offset imports. In financial services, the most substantial and profitable of our service industries, American companies have already felt the bite of foreign competition and loss of market share. European and Japanese firms, flush with capital garnered through trade surpluses, have moved aggressively to establish themselves on our shores.

Nations, like individuals, should not put all their eggs in one basket. No single industry or sector, however great its importance, can provide future generations of Americans with economic security. America's best strategy is to foster a variety of world class competitive industries to keep the United States economy growing in the years ahead.

Though the erosion of market share to imports is common to nearly all industries, the difficulties facing each sector vary. Some sectors suffer from low investment, lagging technological innovation, or poor industrial organization. Some face tough wage competition, while others confront government-supported foreign firms, targeting strategies, or dumping of goods because of overcapacity. The decline of one industry often has a ripple effect on others. Semiconductors and steel, for example, are essential products for many other industries (their problems can also impact national security). The point is that industries are interdependent. Any effort aimed at rebuilding a competitive America should be predicated on that reality.

The idea of explicit industry-level approaches for improving competitiveness was first raised in the late 1970s and resulted in a variety of proposals for industrial policy. One proposal widely debated was a Reconstruction Finance Corporation which would have provided industries with new investment funds. It was also suggested that the United States set up a Department of International Trade and Industry, modeled on Japan's MITI. These proposals provoked the criticism that they called for a degree of centralization and planning that was inconsistent with the strong U.S. tradition of decentralized solutions to problems. And many proposals failed to build on existing government avenues which could be better used to regain competitiveness.

The impetus for a national industrial policy faded with the economic recovery in 1984. But the issue of what happens to industries remains with us. Without a way to bring macroeconomic, trade, and structural adjustment policies down to the level of industries, the level at which competition actually takes place, these policies will not meet their goals. And if we are to develop a coherent strategy and put it into action, we must have cooperation and communication between government, industry, labor, and the public. We must also have clear goals for such initiatives and explicit criteria for evaluating their success.

In the pages ahead, we examine a cross-section of industries. The five sectors reviewed—apparel, steel, telecommunications, financial services, and food—reflect a wide range of American business, from traditional to emerging industries. We chose these industries because they are important to New York State's employment and production base. Each offers specific lessons to consider in the creation of new policies for increasing competitiveness.

Apparel: The First Target

The apparel industry first served as a cornerstone of the industrial economy in the northeastern U.S. It quickly evolved from a regional to a national industry as the American economy and market developed.

After World War Two, the U.S. apparel industry grew and prospered for about twenty-five years. It found an inherent competitive advantage in its close link with the American textile industry. The apparel industry provided a large, stable demand for textiles; it offered sufficient returns for investments in new technology that automated the textile industry. In turn, the textile industry provided relatively inexpensive, high-quality fabric.

Along the way, the industry achieved significant advances in labor standards—employment security, health and retirement benefits, improved working conditions. Even today, after years of decline, the apparel industry remains an important source of jobs. Together, textiles and apparel are still the nation's largest sector of nondurable goods manufacturing, employing approximately 2 million workers in 1985—more than 10 percent of all manufacturing jobs. Of these, the apparel industry employed approximately one-half.[5]

During this century the textile industry has been substantially altered by advances in automation. Dramatic gains in productivity have produced a capital-intensive industry highly concentrated in relatively few large firms taking advantage of economies of scale in the large domestic market. Since the war the industry has been challenged by the growth of the textile-apparel sector in the Far East, but it has so far survived by moving into additional products besides apparel and by achieving greater gains in productivity through further investments in automation.

Most recently, the textile industry was on the ropes, again, in the early 1980s, but under the shelter of import restrictions, it has made billions of dollars of investments in modernization that further boosted productivity and further consolidated the industry. Aided by the fall in the dollar, the industry has emerged profitably, and 1986 and 1987 have proved to be the best years in memory for those still in the industry. This recovery has been good for owners, shareholders, and those workers who still have jobs, but it was gained at considerable hardship for those workers whose jobs were eliminated by the layoffs and plant closings that accompanied the increase in productivity.

In most cases the apparel industry has not found similar developments to take advantage of, and has felt the same pains in international competition with little of the success.

Apparel is a labor-intensive industry. Skill requirements are low, as are barriers to entry. It is not difficult to open an apparel factory, or move that factory to another country. Transportation is relatively cheap. These characteristics made the apparel industry an easy target for foreign producers, as well as making it easy for U.S. companies to move their factories abroad to reduce costs.

The apparel industry has felt the impact of international competition for many years. By 1986, the deficit in apparel amounted to 10.4 percent of the overall U.S. trade deficit.[6]

Foreign competition in apparel has driven the return on investments below the average for all manufacturing, and has caused a steady decline in employment and real wages.[7] Between 1973 and 1985, employment plunged 27 percent as imports gobbled up the domestic apparel market.[8] (See Chart 6.3.) A 1986 USITC study suggests that possible job loss from trade between 1980 and 1984 was greater in apparel than in any other industry.[9] Only about half of the 170,000 apparel workers who lost jobs between 1980 and 1985 found new jobs by January 1986.[10]

Japan was the first to develop an export-oriented apparel industry. The Japanese successfully demonstrated that domestic development could be accelerated by focusing on exports. When the competitive consequences of this were first felt in the 1960s, the U.S. believed it could manage the impact. Instead, newly developing countries jumped into the apparel market, and the decline of the American industry worsened.

THE RISE OF THE THIRD WORLD
Following the Japanese model, many developing nations have adopted policies to nurture the apparel industry. For instance, most of Taiwan's textile and apparel mills are located in special export-processing zones permitting duty-free imports of equipment and raw materials. In Pakistan, where the majority of industrial jobs are in textiles and apparel, the government lends

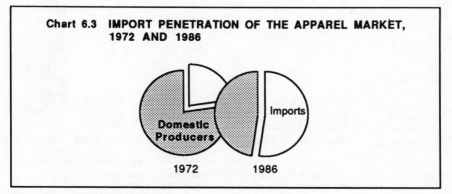

Chart 6.3 IMPORT PENETRATION OF THE APPAREL MARKET, 1972 AND 1986

Domestic Producers

Imports

1972   1986

Source: Fiber and Fabric Coalition

foreign exchange to firms to help them buy foreign production equipment. These imports are exempt from customs duty.[11]

Paying their workers from 3 to 25 percent of a U.S. apparel worker's wages, the nations of Southeast Asia and China all provide tough, low cost competition for U.S. producers. In Taiwan, Hong Kong, South Korea, and China, for example, wages per hour range from $0.21 to $1.89.[12] (See Chart 6.4.)

Many Third World governments bolster their apparel producers by requiring few fringe benefits and ignoring the rights of workers. As the International Labor Organization (ILO) has observed, "governments often play a much greater role in labor relations . . . since they fear that the free play of labor relations may adversely affect the economic development of the country and even its political stability."[13] As a result, most workers in developing nations are not organized into unions. They have no protection against long hours and health hazards—protection American workers gained as basic rights much earlier in this century. Foreign producers often use cottage workers who are generally paid much less than factory workers. And factory workers in some countries work as much as sixty hours a week at straight-time pay.[14]

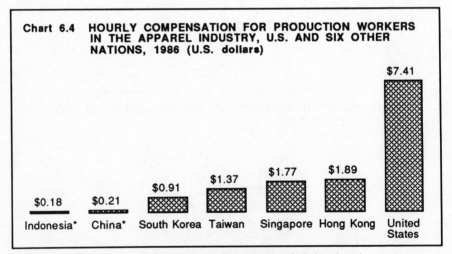

Chart 6.4   HOURLY COMPENSATION FOR PRODUCTION WORKERS IN THE APPAREL INDUSTRY, U.S. AND SIX OTHER NATIONS, 1986 (U.S. dollars)

Indonesia*	China*	South Korea	Taiwan	Singapore	Hong Kong	United States
$0.18	$0.21	$0.91	$1.37	$1.77	$1.89	$7.41

Source: U.S. Department of Labor, Bureau of Labor Statistics, except for Indonesia and China, from Cuomo Commission on Trade and Competitiveness, *Apparel Study*

Data for Indonesia and China refer to 1984, while the other data are for 1986.

Many companies routinely use child labor. A 1985 ILO study for the Thai government traced the recent increase in nonfarm work by Thai children to the country's export boom: "Manufacturing industries employing a large proportion of child workers are those which expanded very rapidly as a result of their export potential." Though many nations legally restrict child labor, most laws are flexible and easily skirted. South Korea's labor standards law requires only that children under age 13 have work permits and parental permission. Philippine children earn 1 to 5 cents an hour for sewing in their homes; most of the children work between 15 and 30 hours a week.[15]

American-based firms have searched for ways to compete, but have found that superior U.S. productivity only partially reduces the low-wage advantage. This table illustrates the problem:

Production of a Man's Shirt [16]

	Avg./person/min.	Compensation/hr. (in U.S. dollars)	Compensation/ shirt
U.S.	14	7.53	1.76
Taiwan	19		
Hong Kong	20	1.40	.46
South Korea	21	1.53	.53
India	23	.40	.15
Sri Lanka	24	.35	.14
Bangladesh	25	.25	.10

Though American workers are 26 to 44 percent more efficient than their counterparts, their wages are seventeen times as high as those of workers in Bangladesh. To reduce the labor cost to Bangladeshi standards, U.S. wages would have to fall to 45 cents an hour—or U.S. productivity would have to rise about 900 percent, from 4.29 to 45.25 shirts per hour.

STEMMING THE LOSSES: TRADE POLICY

American trade policy for the past thirty years has not kept the industry vital. The present U.S. trade regime in apparel began with bilateral agreements with the Japanese in the mid-1950s and evolved into the "Multi-Fiber Arrangement," or MFA, the latest version of which was negotiated in 1986. The MFA sets guidelines by which developed countries can bilaterally negotiate import controls and recommends an annual import growth rate of 6 percent. Today, thirty-five nations trade under agreements within the MFA.

In the most recent round of negotiations, European nations have applied the guidelines strictly, limiting import growth to 6 percent. In the U.S., the combination of a strong dollar, a more liberal import policy, and lax enforcement has overwhelmed domestic producers; MFA-regulated imports ballooned by 30 percent in 1983 and 32 percent in 1984, before falling to 7 percent in 1985. In 1986 those imports soared by more than 17 percent.[17] (See Chart 6.5.)

A basic problem with the MFA is the ease with which apparel makers can set up shop in a country less restricted by the Agreement. Indeed, the Congressional Budget Office suggests that U.S. trade policy has bred a generation of apparel "Marco Polos," moving from country to country in search of places where import quotas do not yet apply.[18] These companies also look for fabrics that do not yet fall under regulation. For example, garments made from ramie fiber came into fashion in Amer-

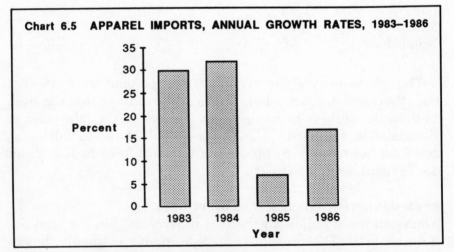

Chart 6.5 APPAREL IMPORTS, ANNUAL GROWTH RATES, 1983–1986

Source: U.S. Congress, Office of Technology Assessment

ica, not coincidentally, at a time when foreign producers dumped huge numbers of ramie-cotton blends on the American market and *before* the fiber was brought under quota regulation.

In 1982, 72 percent of all American textile and apparel imports were covered by our agreements.[19] Under the MFA, imports even of restricted goods can increasingly seize market share. The arrangement permits quotas to grow 6 percent annually even if domestic demand grows less—which in recent years it has.[20]

While U.S. trade policy in apparel has moderated the flow of imports and been essential to the U.S. industry's survival, it has not provided the industry with an active strategy to respond to global competition. The history of the industry in the last thirty years illustrates the limits of using trade policy as a substitute for competitiveness strategy.

Are there policies which would help the U.S. maintain its industry at the present scale, other than costly, short-sighted protectionist measures? The Commission's analysis of this industry found four fundamental issues which will shape any discussion of the industry's competitiveness and future as a source of employment: technology, competition based on low wages and poor working conditions, economic growth abroad, and trade policy.

Advances in technology cannot by themselves make up all the cost advantages of many competitors. But if we regain an edge in new technologies, domestic producers are less likely to fall further behind foreign producers. Steady advances in apparel productivity have been seen, but they have not reached the level and impact of change of some other industries, such as textiles. Further automation in production has an essential role to play, though it would also require economic adjustment measures to help with those who might be displaced from their jobs. Alternative production processes such as "quick response" which tie the textile supplier, apparel producer, and retailer into a speedier production process can also help the industry, particularly to exploit its advantage of being close to the world's biggest market for clothing.

Unfortunately, federal support for automation has not kept pace with efforts by other governments. The U.S. government has given the industry $11.7 million to develop an automated apparel production system. This investment pales alongside the Japanese government's $100 million commitment to a similar project.[21]

No doubt future gains will be made, especially if the industry gets more technological assistance from government, but these alone cannot hope to match the advantage of significantly lower wages. This is particularly true today as new technologies rapidly spread around the globe. A realistic strategy to help the U.S. apparel industry survive would require economic and trade policies that encourage cooperative efforts at economic growth in other countries, rather than merely moderating international competition as the MFA does.

The third element of the apparel issue is the effort to eliminate the problem of destructive competition based on child labor, wage exploitation, and suppression of human rights. Recent amendments to U.S. trade law have taken steps toward that end; such efforts should be strengthened to help industries like apparel.

The domestic industry's future will also depend on proper trade policy, particularly because apparel production continues to be a route for Third World development.

The MFA notwithstanding, the U.S. has maintained a relatively open market compared to its trading partners. Because the restrictive measures of other MFA signatories are more stringent than ours, the U.S. has disproportionately absorbed the exports of developing countries.

The industrialized nations of the European Economic Community are far less open to apparel goods produced in the Third World. Since 1983, EEC restrictions have been strengthened under the MFA's "reasonable departures" clause. As a result, their policies appear to be shunting Third World exports to the U.S. Imports from Hong Kong, Taiwan, South Korea, and the People's Republic of China in 1986 totaled:[22]

U.S.	U.K.	Germany	Italy
$17 billion	$1 billion	$1 billion	$59 million

Developing nations also strictly regulate home markets: a GATT survey found that tariffs in twenty-one developing countries ranged from 25 percent to 75 percent.[23] For example, the Philippines maintains a 100 percent tariff on garment imports and permits duty-free importing of textiles used to produce clothing for export. Meanwhile, tariffs in South Korea will continue to average 30 percent even after a reform package to cut general tariff rates to industrialized nation levels takes effect in 1988.[24]

In a recent study, the Federal Office of Technology Assessment identified the following proposals for improving apparel trade policy, with the caveat they be considered within the context of overall U.S. trade policy: (1) expanding the MFA to include fibers not presently included; (2) negotiating increases in tariffs; and (3) establishing an import licensing system to prevent overshipments of imports.[25] Additional reforms could also be instituted—a more systematic approach, restoring overall and group ceilings, and selling off import licenses. These limited steps can enhance the MFA's ability to achieve its goals.

However, we ought to consider whether the aims of U.S. trade policy should be more ambitious. Ideally, such a policy would enhance cooperative efforts at growth, rather than merely moderating predatory or destructive competition.

As the U.S. faces its third generation of low-wage apparel competitors, we should consider a broader vision of trade policy than the MFA. Such a regime would include:

1. An economic adjustment policy for both the industry and its workers.

2. A multilateral vision of which countries truly need access to the U.S. apparel market for orderly development, and a policy that assists those countries which receive access to our markets to improve working conditions in their industries.

Imports of apparel will continue under the current MFA for the foreseeable future. Our immediate policy must therefore address the economic adjustment needs of the industry and its workers in order to reduce the hardship and economic losses caused by foreign competition. This issue is common to all industries faced with foreign competition and should be addressed in the context of overall trade policy.

Steel: Ready for a Resurgence?

The steel industry, like the apparel industry, has long felt the impact of international competition. But unlike apparel, steel is a high-wage, capital-intensive industry with very high barriers to entry.

The steel industry in the U.S. was once the world's largest, emerging from World War Two as the undisputed leader in international steel production. The war had greatly increased the demand for steel and left the U.S. industry with the capacity and technological superiority needed to fill the vacuum created when Europe's steel industry was destroyed. By 1950, U.S. companies produced 45 percent of the world's steel.[26]

In Europe and Japan, postwar reconstruction spurred the development of domestic steel industries. Hostility often characterized U.S. government-industry relations, but the European and Japanese goverments cooperated with steel companies, aiding growth with financial support. These governments also stimulated growth with export policies designed to exploit the U.S. market; the first cracks in the wall of U.S. steel dominance appeared in 1959 when imports exceeded exports for the first time in the century.

In the decades following the war, the U.S. failed to keep pace with new technology. While U.S. steelmakers continued to invest in the established technology, the open-hearth furnace, European and Japanese firms, encouraged by their governments, put money into technologies that rendered the open-hearth method obsolete. In the 1950s it was the basic oxygen furnace; in the 1960s and 1970s it was continuous casting, a process that eliminated several steps, and costs, in steelmaking.

This U.S. technology lag continues—in 1986, U.S. firms produced 52 percent of their steel by continuous casting, compared to 93 percent of Japanese production and 78 percent of European production.[27] (See Chart 6.6.)

Historically, the U.S. industry limited the costs of raw materials by owning iron ore fields and by building plants near inland deposits. When these deposits began running out in the 1960s, steel companies invested in new fields of lower-quality ore in North America; shipping costs to inland locations prevented the importation of higher-quality Australian and Brazilian ore. In Japan, however, it was an entirely different story. Since Japan lacks ore deposits, the Japanese built steel plants on deepwater ports serviced by a fleet of ships commissioned to bring ore from Brazil and Australia. Thus the Japanese turned a comparative disadvantage in raw materials into a significant edge.

Wage competition has added to U.S. steel's troubles. The U.S. industry's labor costs were higher than those in Japan and Europe during the 1960s and 1970s. Overall the industry's labor market strategies were slow to recognize the growth of global competition. Many long-term contracts were hailed as innovative breakthroughs at the time they were signed. With hind-

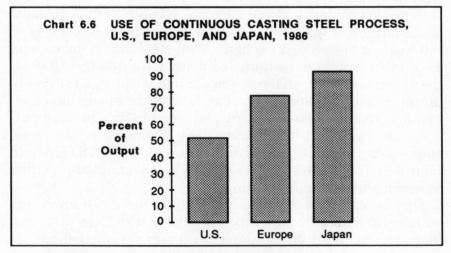

Chart 6.6 USE OF CONTINUOUS CASTING STEEL PROCESS, U.S., EUROPE, AND JAPAN, 1986

Percent of Output

Source: Peter F. Marcus and Karlis M. Kirsis, *World Steel Dynamics*

sight it is evident these contracts made it hard for American producers to cut costs and alter inefficient work rules to meet the new competition. But while wage differences were part of the European and Japanese advantage, they were not, ultimately, decisive.

In the 1970s, developing countries joined the challenge to U.S. industry, assisted by the diffusion of steelmaking technology and advances in transportation. Brazil, South Korea, and other newly industrializing nations, following the Japanese model, used state support and import restrictions to nurture export-driven steel industries. These factors, combined with labor costs which in some cases are one-tenth of those in advanced industrialized countries, have given Third World producers the ability to compete aggressively worldwide. Analysts project that developing nations will supply 24 percent of the West's steel by 1990, up from 9 percent in 1973.[28]

Many nations regard steel as a basic, vital industry and devote great amounts of financial and political support to developing and maintaining their steel industries. Unfortunately, these development-through-steel strategies were built on overestimates of growth in world steel demand. Growth has been less than anticipated, and the world has now come face to face with the problem of chronic overcapacity.

In the environment of overcapacity, when governments have made large investments in steel facilities, the political cost of retrenching has proved too high. Most steel-producing nations have maintained production, and many have dumped steel on the world market at whatever price it will command, especially during economic slowdowns. The Europeans finally did agree to a first round of managed cuts, financed by the governments and the European Coal and Steel Community. But they stopped far short of needed reductions, and the efficiency of their remaining plants was increased by government-provided research and development funds.

The casualties in this environment are not those producers which are the least competitive, but those which are protected least. Overcapacity has endured, and the U.S. market has remained the principal export target of that overcapacity.

STEEL AND TRADE POLICY: OFF-AGAIN, ON-AGAIN

During the last two decades, the U.S. enacted three periods of import relief. In each succeeding period the industry sought protection from dumping. In the late 1960s, when imports were rising and domestic demand declining, U.S. steelmakers and the union lobbied strenuously for import restrictions. In 1968 the Europeans and the Japanese agreed to quotas called "voluntary export restraints" (VERs). The VERs were renegotiated in 1972 and lasted another two years.

During the economic slump of the mid-1970s, the U.S. steel industry initiated a series of antidumping lawsuits against foreign competitors. The Carter Administration instituted the "trigger price mechanism" (TPM) program. The TPM was intended to identify and prevent steel dumping, but because of political considerations related to U.S. defense commitments in Europe, the program only moderated the amount of European steel dumped. The Reagan Administration canceled the TPM program in 1982, but two years later, faced with protests from steelmakers charging a new spate of dumping and suffering from a rising dollar, the U.S. negotiated "voluntary restraint agreements" (VRAs) with major steel exporting countries. The VRAs will run until 1989, and steelmakers have already begun pressing for their renewal.

Despite these restraint programs, steel imports climbed from less than 14 percent of the domestic market in 1975 to 23 percent in 1986.[29] (See Chart 6.7.) The impact on U.S. steel producers has been compounded by the declining fortunes of all U.S. manufacturers, especially during the years of the overvalued dollar. The worsening deficit in indirect steel trade—steel-consuming products such as cars, appliances, and heavy machinery —has further transferred domestic steel demand to foreign producers.

Looking back over the past twenty years, we see that each new crisis in steel prompted a reluctant, short-range, and uncoordinated response from the U.S. government. And in each case U.S. companies failed to recapture the market share lost to foreign firms. The government has not addressed the problem of enduring worldwide overcapacity, nor has it required or

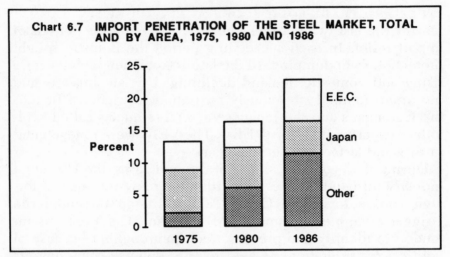

Chart 6.7 IMPORT PENETRATION OF THE STEEL MARKET, TOTAL AND BY AREA, 1975, 1980 AND 1986

Source: Peter F. Marcus and Karlis M. Kirsis, *World Steel Dynamics*

helped the industry to modernize and take other steps to improve its ability to compete.

Left on its own, the industry has gone through a severe adjustment which has been especially painful to steelworkers and their communities. In the face of chronic overcapacity, a restricted import share of 23 percent of direct steel trade, and the declining competitiveness of its manufacturing customers, the industry's adjustment has focused on reducing its least efficient capacity. Since 1982, the U.S. has reduced its steelmaking capacity 27 percent and cut its work force in half.[30]

Today, after several years of retrenchment, American steel is in a position to begin recapturing its share of the American market. The decline of the dollar to its 1980 level has given the U.S. steel industry among the lowest costs-per-ton of the industrialized countries. The U.S. integrated steel sector now ranks number one in the world in labor productivity or man hours per ton of steel. (See Chart 6.8.) And the long-standing friction between management and the United Steelworkers of America has given way to cooperation and compromise. After losing $12 billion between 1982 and 1986, most major U.S. companies posted modest profits for 1987.[31]

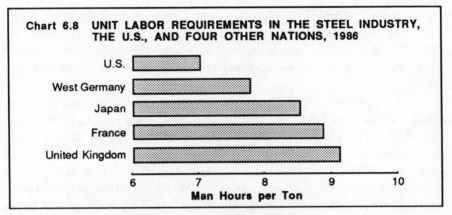

Chart 6.8 **UNIT LABOR REQUIREMENTS IN THE STEEL INDUSTRY, THE U.S., AND FOUR OTHER NATIONS, 1986**

Man Hours per Ton

Source: Peter F. Marcus and Karlis M. Kirsis, *World Steel Dynamics*

SPECIALITY STEEL AND MINIMILLS: A HOPE?

Despite these gains, no easy time lies ahead for the industry. This can be seen in two cases—specialty steel, which by any standard should compete successfully in today's market, and minimills, which some have said are the future of American steel. Both kinds of producers are plagued by the underlying problems of global overcapacity and foreign government support for steel.

Specialty steel firms are efficient, modern producers of high-value products appropriate to advanced industrial economies. They are unexcelled by foreign producers in efficiency, quality, and cost. The industry spends heavily on research and development to maintain modern production and ensure future competitiveness. Cooperative labor relations have maintained cost competitiveness in international markets.

Despite this, specialty steel producers have for years faced declining profits and calls for capacity reductions. Formerly significant producers of export earnings, they now confront closed markets abroad.

Critics of steel's integrated sector—those producers which process steel through all phases of production—minimize the impact of integrated steel's decline and proclaim minimills as the competitve future of American steel. As the name implies, minimills are much smaller than integrated mills. They use

147

steel scrap rather than iron ore, and process steel through electric arc furnaces and continuous casters. Enthusiasts believe that technological advantages, low capitalization costs, and high productivity make minimills the natural successor to integrated steel.

So far, unfortunately, minimill production is restricted to a limited range of low-end products, making up just 14 percent of the U.S. market. Most minimills are struggling to survive the overcapacity that presently plagues the market. Those few firms installing new technology are still five or ten years from knowing whether the process will be sufficiently cost-effective to sustain their cost advantage—and still farther away from proving to major customers that they can reliably supply the volume and consistent quality required.

STEEL AND GOVERNMENT

In the face of such gloomy prospects, would it be possible to reverse the increase in the steel trade deficit? The Commission's analysis points toward a positive answer, but only if we accept the basic reality facing U.S. producers: government policy abroad, as much as the market, will determine the shape of the world's steel industry in the years ahead.

In the debate which has now started on the future of the industry, capacity reduction is the favored approach by many inside and outside the industry. The Commission study found that this approach would risk permanently surrendering a significant share of the American market to foreign producers. No other advanced nation has shown the same degree of willingness to withdraw unilaterally from some part of its domestic market. Indeed, both Japan and Europe have current capacities, as a percentage of their domestic steel use, that are far above that of the U.S. Japan has twice as much steel capacity as it ultimately uses at home. Nearly half its steel production is exported, directly or indirectly in manufactured goods.[32] In Europe, current steel capacity is more than 140 percent the level of steel ultimately consumed in European countries.[33]

In contrast, the United States produces only 71 percent of the steel ultimately consumed in America.[34] The U.S. is the only major industrialized economy in the world that cannot produce all the steel it uses. Japan is planning real cuts in its production capacity, but these cuts will still leave Japanese steelmaking capacity at a level far higher relative to domestic use than the U.S. While European countries have promised another round of capacity reductions and an end to government subsidies, those plans have repeatedly been pushed back.

The industry's current good fortune also illustrates the problem with focusing on capacity reductions. The recent surge in domestic demand drove up prices and profitability, but caught many producers unaware. Already there are complaints of shortages of certain steel products. Officials in the industry admit that they may not have the capacity to meet a sustained recovery in demand. Capacity reductions in the face of growing domestic demand may ultimately give further domestic market share to foreign producers.

Capacity reduction is also expensive. Some companies now use bankruptcy as a way to shift the high costs of plant closings to the federal government by placing the burden of paying pension benefits on the federal government's Pension Benefit Guarantee Corporation (PBGC). PBGC is already facing claims of $2.6 billion by two major bankrupt (but still operational) steel producers. The pressure on others to follow suit threatens to unload on the PBGC an even greater burden.

Further capacity reductions will not solve the steel dilemma. Instead what we need is a U.S. policy that is practical about our competition and able to deal with the fact that Europe, Japan, and the developing nations make great use of nonmarket forces such as high domestic import restrictions, informal market-sharing devices, and government subsidies and ownership.

We also need a policy which honestly acknowledges that the federal government will be involved in the steel industry one way or another, as it has in the past, and that we must be clear about the most effective and efficient policies. It is likely that if government brings more realism to its role and has a clear set of objectives in working with the industry, the nation will probably reach its goals for the industry more quickly, less painfully, and more efficiently. For example, the realistic and active approach would emphasize the need to tie negotiation of access to the U.S. market to overcapacity, and the need to restore sensible balance to world steel production and demand.

The Commission has identified four basic goals that would define a national commitment to a more competitive industry: restore the industry to long-term, reasonable levels of profitability; assure U.S. customers an adequate supply of high-quality, competitively priced steel; minimize the steel trade deficit; provide an adjustment program so that individual workers and their communities do not bear unfair burdens in the process of restructuring.

The issue of the future of the steel industry will be taken up in 1988 and 1989 in the debate over the extension of voluntary import restraints. It would make sense for the federal government to call together a task force of all the relevant parties— industry, labor, steel consumers, and the relevant agencies— and start a dialogue on the industry's future. Such a dialogue would include the question of what management and labor would have to do, the proper incentives for further modernization, the costs and benefits of new policies for the industry, and what to do for the communities impacted by changes in the industry. New policies should be consistent with our earlier discussions on temporary import restrictions and the requirements of effective programs to increase the competitiveness of an industry.

Food Manufacturing: Holding the Market

The history of the U.S. food-manufacturing industry in international competition is largely a success story. Imported food products account for only a small portion of our huge domestic market. Even so, in the 1980s we are running a trade deficit in processed, i.e., manufactured, food. Today, imports are approximately 150 percent of the value of exports.[35]

The food industry compared to apparel and steel falls in the mid-range in terms of wage levels and capital investment. It faces no immediate threats from lagging technology or from closed markets abroad. The deficit has been caused primarily by three factors: the globalization of production, which took U.S. multinationals to other countries offshore to produce goods for domestic and foreign markets; the high value of the dollar; and the progress made by other countries in the agricultural sector.

The early success of this industry was, in large measure, the legacy of past public policies aimed at agriculture, including programs such as the agricultural extension service. Abundant output and high productivity in agriculture assured the food manufacturing industry a plentiful, low-cost, reliable supply of the industry's basic input—food. The nation's superb transportation system efficiently delivered food from farms and fishing docks to the factories, then stores, then on to the consumer.

Public policies played a critical role in the emergence of large, relatively homogeneous markets. And continuing advances have led to ever-expanding markets. These markets and the ability to supply them enabled the industry to exploit economies of scale and develop into a modern, well-capitalized industry.

With profits and knowledge gained from their insulated home markets—insulated by distance, cost advantages, and relatively early development—U.S. food-manufacturing giants successfully ventured into foreign direct investment. Today, overseas investments by U.S. firms are substantial. Overseas interests provide about one-fourth of the major U.S. food firms' income.[36] For the most part, U.S. multinationals prefer to locate abroad rather than export from the United States, primarily to be close to both markets and agricultural supplies and to take advantage of cheaper labor. At the same time, many of these firms are responsible for much of the food imported into the U.S.

A very high proportion of U.S. food imports is through intrafirm trade, in which a domestic U.S. subsidiary imports directly from a subsidiary of the same company abroad. This practice amounts to about 40 percent of all manufactured food imports, and as much as 77 percent of imports from Mexico.[37] It accounts for most fruit and vegetable imports. Clearly, this contributes to our current trade deficit. Combined with the successes of foreign companies, especially in specialty foods, intrafirm trade has caused our imports to rise. We now import over $18 billion in food products from other countries.[38]

Conversely, our exports have grown slowly. Developing countries such as India and Brazil now produce their own agricultural products. This has taken away one of our major export markets: packaged cereals and grains. And slow world growth has delayed the onset of new markets in developing countries for higher-valued food products.

These trade figures in no way mean that U.S. food companies are not competitive. In fact, the food products deficit is nearly the smallest among the top twenty manufacturing industries. But long-term trends in competitiveness have shown that we cannot expect past advantage to guarantee future success.

Because of the shift in international food trade to higher-value products, the value of the food in a food product dropped from three-fourths of the product price in 1947 to less than half in 1977 and is probably even lower at present.[39] As foodstuffs became less and less a cost factor in food products, the advantage of America's low-cost agriculture has lessened. Because the U.S. exports are mainly low-value-added products, not specialty foods, the Green Revolution abroad has provided substitutes for U.S. exports. The U.S. cost advantage has been met and matched by foreign nations.

Imports already account for about one-third of the specialty food markets.[40] This trend may continue as new preservation and packaging technologies reduce import costs and permit affluent tastes to seek more exotic foods. Greater competition in both imports and exports is likely in the future.

The successes of the food industry illustrate two policy lessons. First, an industry's links to other sectors can determine its world-class status. Without the wonders of our agricultural sector, U.S. food manufacturers would not be the world leaders they are. Second, active government policies made it possible for American agriculture to become so competitive. Positive government action in one sector of the economy has repercussions in other economic sectors.

In the short term, the food industry would benefit primarily from help at the macroeconomic level. The process of restoring our trade balance through dollar devaluation seems to be slowly underway. California wines, for example, are once again competitive with French wines. If we promote growth abroad, especially in Latin America, our exports should rise.

Finally, we need to be sure that federal agricultural policy remains cognizant of how policy changes in agriculture can impact the food manufacturers.

Telecommunications: Connecting to the Future

With the rise of the information society, telecommunications are more important than ever to American competitiveness. What was once just "the telephone company" is now a basic part of the nation's infrastructure. Its importance will only grow in the next century.

This industry stands in sharp contrast to apparel, steel, and food in one major way—it is a "sunrise" industry, and has been throughout the 1970s and 1980s. It is a higher-technology industry than steel, earns high profits, pays better wages than food manufacturing, and is capital-intensive. With such conditions, why do we face a mounting trade deficit?

The first factor to consider is the role of U.S. government policy. Until the 1970s, the U.S. treated telecommunications and its equipment as a basic need. A government-regulated monopoly provided virtually the entire continent with affordable service which was significantly better than service in the rest of the world. Telephone equipment was built in America. Technology and engineering skill seemed homegrown.

Under government regulations, AT&T provided full service across America. Until 1984, AT&T served 80 to 90 percent of the market for local exchange service and long distance.[41] It had a monopoly on equipment. AT&T was perhaps the most vertically integrated telecommunications corporation in the world, providing everything from switching equipment to local service. This promoted stability, and expensive research and development—the work of the Bell Labs—was sustained by the broad financial base of the Bell System.

Competition began with the first wave of deregulation in the 1970s. The Federal Communications Commission allowed consumers to connect non-AT&T equipment to the Bell System, and barriers to the imports were lifted. Imports began to grow, particularly in the early 1980s when the dollar was high.

In 1984, in a settlement of the Department of Justice's antitrust suit, AT&T agreed to divest itself of its local operating companies, leaving AT&T with long-distance service, equipment manufacturing (Western Electric), and the Bell Labs. At the same time, the FCC, in addition to eliminating AT&T's manufacturing monopoly, created new competition for the company in long-distance markets. Today, AT&T and the operating companies are radically different from what they were five years ago, and operate within a vastly restructured environment.

Since January 1984, competition in the U.S. telecommunications equipment market has exploded. AT&T has rapidly lost market share to foreign manufacturers. According to Alfred Sikes, Assistant Commerce Secretary for Communications and Information, before the divestiture of AT&T the U.S. was a net exporter of telecommunications equipment; in 1986 the U.S. imported twice as much equipment as it exported.[42]

Arthur Andersen and Company projects that foreign competition will grow, and that foreign manufacturers will gain a 28 percent share of the U.S. telephone market by 1990.[43] A study by Bell South indicates that foreign competition has already had a tremendous impact on employment; the study estimated that loss of business to foreign manufacturers has cut at least 15,000 jobs from the U.S. communications equipment industry in recent years.[44]

Meanwhile, continued regulation of telecommunications networks abroad will block growth in our exports. Our exports at present are minimal. Until the mid-1970s, exports made up less than 3 percent of the value of industry shipments. The ratio did rise to 6.2 percent in 1986, but then began to decline.[45]

Britain, West Germany, and Japan all exclude U.S. equipment and service providers to a significant extent, though in different ways. Britain simply has an informal "Buy British" policy; West Germany has a legalized cartel, the Central Association; and Japan either prohibits foreign ownership or restricts entry to its markets. While the potential foreign market is huge, the U.S. telecommunications industry is unlikely to capitalize on it without a substantial change in current policies.

Though U.S. telecommunications manufacturers have occasionally penetrated foreign markets, most sales have been relatively small and have often been made through U.S. subsidiaries abroad. Foreign companies sometimes use obstacles to their markets as a way of acquiring U.S. technology. For instance, the Corning Glass Company, which holds basic patents on fiber optics technology, was for a long time prevented from selling its fiber optics in Japan. In the end, the only way Corning could enter the Japanese market was to license patents to its Japanese competitors, thereby losing its technological advantage.[46]

Given the importance of telecommunications, it is highly unreasonable to assume that we will see any significant market openings overseas. With policies so different from those of our competitors, the industry's troubles could get worse. The fact that we opened our market to foreign firms without demanding reciprocal access to their markets can only be called a competitive blunder. When the U.S. deregulated AT&T, it jeopardized not only the U.S. telecommunications industry, but our future control over the whole infrastructure.

Without treating our industry as other governments do, the U.S. risks abandoning its technological lead. Deregulation gave the American consumer, particularly business users, the short-term advantage of having many companies competing to supply advanced equipment quickly. But that advantage may be short-lived. The next generation of industry growth will be in markets now protected. Foreign firms can apply the technological knowhow they gather in our market to new systems and products, gaining another generation of product development at low cost. It is possible that the U.S. industry could find itself unable to participate in the next round of growth and product development, perhaps lacking enough market growth to fund R&D adequately.

What policy changes are needed to avoid such a future? While it is unreasonable to expect that the U.S. will reverse the deregulation of the past fifteen years, and that other countries will open their markets, we can reasonably suggest that a major shift in our policy framework is possible as well as essential.

To make sure that the telecommunications infrastructure does not become dependent on foreign manufacturing, U.S. policy should amend its largely regulatory focus to include a concern for competitiveness. Retaining and bolstering domestic market share should be a prime objective. Policy should be made for the long term and aim toward market share and technological prowess. Telecommunications equipment policy must be closely tied to the policy for services.

At present, the plethora of decision-making agencies frustrates the making of coordinated policy. Telecommunications policy is formed mainly by the FCC, an independent government agency whose commissioners are appointed by the President. But other agencies make policy, too. In the executive branch, the Commerce Department's National Telecommunications and Information Agency coordinates the President's overall telecommunications policy and works with the U.S. Trade Representative and the State Department on international telecommunications negotiations. The Antitrust Division of the Justice Department oversees much of the telephone industry through its enforcement of the AT&T divestiture. The federal courts (through rulings) and the Justice Department and Federal Trade Commission (through regulation) affect the industry's competitive behavior and structure. Finally, Congress itself, which established the FCC's authority in legislation, continues to signal its concerns to the FCC through bills, resolutions, hearings, and the budgetary process.

Some reorganization of relations among existing institutions could help, as we frame a competitiveness strategy. Government must make sure to incorporate ideas and energy from both business and labor.

In the long run, this is an industry well poised to compete. Our goal should be to make sure government does not handicap the industry at home or abandon it abroad through failed trade negotiations.

Financial Services: The Competition of Capital

The financial services industry—banking, brokerage, and insurance—is the quintessential industry of the information age. It has grown tremendously in recent years, seemingly confirming the rise of the service sector over manufacturing. Yet the present condition of the industry demonstrates that the American competitiveness problem is not restricted to our manufacturing sector. Far from having its future secured in the emergence of a postindustrial economy, financial services may face a competitive challenge every bit as serious as that which plagues manufacturing.

This challenge is in many respects the second wave of our declining manufacturing competitiveness. The changing economic and political environment which led to the decline of manufacturing has also transformed the financial services markets. These changes fueled the growth of the industry worldwide, a development that U.S. financial services were at first well positioned to capitalize on. But the outcome of our industrial decline and our inadequate response to it have ultimately served to strengthen our international competition. Propelled by international industrial success, the Japanese are also the inevitable, formidable competition in financial services.

The future prospects of the American financial services industry are of particular concern because the industry plays such a crucial role in marshaling the capital strength of the nation's economy. To an America deeply in debt and trying to restore its economic vitality, the industry's role is especially critical. Ironically, the transformation of the industry has produced a finance sector very independent of the nation's real economy. There is no longer any necessary coincidence of interests and fortunes, especially in the short term, between the finance industry and the nation's real economy. This makes developments in the industry and our response to them all the more crucial.

Since the mid-1970s, financial services firms have faced market changes unlike any they encountered during the previous thirty years. Among the forces driving these changes is the instability of interest rates. Steep inflation and high, volatile interest rates in the 1970s and early 1980s caused consumers to protect their savings by seeking higher returns. This forced banks to compete on price as well as quality of service. Corporations also sought greater returns, moving their funds from commercial banks to investment banks and into new financial markets abroad.

At the same time, borrowers began to look for products and services their traditional lenders were unable to provide or were prohibited from providing. Increasingly, corporations turned from banks to the securities market to satisfy their borrowing needs.

Volatile interest rates and the defection of customers had a serious impact on commercial banks and savings and loans. The flow of inexpensive, stable deposits was reduced, while the commercial banks' highest-quality, lowest-risk borrowers were doing business elsewhere. The phased-in deregulation of interest rates in the late 1970s and early 1980s helped banks some, but not before securities firms had established themselves as competitors.

With the spread of competition, the emphasis in financial services has shifted from long-term safety and stability to profitability. This has important consequences for competitiveness. It may make the funding of long-term investment more difficult because firms are preoccupied with short-term returns. Banks have always played a special role in the economy by changing "liquid" deposits of consumers and companies into "illiquid" or long-term investments and assets. Economic endeavors that contribute the most to a prosperous future depend on access to long-term funds. Yet changes in the financial services industry may be weakening the banks' ability and/or willingness to provide those funds.

On the world scene, most analysts agree that the primary challenge comes from the Japanese. To a large degree, Japan's competitive prowess was built directly on the success of its export manufacturers, which have produced huge and growing pools of capital. Japan had a trade surplus of nearly $80 billion in 1987,[47] and may by the end of the century accumulate as much as $1 trillion in external assets.[48] Japan's move into global finance has also been aided by the U.S. government's need to borrow funds abroad and by the appreciation of the yen compared to the dollar.

One of Japan's competitive advantages is the overwhelming size of its firms. Seven of the largest ten banks in the world are Japanese,[49] and the highly concentrated Japanese securities industry boasts the world's largest securities firms. To be sure, the rankings and earnings of international firms are affected by stock prices and the yen; still, the presence of Japanese firms at the top of international rankings reflects real clout—and a real competitive challenge for the U.S.

American competitors and government officials complain of unfair advantages in the Japanese regulatory structure. The sheltered Japanese market reduces competition for the large firms, allowing them to charge more at home to subsidize foreign operations. At the same time, a lower capital reserve requirement reduces their lending costs and allows them to underprice their more strictly supervised British and American rivals.

Japan also has plenty of low-cost capital, thanks to its high savings rate and still-regulated deposit interest rates. But in the end the most important advantage, aside from the strength of Japan's economy, may be Japanese financial firms' ability to absorb low returns. That has been the key to Japan's strategy of building market share. Especially in the case of the banks, Japanese shareholders have been willing to accept returns that are low by present American standards.

Based on these advantages, Japanese financial firms are making inroads. In 1986, Japanese firms issued 56 percent of the letters of credit in the U.S. market, and reportedly accounted for almost 40 percent of the commercial and industrial loans outstanding at foreign banks.[50] They financed $60 billion of new U.S. Treasury issues (about one-third of our budget deficit), and have become major players in the municipal finance business, a market several American firms are abandoning.[51] The Japanese are investing directly in U.S. financial services. According to the New York Federal Reserve, the Japanese have made major acquisitions or investments in eight U.S. financial firms ranging in value from $131 million to $3.1 billion. They have also made their first moves into retail banking. In California, four of the top ten largest banks are Japanese-owned.[52]

The U.S. also faces competition from German, Swiss, and British banks. American commercial banks are at a competitive disadvantage because unlike European banks they cannot engage in investment banking in their home markets. Europe's universal banking tradition has produced powerful national banks active in all banking businesses within their nations, a striking contrast to the U.S. system of 15,000 commercial banks scattered within fifty jurisdictions. Size provides European firms with a substantial capital base and lower risk through diversification of assets and liabilities.

COMPETITION THROUGH REGULATION

Just as the market for goods has become global, so has the market for capital. The U.S. financial services industry confronts growing international competition governed by an array of differing national policies whose results, consciously or not, often handicap American firms. These varying policies risk the stability and reliability of the world's financial system. A globalized industry has outgrown the ability of individual nations to guide it. If we are to achieve national competitiveness and international financial stability, new forms of international regulation are essential.

The Crash of 1987 served as a warning that the imbalance created by our trade and fiscal deficits cannot continue without further rocking of the financial system. It also signified that change has outpaced our present institutions. New risks and volatility have accompanied innovations in the financial markets. Since these innovations are probably here to stay, we must examine them thoroughly so that the new risks can be better regulated. We should also carefully consider further institutional reform to reflect the new realities of the market.

Commercial banks (deposit-taking institutions) and investment banks (banks primarily for investors) have entered each other's markets in response to changes in demand by customers. Many analysts have proposed a new set of regulatory rules based on products or markets rather than on institutions. They would allow commercial banks to engage in some investment banking activities and vice versa, but only so long as the consumer remains protected. That would mean keeping consumer banking and institutional/corporate banking separate within the same firm.

Even as the debate on domestic regulation proceeds and is sorted out, it is evident that on the international level we should establish formal guidelines to standardize accounting procedures and capital requirements for banks in different countries. Steps already being taken should be encouraged; financial markets will be strengthened only when everyone begins playing by the same rules. We should also promote U.S. standards of disclosure as a basis for global standards. Better information means better knowledge of risk—and more stability. In an earlier chapter we discussed the reforms for international monetary stability. These reforms and the revival of the goods-producing sector of our economy through a competitiveness strategy can do much to help financial services in the long run.

The Lessons Learned

The case studies demonstrate that America's competitiveness difficulties are broad based and arise from a variety of factors which differ from industry to industry. Our competitiveness problems are across-the-board, from labor-intensive industries to high-technology and service industries, and are the result of a variety of factors, of which the high value of the dollar between 1980 and 1985 is only one. No industry is safe from the pressures of a global economy. Our technological edge has not kept foreign producers from digging into our telecommunications equipment market, nor has America's move into a "service economy" meant that our financial services industry has remained unscathed. Even our continued advances in agriculture have not kept foreign competition from our food processing sector.

The major competitiveness problems vary from industry to industry. Apparel suffers from low-cost, low-wage competition.

In many sectors, including steel, competitive outcomes have been significantly influenced by the protectionist and promotional policies of our trading partners. Telecommunications shows the disparity between the regulatory mentality in this country and the producer strategy abroad. Domestic policy choices, such as the decision to break up AT&T and deregulate the domestic telecommunications network, must be considered in light of their international ramifications. We overlooked the opportunity to use access to our newly opened telecommunications market to gain access for U.S. producers to protected telecommunications markets abroad. We should not make similar policy mistakes in other industries in the future.

Despite the differences between industries, it is clear that general programs to do more manufacturing research and development and to develop new technologies would be very helpful to our overall competitive position. Among the other general lessons that we have learned from our study of these five industries are the following:

1. *A competitiveness strategy at the industry level can be an important complement to our trade, macroeconomic, and regulatory policies.* In terms of trade policy, protection from imports alone will not restore an industry's competitiveness. In the absence of viable policy alternatives, we are likely to do as we have done in the past: resort to protectionist responses which offer little hope of long-run competitive success. Too often we have provided protection for industries without requiring them to adjust to a new environment. In the apparel industry, thirty years of protection under traditional trade policy has not revitalized the industry. In the case of steel, protection without an adjustment program has increased inefficiency and hardship, squandering the time that was bought with protection. In terms of macroeconomic policy, the promotion of growth abroad will not ensure U.S. export strength unless U.S. industries are made more competitive. For example, it is not clear whether food processing will automatically remain competitive in growing world markets, given the rapid development abroad of new technologies and lower-cost processes. Finally, in terms of regulatory policy, the folly of taking action

to restructure a major domestic industry without regard to the consequences of international competitiveness is very clear in the deregulation of our telecommunications industry. New initiatives in trade, macroeconomic, and regulatory policy are likely to be more effective if done with a simultaneous initiative with the industries involved.

2. *Industries are interdependent, and a broad base of industrial activity is necessary for a healthy economy.* No industry is an island. Success in one sector can bring prosperity to another, which in turn can further the success of the first. For example, telecommunications grows and innovates, it helps financial services to grow faster—and that, in turn, creates a larger market for telecommunications equipment. The same relationship exists between auto manufacturing and steel, and between countless other industries.

This synergy can be a tremendous source of economic strength. Industries with many links to other industries are the building blocks of our national economy. It is also important that we take a long-term view of industries which will form the infrastructure of our future, and coordinate policy to ensure their health.

Realistically, the U.S. cannot hope to be competitive in all industries, nor can it employ the tools of government to ensure production and employment in all economic sectors. Therefore, in developing a national competitiveness strategy, we must address the issue of how to gauge the strategic importance of various industries. The studies suggest that industries have strategic importance if their continued health is vital to maintaining general employment and to sustaining the well-being of other sectors, specifically in providing relevant inputs and infrastructure to other industries. Economists often stress the view that high rates of return for capital and labor, relative to the world economy, give an industry strategic value, especially to the degree that the industry provides a large share of these returns to the nation's citizens. Whatever the definition, we need to reach a national consensus on how to evaluate the strategic importance of the various parts of our industrial base.

3. *Developing workable competitiveness strategies is possible only if business, government, labor, and the public cooperate.* In each of the five industries, we have identified the competitiveness issues and the problems facing the industry. We have outlined the initiatives which could be undertaken by those sectors to help reduce our trade imbalance and help to improve our total trade balance. But the ultimate development and implementation of any competitiveness plans will require real cooperation between business, government, and labor, not simply studies by commissions.

4. *Industry adjustment plans should be mandatory when trade relief is requested.* To ensure the vitality of domestic industry, the submission of an adjustment plan and revitalization strategy should be mandatory for any industry which benefits from import limitation. Under the trade bill passed by the House of Representatives, industries petitioning for import relief "may submit" a statement of proposed adjustment measures to the ITC and the USTR. While this is a step in the proper direction, the optional nature of these statements increases the likelihood that the period of import relief will not be used constructively by an industry.

Requiring an industry to develop a strategy does not mean that government will be telling an industry what it must do. It does, however, place an appropriate responsibility on an industry for its continued well-being. When an industry looks to the federal government for financial assistance in restructuring, it should meet five criteria: (1) the industry should be strategic, one whose continued health is vital to the well-being of other industries and the maintenance of employment; (2) the protection should come in time to do some substantive good; (3) government intervention should be supported by leaders in labor, industry, and experts; (4) the program for restructuring should be specific, have a clear end point, and include sufficient capital, management talent, and labor resources; and (5) in those cases where the industry is likely to decline no matter what is done, a program of economic adjustment is needed for the workers and communities impacted.

5. *Broadly based task forces to help develop long-term trade strategy should be established.* To develop a coherent, long-term trade strategy and implement it, we must have cooperation and communication among relevant government agencies, experts, industry, labor, and the public. We recommend the organization of strategic task forces to analyze economic trends and market opportunities in specific sectors, monitor technological change and trade practices, and develop plans for industry adjustment and flexible response to the changing economic environment. Such task forces would be similar to the private advisory committees used effectively in the past as consensus-building mechanisms for multilateral trade negotiations, but they would have a broader mandate.

We should give special attention to forming task forces in industries that have strategic importance, the expertise to institute change, and a demonstrated willingness by management and labor within the industry to make necessary reforms.

The Road Ahead

As dark as the horizon for American industry may sometimes seem, there are some beneficial trends. In the manufacturing sector, productivity has been growing, on average, at a healthy rate throughout the 1980s. Manufacturing has held its ground as a contributor to the economy, and still constitutes about one-fourth of the nation's GNP.

While the lower value of the dollar is no substitute for sector-specific competitiveness strategies, it has helped some producers compete, particularly when their competitors are primarily Japanese or European. It remains to be seen how wisely these industries will use their present advantage to invest for the long term, but at least the opportunity is there.

Some industries are not relying on macroeconomic changes to solve their problems. Instead they are taking an activist approach. In response to the beating they took from their Japanese and Asian competitors in the mid-1980s, U.S. semiconductor manufacturers have pooled their resources to form a consortium—Sematech—as a vehicle for joint research and development. This coordinated effort, toward which the federal government has contributed, may generate advances in generic technology from which commercial products can be developed. Implicit in Sematech's formation is the recognition by the manufacturers that macroeconomic policy is not enough. Rebuilding the industry's competitiveness requires new thinking and cooperation.

Greater cooperation has made strides not only within industries, but within companies. Workers and managers around the nation are discarding certain labor-management conventions and embracing the notions of cooperation and participation. By giving those who do the work a greater say in how the work is done, companies are reaping the benefits of greater productivity, production innovation, and higher worker morale. Of the many seedlings of change in the broad field of American industry, perhaps no other deserves our care and attention more than this movement toward participation and cooperation.

The test of these new strategies (and of how well we have learned the lessons of our recent industrial experience) will be the success we achieve in regaining shares of our own market and in reducing our trade deficit.

Building and maintaining industries is what international competition today is all about. This is how other nations are playing. If we want to stay in the game, we should do no less.

CHAPTER SEVEN

Americans in the Workplace

MILLIONS of Americans grew up thinking a skilled or semi-skilled job with good wages and benefits was a realistic goal and the ticket to the middle class. Even if these jobs were not always interesting or fulfilling, they were a source of hope for the future and a cornerstone of the most productive economy in history.

That idea is changing because more unemployment, more part-time jobs, fewer wage increases and fringe benefits, and less job security have decreased the quantity of work and pay available to many, though clearly not all, Americans.[1]

As we discussed earlier, the way America consumes, both individually and as a society, is also changing. Our society consumes increasing amounts of tax revenue to pay interest on past debts. We make fewer long-term investments in our future prosperity.[2]

The American Formula and the Workplace

The roots of how America produces and consumes—what we have called the American Formula—were the tremendous gains in productivity achieved by mass production techniques such as the assembly line and "scientific management." Under these methods, production was divided into smaller and smaller units, with each worker given a fixed place within the process. A hierarchical management structure transmitted direction from the top to the shop floor.

These techniques made possible a quantum leap in overall production levels.[3] But this potential was not realized until the 1930s and 1940s, when the U.S. began to implement the idea that rising production was possible only if our economic and social policy promoted the demand for goods, or consumption.

This strategy for prosperity was executed in many ways, among them the passage of the National Labor Relations Act. The NLRA established a social contract in which the employer would develop and implement a business strategy to make revenues and profits, while workers would collectively bargain for their share through unions. The unions negotiated labor contracts, which set forth work rules, the seniority system, the right to have grievances heard, and other measures to help bring fairness to the workplace. Contracts also recognized management's right to run the business and make strategic decisions.

Most people believe modern labor relations worked well for over three decades, regulating the way work was done and distributing to workers a share of the output.[4] Indeed, nearly everyone understood and supported the idea of a positive relationship between rising production and rising consumption, and the role labor relations played in that formula.

Looking back, we can see that the success of this system depended in part on the fact that American companies did not have serious competition from abroad. For the most part, domestic competition did not provoke the reduction of workers' wages or affect their living standards and consumption.

The world has changed. Many employers have become vigilant cost-cutters because of international competition, even at the risk of depressing overall living standards. Wages have once more been tossed on the bargaining table. This trend will continue and millions will face, some for the first time, the "fight or flight" situation that numerous industries have experienced in the past fifteen years.

We believe that most Americans would rather fight to be more competitive than flee in the face of foreign competition. This attitude is a great asset and a cornerstone of a realistic pro-competition strategy.

The devaluation of the dollar, leading to a decline in the price of American products compared to our competitors, has in some ways made us more competitive. And there is a resurgence in productivity now underway as more and more U.S. plants invest in new equipment and change their methods in order to improve their efficiency.[5] (See Chart 7.1.)

But a realistic competitiveness strategy should not rely too much on the value of the dollar. In the global economy, control of the dollar's value depends as much on foreign investors and central banks as on the actions of our government. How we produce, by contrast, is entirely under our control, and every American can play a role in its reform.

The Profits of Participation

The way Americans work is changing, and none too soon. In many workplaces, the hierarchy, chain of command, and division of labor have been replaced by a more collaborative approach. Experiments in new ways of organizing work, both manufacturing and services, have blurred the lines between managers, supervisors, workers, unions, and shareholders.[6] Driven by a growing national awareness of the need to improve quality and productivity, this trend has the potential to transform the way most people do their jobs—and to help reestablish America's economic leadership.

The experiments of the last ten years have shown that important gains in productivity can result from a commitment to promote new relationships among workers, managers, unions, and shareholders. Companies across America are finding out about this new approach and the "profits of participation."[7] It is the Commission's position that increasing the quantity and quality of employee participation is one of the most important actions that the nation can take to restore competitiveness.

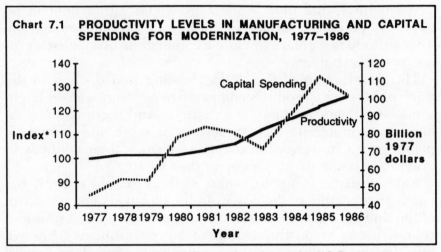

Chart 7.1 PRODUCTIVITY LEVELS IN MANUFACTURING AND CAPITAL SPENDING FOR MODERNIZATION, 1977–1986

Source: for productivity, U.S. Bureau of Labor Statistics; for capital spending, U.S. Department of Commerce and DRI–McGraw Hill

*1977=100

Productivity and Participation: Some Recent Success Stories

In New York State and throughout the nation, many companies and unions have adopted innovative approaches to meet the challenge of global competition. Many of them have focused on the quality of work life and aim to improve employee satisfaction. But even more important are the programs which improve competitiveness, quality, and the employee's economic security. For example, a number of companies now use the "cost study team," a joint labor-management group with the mission to make products at more competitive prices.[8] Other new types of participation include giving employees a part in making company strategy, and giving workers a piece of the action and responsibility through employee ownership.

CUTTING COSTS AND SAVING JOBS: XEROX
Xerox dominated the photocopier business from the 1960s, when it pioneered the production of xerography machines. But

from a peak market share of 93 percent, Xerox declined to a 42 percent share in 1981, as companies like Sharp, Canon, Ricoh, and Kodak emerged as competitors. In the early 1980s, cost-cutting was the order of the day at Xerox. After a year-long study, the managers of a large Xerox plant in Rochester, New York, decided that millions of dollars could be saved by outsourcing items built in the plant's wire harness department. Every job in the wire harness department would be eliminated.

The Amalgamated Clothing and Textile Workers Union (ACTWU) proposed instead a joint labor-management cost study team to find ways to reduce costs and save the jobs. Xerox accepted the proposal. A labor-management team was formed and trained in cost accounting and problem solving. After a six-month study, the team recommended changes in equipment, workflow, operations, the organization of work, and the elimination of overhead. Many of the recommendations required ACTWU and Xerox to negotiate changes in work rules. The team surpassed the target set by management of $3.7 million in cost savings. The wire harness works was kept at the Rochester plant and the jobs were saved.

The ACTWU pushed to include the cost-study-team concept in its 1983 agreement with Xerox. It was a wise move; in 1984 the company declared three more products uncompetitive. New teams were established to follow the path of the wire harness team and cut costs.

The three teams had tougher goals to meet than the first team. Each came close enough to its benchmark goals that the work was retained, though one team fell significantly short of its goal. Setting benchmarks is difficult, because of uncertainties in assigning dollar values to manufacturing and supplier costs. Even more serious is the problem of obtaining good price quotes from other companies producing a similar product. For example, it is difficult to know whether volume considerations and "lowballing" by vendors are creating falsely low bids in the hope of future work.

In 1986, Xerox again decided that the wire harness operation was uncompetitive. This time the cost study team had to find ways to reduce costs by 40 percent. The team, aware of the impossibility of competing with the low wages paid by Mexican suppliers, took a new approach. They decided to compare their work on the basis of quality, not just cost. A major effort was made to compute the cost of quality and to compare it to the proposed vendor's quality.

The issue of quality was persuasive to management, and the second wire harness team succeeded in keeping the jobs in Rochester. In addition, workers in the wire harness area were given the right to bid on all new work in the plant; they now are given first preference if they can bid within 5 percent of the lowest outside bid.

Cost study teams at Xerox have saved money and jobs. They have given the union a greater voice in management operational decisions, particularly on outsourcing, and they have given the union and management a way to work together regularly. So far the teams have shown that they can meet the competition, especially in quality and delivery. In the long run, it will be a challenge to keep the cooperative process going as management turnover occurs and corporate prerogatives change. Xerox is a worldwide corporation, and the possibility of outsourcing will continue.

Employee participation at Xerox has led to a better use of the workers' wealth of expertise and creativity to make better and more competitive products. It has improved the decision-making process. A new appreciation of the skills of the work force has led to the incorporation of employee participation as a basic operating philosophy throughout the company.[9]

TRICO

In November 1985, Trico Products, a leading manufacturer of original equipment windshield wipers and assemblies, announced it would close two of its Buffalo plants and construct new "twin" plants in Matamoros, Mexico, and El Paso, Texas. The plan called for layoffs of 1,100 of the company's 2,600 workers at Buffalo.[10]

This decision was based on the idea that only lower labor costs could make the company more profitable. Like dozens of U.S. firms, Trico saw its solution in the "Maquiladora" system under which low-wage, unskilled Mexican workers assemble products from U.S.-made parts, which are then shipped back to distribution facilities in Texas.

Trico's announcement prompted New York State's Director of Economic Development, Vincent Tese, to ask the union at Trico, the United Auto Workers, to work with management to find ways to mitigate the loss of jobs. Outside consultants, skilled in employee participation and the cost-study-team process, helped assess the company's needs and find ways to achieve the cost savings Trico envisioned through the Maquiladora system. Shop floor workers, cooperating with foremen and middle managers, thoroughly examined Trico's major departments in terms of layout, technology, and production planning. Other consultants studied the feasibility of a new plant for Trico in Buffalo.

The study concluded that Trico had problems with overall operating costs, not just labor costs. Changes were proposed in operating structure and procedures, including the creation of joint labor-management work committees. The study and the incentive package prepared by the state, which included construction of a state-of-the-art manufacturing plant, were estimated to achieve $30 million in annual savings and to eliminate the need for the move to the Southwest.

During this time, Trico and the UAW also conducted negotiations on a new contract. After lengthy negotiations, the company agreed to pursue some study recommendations, including modernization and centralization of operations at its main Buffalo plant.

Under the new contract, 300 of the jobs scheduled to move to Texas remained in Buffalo. The labor-management committees were included in the contract. In addition to this unique agreement, the new pact broke with recent patterns by not requiring wage or benefit concessions from workers. Finally, based on the Trico model, the state established a new Industrial Effectiveness Program to help companies and their employees throughout the state work together to become more competitive.

Participation and New Products: The Ford Taurus

Ford Motor Company found that encouraging greater communication between the people engaged in research and development and those involved in production could step up the pace of product development and improve quality.[11]

The Ford Taurus, the auto industry's success story for the 1980s, was the result of white-collar and blue-collar employees working together at every step of the car's development. A team approach brought different groups of workers together in a streamlined process.

The Taurus was conceived in 1980 when Detroit was deep in recession. To Ford's executives, "it was painfully obvious that we weren't competitive with the rest of the world in quality," says John A. Manoogian, then Ford's chief of quality. "It became our No. 1 priority." Representatives from all the various units—planning, design, engineering, and manufacturing—worked together. Because all these usually unconnected groups were intimately involved from the start, problems were solved before they became crises.

Ford asked assembly-line workers for advice before the Taurus was designed, and used many of the suggestions. After workers complained they had trouble installing car doors because the body panels were formed in too many different pieces—up to eight to a side—the Taurus door was redesigned with two pieces. One employee suggested that all bolts have the same size head so workers wouldn't have to change wrenches. "In the past we hired people for their arms and their legs," says Manoogian. "But we weren't smart enough to make use of their brains." The Taurus team worked so well that Ford decided to apply the concept of participation across the board.

Participation in the Service Sector

Although many manufacturing companies have turned to worker participation to boost productivity, the "postindustrial" service sector had also discovered the benefits of employee participation.

Like many information-based companies, the Shenandoah Life Insurance Company sought to improve productivity and profitability by taking advantage of the advances in computer technology that revolutionized the American workplace in the 1980s. Although the company installed a multimillion-dollar computer system, the investment did not pay off in increased efficiency. A typical policy conversion still involved thirty-two clerks and took more than a month to complete.[12]

Realizing that internal bureaucracy had thrown a monkey wrench in the company's high-tech plans, management initiated a radical reorganization based on worker participation and teamwork. Shenandoah did not abandon the computer system but integrated it into a new synergistic relationship with the workers.

Under the old system, clerks processed claims on a "paper assembly line," with separate departments performing distinct tasks. The company reorganized clerks into teams of five to seven members with each team responsible for all aspects of claim processing.

Participation paid off. The company cut processing time dramatically and increased productivity by 50 percent. Employees reported a greater sense of job satisfaction that came from learning new skills and an increased say in their jobs.

Aetna Life and Casualty Company has established a similar program as part of a "bossless" management system in its Rocky Hill, Connecticut, office. Team members set productivity goals and decide who will perform certain tasks each week. Whereas workers were responsible for only one aspect of claims processing in the past, they now learn all aspects of the process and trade jobs as needed. Each team decides hiring and firing policies, evaluates members' performance, and performs other duties that were traditionally the prerogative of the office manager. The Travelers Corporation has instituted a similar pilot program, though teams do not decide hiring and firing policies.[13]

Blurring the Lines: Employees as Managers and Owners

Worker participation is only one example of the changes underway on the production side of the American Formula. The
boundaries between employers and employees are also being
blurred by the spread of joint approaches to strategic decision
making.

In return for wage and work-rule concessions, workers have
asked for—and received—a voice in the way companies are
run. Union representatives now sit on the board of directors at
Kaiser, Wheeling Pittsburgh, and other steel companies. And at
LTV, steelworkers have joined management on the steelmak-
er's central planning committee to develop long-range strategy.
This phenomenon is also occurring in transportation and other
industries.[14]

Perhaps the most dramatic example of the worker's new role
is the concept of employee ownership. About 8 million workers
belong to Employee Stock Ownership Plans. Employee-owned
companies include high-tech firms, insurance companies, manufacturers, and service sector firms. The number of ESOPs is
growing at a 7 to 8 percent annual rate.[15] (See Chart 7.2.) The

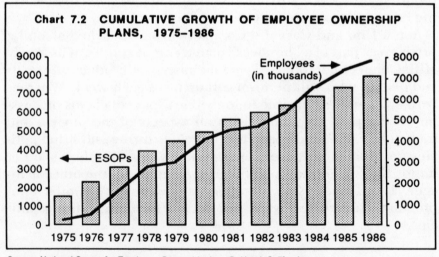

Chart 7.2 **CUMULATIVE GROWTH OF EMPLOYEE OWNERSHIP
PLANS, 1975–1986**

Source: National Center for Employee Ownership, Inc., Oakland, California

forms of employee ownership vary widely, from the large corporation, in which employees receive stock through a profit sharing plan, to small businesses organized as cooperatives, in which each employee owns an equal share and has equal responsibility. What is common among almost all enterprises with employee ownership and participation is above-average productivity levels.

The cases we describe below show the many ways employee ownership helps workers gain responsibility and makes their jobs more rewarding and meaningful. The Commission recommends that employee ownership be made a central part of state and national economic strategies. Federal law already provides sufficient tax incentives. What we need now are programs in training, education, technical support, feasibility studies, and financing. Some states have already initiated such programs and these efforts should be encouraged and expanded in order to help realize the tremendous potential offered by employee ownership.

COOPERATIVE HOME CARE ASSOCIATES

Cooperative Home Care Associates (CHCA) is the largest low-income worker cooperative enterprise in the nation.[16] Its 150 employee-owners provide clinical, personal care, and related home health care services to homebound patients in the Bronx and upper Manhattan.

CHCA was started in January 1985 to obtain better wages and benefits, working conditions, job stability, and career opportunities for low-income minority women, and to ensure high-quality home care services for elderly and disabled patients.

CHCA provides reliable, personalized home care; opportunities for workers to learn and grow as members of a professional health care team and a worker-owned company; the highest levels of salaries and benefits for home care workers in New York City; and a workplace which fosters teamwork, the sharing of ideas, and a supportive management staff.

At CHCA every worker owns an equal share in the company and earns a portion of any profits the company makes. Worker-owners elect the board of directors and the grievance council, and serve on board committees which develop company policy.

CHCA's home health aides participate in monthly team meetings in which they analyze and solve problems. Paid in-service training sessions are held regularly to reinforce and build skills, and aides receive extensive administrative and nursing support while on case assignment.

Workers regularly attend worker-ownership training sessions. At these meetings they learn their rights and responsibilities as worker-owners and learn how CHCA functions as a business. Home health aides learn about their company's market, finances, the rationale for its operating policies, and its growth possibilities, and they are taught how to read a financial statement and review a business plan.

In an industry plagued by high staff turnover, inconsistent service, limited skills development, and low wages, Cooperative Home Care Associates has provided stable jobs at above-average pay for its worker-owners and reliable, skilled services for its clients.

CANTERBURY PRESS

At Canterbury Press in Rome, New York, sales have increased 50 percent in the last five years, and the company has added 34 new workers to meet the increasing volume.[17] This privately held printer of periodicals, catalogues, and brochures projects sales of $6.5 million for 1987.

In an industry which has experienced major changes in the last decade, why has Canterbury Press succeeded where other small firms have failed? While the company has kept abreast of technological change in the industry, its success is due in no small part to its innovative ownership structure.

Canterbury Press's eighty-five employees own their company through an ESOP. The plan was established twelve years ago by the owner, Ward West, to divest his 100 percent share of the company. Rather than sell the firm to another printing company—which had made him a substantial offer—and risk the jobs of his loyal employees, West set up an ESOP trust. Over an eight-year period, the trust purchased all of his shares from him.

The purchase of the stock was accomplished through annual tax deductible corporate contributions amounting to 15 percent of annual payroll. The firm has also used the ESOP to borrow money for expansion and has been able to take advantage of other ESOP tax incentives. Companies borrowing money through an ESOP can deduct both interest and principal payments from their taxes.

Stock is allocated to individual employee accounts based on annual compensation. Since ESOPs are considered employee benefit plans by the IRS, vesting is required. Canterbury Press employee-owners are fully vested after ten years. In 1975, the press's stock was valued by an independent appraiser at $4.13 a share. Today it is worth $15.06. The company estimates that an average employee with ten or more years in the plan has an account balance of $86,000. When an employee leaves the company or retires, the firm buys back his shares.

The ESOP is the company's only retirement plan. "Printing companies as small as we are rarely have pension plans," says Canterbury Press's treasurer, Jerome McCarthy. The ESOP has been a powerful motivator. "When employees see people walking away with $50,000 and $80,000 checks at retirement, they realize that the harder they work, the bigger their check will be when they retire," adds McCarthy.[18]

Canterbury Press employee-owners also receive annual dividend payments on their allocated shares. Last year, total dividend payments amounted to $40,000.

Canterbury employees participate in the management of their company through a quality committee of representatives from each department. It meets independently of management to discuss production issues, personnel policy, and other concerns. The head of the quality committee sits down regularly with the company president to make recommendations and suggestions. McCarthy says that since the ESOP was instituted, "quality has improved, and in the printing business, that's what gives you the edge."[19]

SEYMOUR SPECIALTY WIRE
For 107 years, workers at the Seymour Specialty Wire Company's plant on the Naugatuck River produced the brass alloys needed to make eyeglasses, jewelry, auto parts, keys, zippers, and pot scrubbers sold around the world. In 1984, Bridgeport

Brass, as the company was called then, was about to become another casualty in the wave of plant shutdowns which had beset the Naugatuck region for twenty-five years. Instead, the plant's employees took matters into their own hands and engineered an employee buy-out of the plant.[20]

The buy-out effort was led by the local plant manager and UAW Local 1827, the union which represents the firm's 172 hourly workers, with assistance from a coalition of church, labor, and community groups formed to ease the effects of plant shutdowns in the Valley. "At first it seemed like talking fairy tales," recalls one fourteen-year plant veteran. "We figured we would have to start over. Then we found out we could buy the place. We said, 'Are you kidding?' "[21]

With funding from the state of Connecticut, the town of Seymour, and National Distillers, the parent company, a study was conducted to determine the feasibility of an employee buy-out. The study determined that the plant could operate profitably as an employee-owned enterprise, and a majority of the employees voted to proceed with the buy-out.

A buy-out committee, chaired by the plant manager and the union president, worked overtime to convert the plant from a subsidiary of a multinational corporation to a democratic employee-owned company. A business plan and a government system were developed with the assistance of consultants, company attorneys, and accountants. Financing for the $11 million deal was based on a loan and a 10 percent pay cut.

The new company has an unusually high level of employee participation. Five of its nine directors are directly elected by SSW's employee owners on a one-worker, one-vote basis. The current board also includes two outside directors, a former plant manager who is now president of the company, and the head of Local 1827, a 31-year-old furnace operator. A recently elected member of the board stated his reason for getting involved: "I don't mind what I'm getting paid right now, I can live, maybe not that great, but I can live. But, in the future, I'm going to have a lot if this place is still around. That's why I'm on the board of directors, because I want this place to be around. I want to make money, and I want to make a change in the way things are going right now."[22]

Paying for Productivity

In all of the examples described in this chapter, employees and managers made a decision to try something different in order to make the enterprise more competitive and the jobs more secure. In each case workers got a chance to put more into their jobs, to participate more fully in the process.

A similar movement is underway, often in the same workplaces, to change how workers are paid. The Commission believes that a strategy to increase worker participation and labor-management cooperation must also experiment with new compensation systems that will give workers a bigger stake in productivity. In a 1983 study reported by Public Agenda Foundation, only 9 percent of American workers (as compared with 93 percent of Japanese workers) believed they would benefit personally from improved productivity.[23] Without significant reform in this area, America will always fall short of maximum gains in productivity simply because employees will lack faith that these gains will not be either used against them or disproportionately benefit others, not themselves. Greater attention should therefore be given to such techniques as the flexible bonus system that would be tied to the creation of value. For example, one of the best programs for bonus compensation is a "gain-sharing program" in which employees benefit from group efforts rather than individual incentive programs which tend to pit employee against employee, leaving the ultimate goal of product quality all but forgotten. These changes are well underway. With support from business, labor, and government, gain sharing, profit sharing, and the bonus will become even more common.

In terms of new products and technology, the Commission recommends that management and labor encourage greater communication between those engaged in R&D and those involved in production. And as part of a company's implementation of technological changes, the views, suggestions, and overall involvement of workers who will be carrying out those changes should be solicited. Although improved employee morale is an important benefit, the crucial fact is that the practical production experience of a company's workers can help management make the most appropriate selection of new technology. Once new technology is in place, workers as well as supervisory management should be instructed fully as to its operation; it is counterproductive to limit employees' knowledge of systems they are supposed to operate and maintain. Companies should also encourage labor-management teams to develop their own proposals for improvements in the production process.

Finally, the new industrial relations must be based on the idea that workers will display greater flexibility in accepting technological change in the workplace. As part of this, the rigidity of some job classifications should be reexamined. In exchange, employers must demonstrate a willingness to offer employment security or in other ways link the benefits of technological progress to the economic concerns of workers.

Toward a New Idea of Consumption

America became known as the world's first consumer society. America's retailers had the flexibility and imagination to make America's marketplace the best in the world. But over the years, major flaws developed in our approach to consumption. The first, as we have seen, was the tendency of policymakers to encourage consumption but not do enough to encourage savings. The second was to encourage private consumption beyond what could be supported by production, and often at the expense of public consumption. Roads, bridges, schools, a clean environment, better health and housing, mass transit systems, and other types of public consumption are really long-term investments that can improve our competitiveness and our quality of life.

Today we need to embrace a new idea of consumption, one that encompasses public "goods" and is not at odds with our level of production. As we discussed in Chapter 5, public consumption can be broadened only in the context of a balanced fiscal policy—we cannot make the long-term investments we need without changes in our ability to raise revenue. At the same time, the potential for revenue is increased by a rising level of production.

To increase our productivity and produce what we are truly capable of producing: that is the great profit of participation. In the final analysis, the success of a collective enterprise—be it a company or a nation—depends on the contribution of the individuals that are part of it. Each of us must be given a chance to participate. Once given that chance, we must do our share.

CHAPTER EIGHT

A Choice of Futures: The Role for Positive Government

The Turning Point

THE word "crisis" has been cheapened by too frequent use, but no other word so well describes America's present situation. Originally, "crisis" meant turning point, which is precisely where America stands today. Either we pursue reforms that both strengthen the international trading system and make us more competitive at home, or we risk a long, slow national decline.

The majority of today's Americans grew up after the last great turning point in our history—the fifteen-year period encompassing the Depression, World War Two, and postwar reconstruction. In the long peace and prosperity that followed, many of us came to take the good life for granted, believing that our lives would contain few hard choices and that there would be no serious penalties for national mistakes. America was on an economic escalator.

But today the escalator has slowed, and in some respects begun going backward. Tough choices *do* confront us, and the greatest mistake would be to minimize their seriousness. Unfortunately, political leaders in both parties have for too long ignored the warning signs, squandering irreplaceable assets and precious time for the sake of short-term political gain. Indeed, some say that any political leader is doomed to defeat if he or she tells the American people the truth about the difficult things we must do to secure a prosperous future. Our political system, it is said, rewards only the bearers of glad tidings.

This is the counsel of despair, and underestimates the basic good sense of Americans. Political leaders who have the courage to acknowledge that we face difficult choices in coming years will garner the respect of the American people.

America: A Tale of Two Futures

To convey the urgency and opportunities of our condition, we have developed two scenarios of the year 2000. Neither scenario is a prediction, but both are possibilities.

The first scenario extrapolates present trends. We envision America as it may be when the next century begins, a mere twelve years from now, if we accept our current policies as adequate and do little in the way of fundamental change. The second scenario describes how life could be if the reforms we have called for take place.

Future #1: Economic Decline

Assume that present long-term trends continue. The year 2000 will see a United States dependent on imported goods in most of its vital industries. As Chart 8.1 shows, 41 percent of all goods sold in the U.S. will be imports, including 42 percent of all cars.[1] Thirty percent of our telecommunications, one-third of our steel, and a full 90 percent of all consumer electronics will come from other countries.[2] Unless we can reverse the trend, by the year 2000 we will no longer be a major producer of computers. In 1985 we produced 30 percent of all the computers made in the world; by the year 2000 our share may be as little as 8 percent.[3]

This continuing loss of competitiveness will trigger a decline in our standard of living. As Chart 1.8 showed, over-the-decade average rates of growth have been sliding downward; another

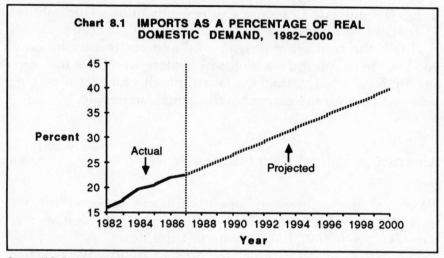

Chart 8.1 IMPORTS AS A PERCENTAGE OF REAL DOMESTIC DEMAND, 1982–2000

Source: U.S. Department of Commerce

Note: Oil imports excluded

decade of decline will leave our average annual growth in the late 1990s at a slow 1.6 percent.[4] This slowdown will ultimately put our standard of living far behind not only those of Germany, Japan, and Sweden, but those of many other industrial societies as well.[5]

If the national debt continues to grow as it has for the last seven years—11 percent per year—at present rates of population and GNP growth, interest payments on the national debt would amount to more than 10 percent of our GNP in the year 2000—or about $2,600 per year for every man, woman, and child in the United States. (See Chart 8.2.) The federal debt would be $9 trillion by the year 2000 and interest payments would consume $750 billion per year. This is clearly not possible, but a doubling of the federal debt to $4 trillion is, unfortunately, not impossible. Annual interest payments on that debt will be over $300 billion.[6] Assuming that foreign holdings grow 1 percent per year, to 25 percent of our national debt, interest payments to foreigners will reach $75 billion a year.[7]

We will lose a large measure of control over our future to foreign investors. Already, average annual foreign direct investment in the United States has risen to record levels. If this

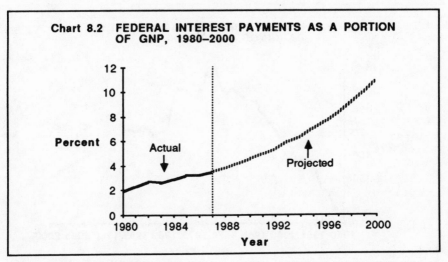

Chart 8.2 FEDERAL INTEREST PAYMENTS AS A PORTION OF GNP, 1980–2000

Source: *Economic Report of the President,* 1987

trend continues, foreign investors will control many firms in key industries and decide what new investments will be made. America may increasingly look like an economic colony, which is where we came in 212 years ago. Foreign interest groups, backed by enormous wealth, will form powerful lobbies that will influence political decisions at every level of government. The spectacle of Toshiba Corporation mobilizing a lobbying campaign to try to stop our government from punishing it for giving secret technology to the Soviet Union will be repeated many times.

Our slow growth and foreign debt will result in lower real wages for American workers. By the year 2000, the average real weekly pay of American workers will be lower than at any time since the Korean War.[8] (See Chart 8.3.) Unemployment will vary between 11 and 12 percent during recessions and between 7 and 8 percent during expansions.[9] One out of six American families—and one out of every four American children—will live below the poverty line.[10] In 1973, almost half of American families earned enough money to afford what the Census Bureau considers a middle-class standard of living. By the year 2000, if present trends continue, only one-third of our families will still be middle-class.[11] By that year, the monthly mortgage

187

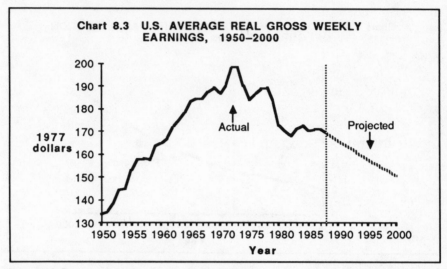

Chart 8.3 U.S. AVERAGE REAL GROSS WEEKLY EARNINGS, 1950–2000

Source: U.S. Department of Labor, Bureau of Labor Statistics

payment for a median-priced home will equal one-half of the median monthly income for a 30-year-old man, up from 21 percent in 1973.[12] We can expect homeownership rates to fall until more than 40 percent of American families cannot afford to buy a home, and homelessness will reach uncontrollable levels.[13] One-third of the population will have no health insurance at all.[14]

Family life will suffer. Falling real wages in the last fifteen years have made common the two-income family. Mothers of preschool children have entered the labor force in ever-increasing numbers—too often out of necessity. But by the year 2000, two incomes will not be enough. Three- and four-income families will multiply as more parents seek second jobs and more children work after school. Over 60 percent of American teenagers aged 16 to 19 will be employed while still enrolled in high school, up from 30 percent in 1960 and 45 percent in 1987.[15]

Educational opportunity will diminish. Four years of tuition and room and board will cost more than $44,000 at a public university and more than $100,000 at a private college.[16] Fewer minority students and students from low-income families will be able to go to college at all, and many middle-class students will have to scale down their college plans from four to two years. Governments, saddled with heavy interest payments, will not be able to provide the additional scholarships and loans that students will need; a college education will once again become the privilege of a select few.

What will be the consequences if these forecasts prove accurate? America will not be able to keep its promises to retirees; social security and Medicare will surely be undermined as domestic spending programs are cut to the bone. As our hard-pressed cities and towns reduce their education funding, the gap between the quality of American education and that of our competitors' education will widen.

The brunt of an American decline will fall on the middle class. A government saddled with immense debts and crushing interest payments will desperately seek to raise revenues, and the largest portion of these will have to come from the middle class; the poor have too little money and there are not enough wealthy people to carry the burden. Even now we are hearing proposals to cut the tax benefits that make middle-class life possible, including the deduction for single-family home mortgage loans. In effect, the middle class will pay more to government and get less from it. Government benefits and services that provide social security for middle-class recipients will be slashed. We can expect major cuts in police, sanitation, mass transit, and education—services the middle class needs to get from state and federal government—if the budget crisis persists. Increasingly, "user fees" will pay for services once regarded as basic. In addition, as the number of older Americans reaches record levels, the demand for government services will rise—without the resources to meet it.

Economic decline will make it harder, not easier, to take the actions necessary to correct the crisis. Austerity and cutbacks will sharpen political competition among society's interest groups and make compromise more difficult, as the protracted budget reduction process in 1987 demonstrated. Even in the wake of a worldwide financial crisis, the White House and Congress nearly failed to reach agreement on a deficit-reduction package. In future years under this scenario, the choices will grow more unpleasant, and interest payments on the federal debt will swallow up more federal revenues, leaving fewer resources for critical domestic and defense programs. Each year it becomes harder to reach agreement on new cuts, and the necessary compromises are being made later and later.

The economic decline and retreat of our nation will have consequences far beyond our own borders. A poorer America will mean a poorer and more dangerous world. The success of democracy in the Philippines, for example, is fundamentally linked with the success of the Philippine economy, and that economy needs substantial, long-term assistance from the U.S. It is improbable that a declining America can provide that aid when we are forced to cut essential programs at home. Israel, Egypt, Latin America, sub-Saharan Africa, and other regions that look to us for assistance cannot expect to receive the aid they need if we fall into economic decline. Our commitments to NATO and Japan are also jeopardized unless we alter our course. Professor Paul Kennedy's warnings about "imperial overstretch"—the growing gap between our obligations and our resources—will become more apparent.

Since World War Two the American economy has been the locomotive of world growth; our consumers have provided demand for products around the world, and, until recently, our savers provided much of the capital. Without a strong and growing American market, even the rapidly growing NICs of East Asia will slip into recession and stagnation. Although we are no longer the only important market economy in the world, we remain the most important source of demand. Our failure to grow will have disastrous consequences for our neighbors and for trading partners around the world. The Third World will suffer the most, as economic problems and political instability will rock governments and societies around the world. This instability will create new threats to America's military security at the same time that our economy will be unable to bear the strains of high defense budgets. The result is likely to be an unpleasant and dangerous world, haunted by a growing threat of war.

This scenario of American drift and decline does not require any dramatic changes to become a reality. We do not need another 500-point crash on the stock market or a collapse of the international banking system in order to see a long-term, gradual decline in our standard of living. This is the kind of future toward which we are currently headed, and unless we carry out major reforms in the next Administration, this is the future that we will reach.

An Economy Built on American Values

This Commission has devoted much of its report to a review of American economic history, because it holds valid lessons and principles for us today. We have built our proposals on the best foundation for America's long-term strength: the values that have guided us this far through our national life.

First among these values is our commitment to the democratic process. Although often criticized as too slow and too messy to respond to the challenges of the real world, the American democracy often has roused itself in times of emergency.

The American commitment to democracy also reflects our belief that pure market forces do not ultimately determine the direction our society will take. The kind of society we live in and the laws and ethics we live by are ultimately ethical and moral issues. Americans have always believed that these issues should be decided through the democratic process of government, not the market. And while the democratic process can be disorderly and time-consuming, ultimately it generates answers with which the whole society can live. No other process does or can yield this consent.

Growing out of American democratic values is a commitment to diversity and participation. Our ancestors, and we ourselves, have come from every corner of the world. We created a single great nation with so many ethnic, racial, cultural, religious, and geographic differences through participation—giving people a chance, a voice, and the right to participate in the decisions governing their lives. Participation by all does not make us all alike, but it helps to unify us by creating a sense that we all play by the same rules. So increasing the quantity and quality of employee participation, for example, can serve to improve our competitiveness.

So can increased cooperation. Too often we are preoccupied with our differences and fail to see the mutual interests that bind us and the benefits that come from cooperation and creative compromise. America was literally founded through cooperation and compromise. Small states and large states compromised with one another to create the Constitution—a balanced system protecting the rights of states and individuals while creating a strong central government—and the resulting system has worked for 200 years. Once again we must learn to think creatively about cooperation, to find ways we can meet our distinct objectives together.

Americans also cherish the value of compassion, not only because it is morally right, but also because it makes practical sense. A commitment to the poor is often dismissed as the concern of soft-headed sentimentalists, particularly in times of economic trouble. Yet a commitment to those who face hard times is not simply charity: it is a pragmatic as well as a moral necessity.

The underclass, those millions of Americans cut off from our national life and living in near–Third World conditions in the heart of our greatest cities, is more than a human and moral tragedy of immense dimensions. The underclass represents a serious drain on the productive power of our society. Because our society is not prepared simply to let its poorest members starve, the underclass remains a part of our society which consumes, without the opportunity to produce as well. It is in everyone's interest to make the investments in education and services that will bring the submerged one-tenth of our society into the productive mainstream of American life.

Linked to these considerations is our commitment to middle-class Americans, those who must work for a living. These Americans are vulnerable to unemployment, disability, and old age; some of their children need special health care or education.

Another value that must be part of our national economic renewal is a commitment to invest in the future. Across the landscape of American history are many examples of such investments—the canals and railroads of the nineteenth century, the interstate highway system of the twentieth, the land-grant colleges and great public universities, the funding of medical research, federal technical assistance to farmers, and such huge public sources of power as the TVA and Hoover Dam. At this moment in our history, it is wrong to sacrifice tomorrow to protect today's standard of living. From now on, the money we spend must be dedicated toward making us as a nation—and not only as individuals—stronger and more prosperous.

While the Commission does not favor national economic planning, we do believe that government—federal, state, and local—already has within its grasp the ability to affect our economic future, and should exercise it.

Finally, we must also return to a commitment to economic growth, the only workable solution for our society's economic difficulties. Some leaders, alarmed by our drift toward economic decline, have called for a new austerity in government and private consumption as the bitter but necessary medicine that can restore our economic health. Noting that our national savings rate has fallen while consumption has risen faster than production, they argue that we must tighten our belts.

Although austerity sounds virtuous, it is no economic panacea; its side effects can be more dangerous than the original disease. Carefully measured doses of austerity may be needed in certain situations to prevent a much greater dose later on, but its effects should be closely monitored. Austerity, a permanent lowering of living standards, is, after all, what we seek to avoid.

We must instead concentrate on growth. Only growth can generate the funds required for new investment, and can offer investors the profit possibilities that make new investments worthwhile. With growth we can reach constructive compromises in an atmosphere of rising opportunity and generate the productive investments in education, infrastructure, research, and technology that can provide us with a base for stable prosperity in the years to come.

Future growth can be built only on a strong foundation of balanced economic conditions both at home and with our major trading partners. An adjustment in our trade and budget deficits is essential for the long-run competitiveness and security of the nation. A growth-oriented adjustment strategy is feasible, but it will require leadership and determination at both the national and international levels to be realized.

Future #2: Balanced Growth

Future #1 is not ordained. With the knowledge, strength, and experience that we have today, America has the potential to be happier, wealthier, more secure, and more peaceful than any nation in history.

Here, then, is how the combination of a new international order, positive government, rational budgeting, and a new production ethic can lead to an economic renewal by the year 2000.

A NEW INTERNATIONAL ORDER

The export-oriented development strategy currently employed by many countries works well for them individually, but collectively subjects the global economy to increasing stress. These nations now need to turn toward a program of balanced growth in which domestic living standards rise through increased investment and/or increased consumption. Such a program will, in the long run, do more to bring about rapid, sustainable progress in the Third World than export-driven strategies and will avoid a protectionist backlash.

Just as the increased purchasing power of America fueled economic growth after World War Two, increased purchasing power among the Third World's industrial working people can set off a generation of dynamic global growth. In the same way, the First World countries who still cling to the austerity-based policies of the past must allow their domestic consumption to rise and put more real purchasing power in the hands of their citizens. These countries must also continue to open their markets to foreign goods, just as the U.S. has maintained relatively open markets since the end of World War Two.

Our goal is more trade, not less trade. Although we have argued that the U.S. must be prepared to use access to its market as a bargaining chip in international discussions, the long-term goal of open markets is critical for economic growth.

Reforms in international trade will not be easy to achieve, and will involve intricate negotiations in a variety of international forums. GATT, the IMF, the World Bank, and other international organizations represent the opinions of many countries, and they cannot be expected to turn on a dime with every change in American policy. Reforms will involve patient, long-term efforts to understand the views of other countries and to build a consensus around the principles that can stabilize the international trading system.

Despite the difficulties, there is no reason that we cannot make progress. Third World debt restructuring—and in some cases relief—and imaginative programs to finance new investments in the Third World could open new markets for American goods in a matter of months. Within a few years, joint efforts to improve wages and working conditions in the Third World could enhance purchasing power there, while giving American workers and companies a fair chance to compete for the new markets. By the year 2000, the U.S. could be on the verge of a new era in international economic relations, with volumes of trade higher than they are today, protectionist barriers lower, and our trade in much better balance.

POSITIVE GOVERNMENT

International reform can create an opportunity for the U.S., but we will have to act to take advantage of it. The Commission believes that government at all levels—federal, state, and local—has a role to play in restoring our competitiveness and bringing more balance to our fiscal and trade policies, a role that is part of the American tradition of positive government.

From the earliest days of the American Republic, federal and state governments followed policies calculated to foster economic growth. George Washington's Secretary of the Treasury proposed a system of national improvements. Successors set up banks—both public and private—to stimulate new investment and to promote the growth of a system of roads and canals to link the young country together.

Federalists, Democrats, Whigs, and Republicans all advocated extensive programs of government activism in the economy. Abraham Lincoln, the first Republican President, defined the proper role of government in words that still make sense today: "The legitimate object of government is to do for the people what needs to be done, but which they cannot, by individual effort, do at all, or do so well, for themselves."

Another great Republican President took the next step. It was Theodore Roosevelt who put the full weight of the executive branch into regulating the marketplace, distinguishing between constructive and destructive competition. Using better technology, motivating the work force to work more productively, improving the quality of existing goods and bringing new ones to market—these were the techniques of constructive competition, and government encouraged them. On the other hand, exploiting the advantages of monopoly, cutting costs by producing substandard goods, undercutting wages, maintaining unsafe working conditions, or polluting the environment—these negative techniques were gradually subjected to local, state, and federal regulation.

Today, positive government does not mean a single, all-encompassing national industrial plan. But it should mean carefully targeted government action that can build on our economic strengths and help overcome our national problems. Government spending, regardless of how we cut the deficit, will remain a significant proportion of our total GNP; we must learn to use the enormous resource to enhance our society's productivity, not to strangle it.

It is no longer enough, for example, to spend money on welfare when the welfare system can perpetuate itself from generation to generation. It is no longer enough to spend money on unemployment compensation without providing retraining to make our work force more productive. It is no longer enough to provide federal bailouts to weak industries without insisting that labor and management in these industries take steps to bring about their own rapid recovery.

Fortunately, the process of renewal has begun as state governments everywhere have become more involved in using government to promote economic growth. And hundreds of businesses, large and small, are exploring the techniques, often with government support, that can unleash a new wave of technological progress.

A RATIONAL APPROACH TO BUDGETING

Positive government today must do much more than randomly spend money: it must invest money to ensure that our society becomes more efficient.

The President and the Congress fight over spending, but rarely does Washington address the far more important question of investment. How can we ensure that the money we spend now will reduce our costs in future years? What programs will do the most to strengthen economic growth?

The United States government should adopt a rational, businesslike approach to its budget by dividing it into three parts: a consumption budget, an investment budget, and a federal trust fund budget. The consumption budget would include the current operating expenses of the government. The investment budget would consist of expenditures designed to produce long-term returns to the federal treasury. It would resemble the capital budget of any business, with the revenues from items in this budget covering their initial capital costs plus interest over a given period of time. When the economy was growing rapidly, some of the investment budget could go into a sinking fund to reduce the existing national debt; when the economy needed stimulation, more investments could be made to avoid the danger of recessions.

The federal trust fund budget would include programs that help pay for themselves out of specific revenues, among them social security, Medicare, and various government lending programs.

The division of the federal budget into smaller, more manageable entities can help Congress and the President develop more rational budgeting. Each budget would have to be fiscally sound each year on its own terms. A team of professional, independent auditors would constantly review all three segments of the budget to ensure that this requirement was met and bring discipline to the process without choking off needed investments.

The tax system must also raise more money—although this

does not have to mean a more regressive tax system. In Chapter 5 we discussed various revenue proposals, and we may have to select from one or more dishes on that menu.

Positive government using rational budgeting will over time reduce our social overhead and strengthen our economic base. Shrewd investments in infrastructure, education, job training, and research can create new opportunities and increase the earning power of our citizens. We can shrink the welfare rolls and increase the number of taxpayers. We can manage our government more effectively and trim unnecessary and wasteful spending programs—without cutting needed programs or refraining from social investments.

A NATION OF PRODUCERS

To service our foreign debts and restore our competitiveness, we must turn from the psychology of consumption back to a national focus on production.

This change should start in two places: the schoolhouse and the workplace.

There is no better example of a commitment to the future than education. As we have suggested, teachers should have better pay and more recognition—and should be held to the highest standards of performance. With better starting salaries and tuition-forgiveness options available to those who enter the teaching profession, the quality of teachers can improve. Teachers of experience and proven competence should enjoy prestige in their communities—and be paid on a level with other professionals who play a vital role in American life.

Our schools must offer more to their students, and demand more from them. Public education is our most important avenue to economic competitiveness, and deserves the highest possible priority at all levels of government.

America's system of education ought to include high-quality day care and after-school care for the children of working parents. By enabling the mothers of young children to seek employment, the day-care system can drastically reduce the welfare rolls. A rich after-hours program for children can take learning beyond the school day and make "latchkey" children a phenomenon of the past.

Quality education requires a greater partnership between the public and private sectors. In many states and communities, employers and schools can start programs that include on-the-job training for older students, using full-time workers as teachers. We also need an expansion of technical training schools, again with the extensive involvement of the private sector.

A decade of national effort could pay off handsomely. With targeted programs for inner-city school districts, a new trend could appear in some of our great cities: parents of school-age children moving into the cities to take advantage of the cultural and educational opportunities in their public schools.

The workplace can also become a fountainhead of the new producer mentality. New technologies can make us more productive, and new forms of workplace organization can help us discover once again the satisfaction that comes from work well done.

The effects of these changes will be felt far beyond the factory floor. If the production line of the future depends on active worker participation, the relationship between workers and managers will change.

The old-fashioned assembly lines emphasized a hierarchical, top-down management style. The new technologies require a different style. Management will become a two-way street, with more ideas and decisions being made by people directly involved in production. To win the cooperation that can make this system work, corporations must find new ways of motivating and training the work force. Workers must share in the fruits of the new technologies. They must feel more like partners than cogs.

For decades, management and labor have often acted at cross purposes, like two occupants of a lifeboat, each drilling holes in the bottom to teach the other side a lesson. There now exists, however, the opportunity to inaugurate a new era in labor relations, if only companies will understand the new workplace paradigm. If managers treat employees more as economic partners than as external costs, the return to both will increase. For cooperation is both economically and ethically preferable to conflict.

While worker participation and employee ownership help

raise productivity, they even more importantly return control over the future to individual Americans. When workers participate in major decisions, our enterprises produce not only goods, but citizens: people accustomed to responsible thinking about real issues, people who have experience at making decisions and living with the consequences.

Raising productivity is slow and unglamorous work. The big technological breakthrough may get the headlines, but the reality of productivity growth involves thousands of small improvements made on assembly lines and in offices day by day, month by month. No government or central planning agency can call forth this kind of daily effort. In a competitive market economy, managers and workers must develop this effort and attitude in themselves.

To the Next Century

The Commission does not underestimate the difficulties that lie in our path, but neither do we want to exaggerate them.

America is still America. We still have the natural resources and the democratic government that brought us two centuries of prosperity. We still have the population whose genius for innovation and willingness to work made this country the envy and the wonder of the world. We still have a people who will respond enthusiastically to policies which address the needs and concerns of most Americans, policies which give the nation a sense of purpose and mutual commitment, and offer the hope of rising opportunity for all.

It is within our power to renew the promise of American life and choose our future. Freedom, hard work, diversity, participation, and the willingness to change are still values that can again bring us a generation of growth and prosperity.

If we as a nation approach our place in the world with a new realism, if we accept the lessons of global interdependence and work for growth, if we turn our attention to producing with the high degree of efficiency and quality that were once national trademarks, and if we do so in a way that brings greater cooperation between our institutions and greater participation for our people, then we will have built a foundation for prosperity upon which the American house can stand for years to come.

We on the Commission on Trade and Competitiveness hope that our efforts will contribute to the renewal of the promise of the American dream, to accomplish the goal so simply stated by President Kennedy almost thirty years ago: "To get this country moving again."

NOTES

CHAPTER 1

1. U.S. Department of Commerce, Bureau of Economic Analysis, *Survey of Current Business,* June 1987.

2. U.S. Department of Commerce.

3. U.S. Department of Commerce, cited in Claudia Deutsch, "U.S. Industry's Unfinished Struggle," *New York Times,* February 21, 1988, sec. 3, p. 7.

4. United Nations Conference on Trade and Development, *UNCTAD Handbook of International Trade and Development Statistics 1986,* February 1987, pp. 2–11.

5. Council of Economic Advisers, *Economic Report of the President* (Washington, D.C.: U.S. Government Printing Office, 1988), p. 362.

6. Ward's Communications Inc., *1987 Ward's Automotive Yearbook,* 1987, p. 14.

7. U.S. Department of Commerce, International Trade Administration, *U.S. Industrial Outlook 1988* (Washington, D.C.: 1988), p. 38-2.

8. *Survey of Current Business,* June 1987.

9. U.S. Department of Commerce, International Trade Administration, "U.S. Trade Data 1972–1985," December 1986; "Supplement for 1986," September 1987.

10. American Petroleum Institute, cited in Robert D. Hersey, Jr., "Oil Output in U.S. Fell 4.5% in '87," *New York Times*, January 14, 1988.

11. U.S. Department of Commerce, cited in Louis Uchitelle, "Oil Imports a Problem Again," *New York Times*, November 19, 1987.

12. *Survey of Current Business*, June 1987.

13. David M. Gordon, "Private Debt Dwarfs Uncle Sam's," *Los Angeles Times*, January 20, 1987, p. 3.

14. Benjamin Friedman, "Sorting Out the Debt," *New Perspectives Quarterly*, Fall 1987, p. 23.

15. American Farm Bureau Federation, *Farm Bureau News*, December 21, 1987, p. 1.

16. Friedman, op. cit., p. 24.

17. Office of Management and Budget, *Historical Tables: Budget of the United States Government, Fiscal Year 1989* (Washington, D.C.: U.S. Government Printing Office, 1988), pp. 143–145.

18. U.S. Bureau of the Census, *Statistical Abstract of the United States: 1987* (Washington, D.C.: 1986), pp. 293, 295.

19. U.S. Departments of Treasury and Commerce, cited in Walter Mossberg, "Cost of Paying the Foreign Piper," *Wall Street Journal*, January 18, 1988, p. 1.

20. Congress of the United States, Joint Economic Committee, *The Economy at Midyear: A Legacy of Debt*, 1987, p. 18.

21. U.S. Department of Commerce and Dun & Bradstreet Corporation, cited in Council of Economic Advisers, *Economic Report of the President* (Washington, D.C.: U.S. Government Printing Office, 1987), p. 351.

22. *Federal Deposit Insurance Corporation Annual Report*, various years; *FDIC Quarterly Banking Profile*, 2nd Quarter 1987.

23. Robert E. Taylor, "Bank Board Seeks 143 Thrift Mergers in Texas, But Cost of Aid Raises Doubts," *Wall Street Journal*, February 4, 1988; Robert E. Taylor, "Thrifts' Losses Force Industry to Weigh Another Possible U.S. Rescue of FSLIC," *Wall Street Journal*, March 3, 1988.

24. William Dudley and Rob Giordano, "Shake, Rattle, and Roll," *Financial Market Perspectives*, Goldman Sachs & Company, July/August 1987.

25. *Econcomic Report of the President,* 1987, p. 244.

26. Board of Governors of the Federal Reserve System.

27. U.S. Department of Commerce, *Survey of Current Business,* various issues.

28. Ibid.

29. U.S. Department of Labor, Bureau of Labor Statistics.

30. Peter G. Peterson, "The Morning After," *The Atlantic,* October 1987, p. 48.

31. U.S. Department of Commerce, Patent and Trademark Office, cited in "Foreign Gain in U.S. Patents," *New York Times,* February 26, 1988, p. D11.

32. National Science Foundation, Division of Science Resource Studies, *International Science and Technology Update 1987,* March 1987.

33. Lester C. Thurow, *The Zero-Sum Solution* (New York: Simon & Schuster, 1985), p. 186.

34. *Statistical Abstract of the United States: 1987,* p. 147.

35. Ibid., p. 571.

36. "U.S. Trade Data."

37. U.S. Department of Labor, Bureau of Labor Statistics, cited in Nathaniel C. Nash, "Fear over Job Quality Persists Despite Gain in National Rate," *New York Times,* August 8, 1987.

38. Cuomo Commission on Trade and Competitiveness, *U.S. Steel Industry: A Time to Act,* 1988.

39. Putnam, Hayes, Bartlett Inc., *Government Policy and the Domestic Steel Industry,* prepared for the American Iron and Steel Institute, May 1987, p. 21.

40. *1987 Ward's Automotive Yearbook,* p. 64.

41. U.S. Department of Labor, Bureau of Labor Statistics, *Employment Hours and Earnings, United States 1909–84,* Vol. I and II, March 1985; *Supplement to Employment Hours and Earnings,* July 1987.

42. U.S. Department of Agriculture, Agricultural Statistics Board, *Crop Production,* August 11, 1987, A-30.

43. David Sanger, "U.S. Chip Makers Recovering," *New York Times,* May 26, 1987, p. 1.

44. *Economic Report of the President,* 1987, p. 292.

45. U.S. Department of Labor, Bureau of Labor Statistics, "Reemployment Increases Among Displaced Workers," October 14, 1986.

46. National Association of Manufacturers, *U.S. Trade Balance at a Turning Point*, June 1986, p. 11, cited in Congress of the United States, Joint Economic Committee, *Trade Deficits, Foreign Debt and Sagging Growth*, 1986.

47. *Employment and Earnings.*

48. Congress of the United States, Joint Economic Committee, *Working Mothers Are Preserving Family Living Standards*, May 9, 1986, p. 3.

49. Ibid., p. 5.

50. U.S. Department of Labor, Bureau of Labor Statistics, "Usual Weekly Earnings of Wage and Salary Workers, 4th Quarter, 1987," February 1, 1988.

51. State of New York, Task Force on Poverty and Welfare, *A New Social Contract: Rethinking the Nature and Purpose of Public Assistance*, December 1986.

52. Robert Pollin, *Deeper in Debt: The Changing Financial Condition of U.S. Households*, study prepared for the Joint Economic Committee of Congress, October 1987.

53. Katherine L. Bradbury, "The Shrinking Middle Class," *New England Economic Review*, September/October 1986; U.S. Department of Commerce, Bureau of the Census, cited in Kenneth H. Bacon, "The Jackson Message and Economic Angst," *Wall Street Journal*, March 21, 1988, p. 1.

54. *Statistical Abstract of the United States: 1987*, p. 431.

55. "Survey of Consumer Finances 1983," *Federal Reserve Bulletin*, September 1984.

56. Bradbury, op. cit.

57. Sindlinger Economic Services, *The Sindlinger Alert*, No. 1706–08, February 20, 1988, p. 2008.

58. Estimates by the U.S. Departments of Treasury and Commerce, cited in Mossberg, op. cit.

59. *Economic Report of the President*, 1987, cited in Lester Thurow and Laura Tyson, "The Economic Black Hole," *Foreign Policy*, (No.) 67 (Summer 1987), pp. 5, 7.

60. *Global Competition: The New Reality*, Report of the President's Commission on Industrial Competitiveness, Vol. II (Washington, D.C.: U.S. Government Printing Office, 1985), p. 6.

61. *Global Competition: The New Reality*, Report of the President's Commission on Industrial Competitiveness, Vol. I (Washington, D.C.: U.S. Government Printing Office, 1985), p. 7.

CHAPTER 2

1. Walter Laqueur, *Europe Since Hitler*, rev. ed. (New York: Penguin, 1982), p. 16.

2. Ibid., p. 17.

3. Alan S. Milward, *The Reconstruction of Western Europe* (Berkeley: University of California Press, 1984), pp. 28–41.

4. Douglas Botting, *From the Ruins of the Reich: Germany 1945–49* (New York: Crown, 1985), p. 145.

5. Milward, op. cit., p. 18.

6. Ibid., p. 18.

7. Address of Franklin D. Roosevelt to Congress, January 6, 1944, cited in Henry Steele Commager, ed., *Documents of American History*, Vol. 2., 7th ed. (New York: Appleton-Century-Crofts, 1963), pp. 446–49.

8. "The Atlantic Charter," January 11, 1944, cited in Commager, op. cit., p. 451.

9. Quoted in Martin Mayer, *The Fate of the Dollar* (New York: Times Books, 1980), p. 21.

10. Brian Mitchell, *European Historical Statistics 1750–1979*, 2nd rev. ed. (New York: Facts on File, 1981), Table E-1, pp. 378–79.

11. Arthur M. Schlesinger, *A Thousand Days* (Boston: Houghton Mifflin, 1965), p. 654.

12. United Nations Statistical Office, *International Trade Statistics Yearbook*, 1985.

13. Laqueur, op. cit. p. 20.

14. Cited in Mayer, op. cit., p. 21.

15. Organization for Economic Cooperation and Development.

16. See the International Labor Organization's study on the employment effects of transnational corporations in the Third World,

cited in the International Foundation for Development Alternatives News Service, October 30, 1981.

17. John Williamson, *The Open Economy and the World Economy* (New York: Basic Books, 1983), p. 320.

18. Charles P. Kindleberger, *A Financial History of Western Europe* (London: Allen & Unwin, 1984), p. 450.

19. See, generally, Howard M. Wachtel, *The Money Mandarins* (New York: Pantheon, 1986).

20. World Bank, *World Debt Tables of the World Bank*, January 19, 1988.

CHAPTER 3

1. "America's Deflation Belt," *Business Week*, June 9, 1986.

2. Council of Economic Advisers, *Economic Report of the President* (Washington D.C.: U.S. Government Printing Office, 1987), p. 331.

3. Ibid., p. 247.

4. Organization for Economic Cooperation and Development, *OECD Economic Outlook*, Vol. 41 (Paris: June 1987), p. 167.

5. U.S. Department of Commerce, Bureau of Economic Analysis, *Survey of Current Business*, various issues.

6. International Monetary Fund, *Direction of Trade Statistics Yearbook* (Washington D.C.: International Monetary Fund, 1987), pp. 4–6.

7. Ibid., p. 4.

8. International Labor Organization, *World Labor Report 3—Incomes from Work: Between Equity and Efficiency* (Geneva: International Labor Office, 1987), Chapters 1 and 5.

9. World Bank, *World Development Report, 1987* (New York: Oxford University Press, 1987), p. 209.

10. Ibid., p. 209.

11. *Direction of Trade Statistics Yearbook*, 1987, p. 405.

12. Ibid.

13. International Monetary Fund, *Direction of Trade Statistics Yearbook* (Washington, D.C.: 1980), p. 47, cited in Congress of the United States, Joint Economic Committee, *Trade Deficits, Foreign Debt and Sagging Growth: An Analysis of the Causes and Effects of America's Trade Problem*, September 1986, p. 41.

14. United Nations, *UNCTAD Handbook of International Trade and Development Statistics,* 1986, Supplement, pp. 2–14.

15. *Survey of Current Business,* June 1987, Table 7, p. 33.

16. For estimate of 1970 U.S. balance of trade with these countries, see remarks by David C. Mulford, Assistant Secretary for International Affairs, United States Department of the Treasury, before the Asia/Pacific Capital Markets Conference, San Francisco, California, cited in U.S. Department of the Treasury, *Treasury News,* November 17, 1987, p. 4.; for 1987 U.S. trade balance with the Four Tigers, see *Survey of Current Business,* March 1988.

17. National Association of Manufacturers, *U.S. Trade Balance at a Turning Point,* June 1986, p. 13.

18. *Direction of Trade Statistics Yearbook,* 1987, pp. 243, 404.

19. Ibid., p. 243.

20. *Survey of Current Business,* June 1987; March 1988.

21. National Association of Manufacturers, op. cit., p. 13.

22. Robert Bartley, "1929 and All That," *Wall Street Journal,* November 24, 1987, p. 28.

23. *World Development Report 1987,* pp. 134–35.

24. Pat Choate, "Tailored Trade: Dealing with the World as It Is," *Harvard Business Review,* January 1988, p. 91. The data shown in Chart 3.17 were revised slightly by Mr. Choate from those published in the article.

25. *World Development Report 1987,* p. 142.

26. Stephen Marris, *Deficits and the Dollar Revisited,* Institute for International Economics, September 1987.

CHAPTER 4

1. John Berry, "U.S. Economy Still Vulnerable to Shifts in Global Financial Systems," *Washington Post,* March 13, 1988, sec. H, p. 2.

CHAPTER 5

1. *Global Competition: The New Reality,* Report of the President's Commission on Industrial Competitiveness, Vol. II (Washington, D.C.: U.S. Government Printing Office, 1985), p. 7.

2. Quoted in Stephen S. Cohen and John Zysman, "The Myth of a Post-Industrial Economy," *New York Times,* May 17, 1987.

3. Otto Eckstein et al., *The DRI Report on U.S. Manufacturing Industries* (New York: McGraw-Hill, 1984), p. 103.

4. Quoted in Timothy B. Clark, "The Key Is Manufacturing," *The National Journal,* January 10, 1987, p. 74.

5. U.S. Bureau of the Census, *Statistical Abstract of the United States: 1987* (Washington, D.C.: 1986), p. 836.

6. Ibid., pp. 686, 688.

7. Ibid., p. 833.

8. Ibid., p. 735.

9. National Governors Association, Center for Policy Research, *Jobs, Growth and Competitiveness* (Washington, D.C.: National Governors Association, 1987).

10. Ibid., p. 41.

11. Ibid., p. 77.

12. For cumulative increases in defense authorizations, see Office of Management and Budget, *Historical Tables: Budget of the United States Government, Fiscal Year 1989* (Washington, D.C.: U.S. Government Printing Office, 1988); for statistics on the growth of U.S. liabilities to foreigners, see U.S. Department of the Treasury, *Treasury Bulletin,* Winter 1984, p. 143; Winter 1988, p. 118.

13. Peter G. Peterson, "The Morning After," *The Atlantic,* October 1987, pp. 60–61.

14. Ibid., p. 61.

15. John W. Wilson and Otis Port, "Making Brawn Work with Brains," *Business Week,* April 20, 1987, p. 58.

16. *Statistical Abstract of the United States: 1987,* p. 564.

17. Jay Stowsky, *Beating Our Plowshares into Double-Edged Swords: The Impact of Pentagon Policies on the Commercialization of Advanced Technologies,* Working Paper 17, Berkeley Roundtable on the International Economy, April 1986, p. 2.

18. Erich Bloch, "Economic Competition: A Research and Education Challenge," *Research Management,* March/April 1987, p. 6.

19. National Science Foundation, Division of Science Resource Studies, *Federal R&D Funding by Budget Function, Fiscal Years 1986–88,* March 1987.

20. Janice C. Simpson, "A Shallow Labor Pool Spurs Business to Act to Bolster Education," *Wall Street Journal,* September 28, 1987, pp. 1, 27.

21. Jane Perlez, "Banks' Job Program Fails to Find Enough Qualified Students," *New York Times,* June 29, 1987, p. 31.

22. Simpson, op. cit., p. 1.

23. Lester C. Thurow, *The Zero-Sum Solution* (New York: Simon & Schuster, 1985), p. 184.

24. Irwin S. Kirsch and Anne Jungelut, *Literacy: Profiles of America's Young Adult,* National Assessment of Educational Progress, 1986.

25. Louis Harris and Associates, *Survey of the Reaction of the American People and Top Business Executives to the Report on Public Education by the Task Force on Teaching as a Profession of the Carnegie Forum on Education and the Economy,* August 1986.

26. Linda Darling-Hammond, *Beyond the Commission Reports: The Coming Crisis in Teaching,* Rand Corporation, July 1984, p. 6, cited in Thurow, op. cit., p. 186.

27. *Statistical Abstract of the United States: 1987,* p. 571.

28. Thurow, op. cit., p. 187.

29. *Statistical Abstract of the United States: 1987,* p. 147.

CHAPTER 6

1. U.S. Department of Commerce, International Trade Administration, *U.S. Industrial Outlook 1988* (Washington, D.C.: 1988).

2. Ibid.

3. Ibid.

4. Ibid.

5. Bureau of Labor Statistics, *Monthly Labor Review,* Vol. 109, No. 7, July 1986, p. 41.

6. American Apparel Manufacturers Association, *Focus: Economic Profile of the Apparel Industry,* 1986, table 3, p. 10; United States Congress, Office of Technology Assessment, *The U.S. Textile and Apparel Industry: A Revolution in Progress—Special Report,*

OTA-TET 332 (Washington, D.C.: U.S. Government Printing Office, April 1987), p. 80.

7. Carol Parsons, "The Domestic Employment Consequences of Managed International Competition in Apparel," in Laura Tyson, William Dickens, John Zysman, eds., *The Dynamics of Trade and Employment* (Cambridge: Ballinger, forthcoming 1988).

8. American Apparel Manufacturers Association, op. cit., p. 80.

9. Cited in Tyson et al., op. cit., p. 23.

10. U.S. Department of Labor, Bureau of Labor Statistics, "Reemployment Increases Among Displaced Workers," October 14, 1986, tables 3 and 13.

11. American Apparel Manufacturers Association, op. cit., pp. 84–85.

12. U.S. Department of Labor, Bureau of Labor Statistics, unpublished data, September 1987; New York State Industrial Cooperation Council, study of the apparel industry, forthcoming, 1988.

13. International Labor Organization, *World Labor Report 3— Incomes from Work: Between Equity and Efficiency* (Geneva: International Labor Office, 1987), p. 22.

14. International Ladies Garment Workers Union, Research Department, *The U.S. Apparel Industry, 1960–1985, with Special Emphasis on Women and Children's Apparel,* October 12, 1985, p. 38.

15. Joseph Albright and Marcia Kunstel, "Stolen Childhood: A Global Report on the Exploitation of Children," *Cox Newspapers,* June 21–26, 1987.

16. Muzatter Ahmad, "Productivity in Selected Ready-Made Garment Industries," in Dr. Imre Bernolak, ed., *The Integrated Report of an APO Survey in 13 Countries in Asia 1984–85,* forthcoming.

17. American Apparel Manufacturers Association, op. cit., pp. 88–91.

18. Congress of the United States, Congressional Budget Office, *Has Trade Protection Revitalized Domestic Industries?* (Washington, D.C.: U.S. Government Printing Office, 1986), pp. 16, 31.

19. Stanley Nehmer and Mark W. Love, "Textiles and Apparel: A Negotiated Approach to International Competition," in Bruce R. Scott and George C. Lodge, eds., *U.S. Competitiveness in the World Economy* (Boston: Harvard Business School Press, 1985), p. 243.

20. International Ladies Garment Workers Union, op. cit., p. 42.

21. Conversation with Daniel Harrington, Director of the Technical Assistance Division, Office of Trade Adjustment Assistance, U.S. Department of Commerce, January 1988; conversation with Dr. Herman Starobin, Director of Research, International Ladies Garment Workers Union, October 1987.

22. United Nations Conference on Trade and Development, *UNC-TAD Handbook of International Trade and Development Statistics 1986,* February 1987.

23. *The U.S. Textile and Apparel Industry,* p. 83.

24. Office of the U.S. Trade Representative, *National Trade Estimate: 1986 Report on Foreign Trade Barriers* (Washington, D.C.: U.S. Government Printing Office, 1986), p. 165.

25. *The U.S. Textile and Apparel Industry,* pp. 108–10.

26. Donald F. Barnett and Louis Schorsch, *Steel: Upheaval in a Basic Industry* (Cambridge: Ballinger, 1983).

27. Peter F. Marcus and Karlis M. Kirsis, *World Steel Dynamics, Steel Strategist #13,* March 30, 1987, p. 55.

28. Ibid., p. 11.

29. Ibid.

30. Ibid.

31. "Ratings and Reports," *Value Line Investment Survey,* February 19, 1988, pp. 1416–24.

32. Cuomo Commission on Trade and Competitiveness, *The U.S. Steel Industry: A Time to Act,* 1988.

33. Ibid.

34. Ibid.

35. *U.S. Industrial Outlook 1988,* p. 42-4.

36. United Nations Center on Transnational Corporations, *Transnational Corporations in Food and Beverage Processing,* 1981; United Nations Center on Transnational Corporations, *Salient Features and Trends in Foreign Direct Investment,* 1983.

37. C. K. Helleiner and R. Lavergne, "Intra-Firm Trade and Industrial Exports to the United States," *Oxford Bulletin of Economics and Statistics,* 1979, pp. 297–311.

38. *U.S. Industrial Outlook 1988,* p. 42-4.

39. Calculations based on U.S. Department of Commerce, Bureau of Economic Analysis input/output tables for 1947 through 1977. (The percentage figure for food as an input showed a steady decline over that period, and is almost certainly still lower now. The decline reflects both technological change in the food manufacturing process and relative decline of commodity prices.)

40. *U.S. Industrial Outlook 1987*, p. 39-3.

41. Peter W. Huber, *The Geodesic Network: 1987 Report on Competition in the Telephone Industry* (Washington, D.C.: U.S. Department of Justice, 1987), p. 2.3.

42. Speech by Alfred Sikes at USITA, World Bank Seminar, Washington, D.C., December 16, 1986.

43. Arthur Andersen and Company, *New Directions in Telecommunications*, 1984, p. 3.

44. Robert Blau, *Impact of the AT&T Divestiture Decree on U.S. Trade and Employment in Communications Equipment Markets*, Bell South Corporation, September 1986.

45. Tyson, et al., op. cit., p. 30.

46. U.S. Department of Commerce, International Trade Administration, *A Competitive Assessment of the U.S. Fibre Optics Industry*, September 1984, p. 47.

47. U.S. Department of Commerce, Office of Japan.

48. "Unstoppable Japan," *Japan: The Land Where Money Grows*, a supplement to *Euromoney*, April 1987, p. 6.

49. "Global Financial Rankings," *Wall Street Journal*, Worldscope section, September 18, 1987, p. 31D.

50. Dennis Walters, "Stunned U.S. Banks Fear Deeper Market Inroads by Foreign Firms," *American Banker*, February 26, 1987, p. 29; L. Michael Cacace, "Japan's U.S. Presence Grows," *American Banker*, Feburary 26, 1987, pp. 1, 47.

51. M. R. Kleinfield, "Hanging on in the Muni Market," *New York Times*, November 29, 1987, sec. 3, p. 1.

52. "Japanese Banks in California," *Western Banker*, April 1987, p. 13.

CHAPTER 7

1. For more on the American dream in the 1980s, see Frank Levy, *Dollars and Dreams: The Changing American Income Distribution* (New York: Russell Sage Foundation, 1987); and Barry Bluestone and Bennett Harrison, *The Great American Job Machine: The Proliferation of Low-Wage Employment in the U.S. Economy,* Joint Economic Committee, December 1986.

2. For more on consumption and investment patterns, see Alfred Malabre, *Beyond Our Means* (New York: Random House, 1987).

3. Robert S. McElvaine, *The Great Depression* (New York: Times Books, 1984), p. 17.

4. Thomas A. Kochan, *The Transformation of American Industrial Relations* (New York: Basic Books, 1986).

5. "DRI/McGraw-Hill Historical Capital Spending Data," June 1987, p. A-14; U.S. Department of Labor, Bureau of Labor Statistics, *Monthly Labor Statistics.*

6. Kochan, op. cit.

7. "A Work Revolution in U.S. Industry: More Flexible Rules Are Boosting Productivity," *Business Week,* May 16, 1983, pp. 100–10.

8. Forthcoming Commission case study.

9. For more on the Xerox experience, see Peter Lazes and Tony Costanza, "Xerox Cuts Costs Without Layoffs Through Union-Management Collaboration," U.S. Department of Labor, Bureau of Labor Management Relations and Cooperative Programs, July 1984, reprinted from *National Productivity Review.*

10. Industrial Cooperation Council, *Annual Report,* 1987.

11. Russell Mitchell, "How Ford Hit the Bull's Eye with Taurus: A Team Approach Borrowed from Japan Has Produced the Hottest U.S. Car in Years," *Business Week,* June 30, 1986, pp. 69–70.

12. For the Shenandoah story see "Claims Unit Share Power, Workload," *Hartford Courant,* May 11, 1987.

13. Ibid.

14. John Hoerr, "We're Not Going to Sit Around and Allow Management to Louse Things Up," *Business Week,* May 18, 1987, p. 107.

15. National Center for Employee Ownership.

16. Rick Surpin, *Cooperative Home Care Associates: A Status Report,* Community Service Society of New York, January 1987.

17. "Employees Own the Company Through Canterbury Press ESOP," *Hot Off the Canterbury Press*, October 6, 1987, p. 1.

18. Jan Stackhouse, "Employee Ownership Is Good for Business," *North Brooklyn Business Review*, Vol. I, November 1987.

19. Ibid.

20. Gary B. Hansen and Frank J. Adams, "Saving Jobs and Putting Democracy to Work: Labor-Management Cooperation at Seymour Specialty Wire," U.S. Department of Labor, Bureau of Labor-Management Relationship and Cooperation Programs, No. 11, September 1987.

21. Carole and Paul Bass, "A Naugatuck Valley Fairy Tale," *Connecticut Magazine*, 1985.

22. Jan Stackhouse, "Seymour Specialty Wire: An Experiment in Industrial Democracy," master's thesis, New York University, 1987.

23. Daniel Yankelovich and John Immerwahr, *Putting the Work Ethic to Work* (New York: Public Agenda Foundation, 1983).

CHAPTER 8

1. U.S. Department of Commerce cited in Claudia Deutsch, "U.S. Industry's Unfinished Struggle," *New York Times*, February 21, 1988, sec. 3, p. 7.

2. Based on data from the U.S. Commerce Department.

3. Based on data in United Nations Statistical Office, *International Trade Statistics Yearbook*, 1985.

4. Based on data in Council of Economic Advisers, *Economic Report of the President* (Washington, D.C.: U.S. Government Printing Office, 1987), p. 246.

5. World Bank, *World Development Report 1987* (New York: Oxford University Press, 1987), pp. 202–03. (In actuality, the U.S. is second worldwide in per capita GNP, to the United Arab Emirates.)

6. Based on data in *Economic Report of the President*, 1987, p. 246.

7. Ibid.

8. Based on data in *Economic Report of the President*, 1987, p. 293.

9. Ibid., p. 285; see also Hudson Institute, *Workforce 2000*, 1987, p. 56.

10. Ibid., p. 278.

11. *Workforce 2000*, p. 61.

12. Frank S. Levy and Richard C. Michael, *The Economic Future of the Baby Boom*, Urban Institute, December 5, 1985, p. 13.

13. Based on data from the U.S. Bureau of the Census, cited in Michael DeCourcy Hinds, "Owning a Home Recedes as an American Dream," *New York Times*, September 13, 1987, sec. 12, p. 15.

14. Based on data from the Health Insurance Association of America, *Source Book of Health Insurance Data*, 1986 update, p. 4, cited in *The New York State Health Care Delivery and Financing System—Selected Data*, prepared for the Subcommittee on Health Insurance of the New York State Council on Health Care Financing.

15. Based on data from the Bureau of Labor Statistics, cited in "Sweet Sixteen and Ready to Work," *Economist*, January 30, 1988, p. 21.

16. U.S. Bureau of the Census, *Statistical Abstract of the United States: 1987* (Washington, D.C.: 1986), p. 145.

GLOSSARY OF TERMS

balance of payments (surplus and deficit) An account of the difference between a nation's total disbursements abroad and the total receipts a nation gets from foreign sources. Balance of payments includes all the things in the current account (see **current account**) and also payments made to military personnel abroad, foreign aid, loans to foreigners, investment in foreign countries, and income to American companies held in foreign accounts.

"beggar-thy-neighbor" policies Any policy designed to enrich one nation at the expense of its trading partners, based on the idea that trade surpluses are highly desirable. Examples of such policies are protective tariffs which make importers pay an extra sum to sell their goods in the domestic market, and maintaining artificially low exchange rates so that exports are inexpensive abroad and imports are expensive at home.

bilateral negotiations Negotiations conducted between two nations.

Bretton Woods agreement The 1944 accords among the Western powers that established the postwar international economic order of liberalized trade and fixed exchange rates. Major components of the Bretton Woods agreement include the International Monetary Fund and the World Bank.

budget deficit The amount by which a government's total revenue falls short of its total expenditures.

capital flight　The transfer by individuals or corporations of investment funds from one nation to another to escape domestic taxation, inflation, political instability, devaluation, or some other unfavorable political or economic circumstance. Many Latin American countries suffer from capital flight spurred by weak economies and unstable governments.

capital flow　The movement of investment and loanable funds between nations. This includes private and government loans and investment in stocks of companies abroad.

commodity prices　The prices of raw materials such as agricultural products, metals, and fuels that can be obtained on the world market. These goods are generally, but not exclusively, produced by Third World nations and purchased by industrialized countries. Many Third World nations depend on commodity exports to finance development and meet their debt obligations.

current account (surplus or deficit)　An account of the difference between the money value of the total export and import of goods and services of one nation. The current account balance is determined not only by the exchange of merchandise between a nation and its trading partners but by trade in such services as insurance and banking; expenditures by travelers; profits earned abroad; interest; and one-way transactions such as foreign aid or individual gifts.

debt service　Payments of the interest on a debt plus any repayments of the debt itself which are due.

direct investment　Funds used to finance factories, large-scale machinery, and other aspects of production.

dollar devaluation　The decrease in the value of the dollar relative to the currencies of other nations. For example, the U.S. has allowed the value of the dollar to fall versus the yen since 1985. Since the Japanese can receive more dollars for their yen, American exports become less expensive. The government uses dollar devaluation policies to promote exports and discourage imports.

dumping　The practice of selling products below cost to increase market share. Under international trade agreements, dumping is considered an unfair advantage and injured industries may seek import restrictions against producers that dump. In recent years the U.S. has restricted imports of Japanese computer chips after it found that Japanese producers were selling their chips on the U.S. market below their cost of production.

economic integration The creation of one market out of what once had been separate markets. The European Economic Community is an example of the integration of individual markets into a larger system. In recent years, financial services have become integrated into a global system in which many nations' banking and investment businesses interact.

entitlements Government transfers of particular services or benefits to individuals according to law. In the U.S., entitlements can be actual payments such as social security checks and unemployment insurance payments. Other entitlements include in-kind entitlements such as food stamps.

Eurodollar market A Eurodollar is a U.S. dollar held outside of the United States, usually as a deposit in a commercial bank. The Eurodollar market is the term for transactions carried out in Eurodollars. The Eurodollar market is centered in London.

exchange rate The number of units of one currency that can buy a unit of another currency. For example, a yen/dollar exchange rate of 123 means that 123 yen will buy one dollar.

export-driven development A national strategy successfully used by Japan—and now by Third World nations—that finances industrialization by orienting production toward foreign markets. South Korea is a leading practitioner of export-oriented development. It has invested much of its capital in steelmaking, automaking, and other production designed for export to First World nations.

Federal Reserve The central monetary authority of the United States, established by the Federal Reserve Act of 1913. The Fed determines monetary policy through the regulation of the money supply and interest rates.

First World nations Australia, Austria, Belgium, Canada, Denmark, Finland, France, West Germany, Iceland, Ireland, Italy, Japan, Luxembourg, Netherlands, New Zealand, Norway, Spain, Sweden, Switzerland, the United Kingdom, and the United States.

fiscal policy The overall program for directing spending and taxation to achieve economic goals. For example, during a business decline and high unemployment, the government may attempt to avoid recession by increasing spending and/or cutting taxes. The former increases government purchases from the private sector, increasing income; the latter leaves more spendable income in the hands of consumers and/or businesses, which helps stimulate demand. Conversely, in times of overexpansion, the government may try to counter inflation by decreasing spending and/or raising taxes.

fixed exchange rates Limitation by agreement of fluctuation of the value of national currencies. Exchange rates are determined by the value of dominant currencies or, as before 1971, the value of gold.

floating exchange rates Fluctuation of the relative value of national currencies based on international supply and demand. Under this system, the value of each currency is not set, but largely determined by supply and demand on the international market and by governments. For example, if there is more demand for dollars, the price of the dollar will rise.

free trade Trade between nations unrestricted by tariffs, quotas, or other barriers. The recently negotiated agreement between Canada and the U.S. is an example of an attempt at free trade.

General Agreement on Trade and Tariffs (GATT) An international agreement devoted to reducing and eventually eliminating national barriers to trade in goods. Adopted by twenty-two nations in 1947, GATT now sponsors negotiations among ninety-three nations (as of 1983) to reduce tariffs and quotas and covers 80 percent of world trade in merchandise. GATT does not cover trade in services, agriculture, and energy.

Gephardt Amendment This controversial amendment to the 1987 trade bill requires (in its latest incarnation) the U.S. to negotiate with governments that maintain excessive and unwarranted trade surpluses with the U.S. If an agreement to eliminate unfair trading practices is not reached after six months, the U.S. must impose retaliatory duties, quotas, etc. on the offending government. If after a year the foreign government has not reduced its trade surplus by 10 percent, the U.S. must levy additional duties until the surplus is eliminated.

globalization and interdependence The increasing interaction of nations' economies. Goods and services are now bought and sold on a worldwide basis. As markets become globalized, the economic policies of individual nations affect other countries. For instance, a recession in the U.S. could trigger a worldwide recession, as so many nations now depend on the American consumers to buy their products.

gold standard Monetary system in which exchange rates of national currencies are tied to the value of gold. Gold was the basis of the postwar international economic system until 1971, when the U.S. abandoned the gold standard for a floating exchange rate system.

gross domestic product (GDP) GDP measures the value of goods and services produced domestically for final consumption. This includes goods consumed by households and the government, as well as exports, but does not include materials used up in production.

gross national product (GNP) GNP equals the GDP plus the repatriated income from a nation's business, property, and investment holdings in foreign countries, minus the repatriated income received by foreign companies operating within U.S. borders.

intellectual property rights A corporation's or individual's claim on technology, trademarks, and other patented ideas. For instance, a new semiconductor-making process represents an intellectual property right. In recent years, controversy has arisen over the alleged theft of the U.S.'s intellectual property rights by foreign manufacturers—particularly East Asian producers—that duplicate everything from designer jeans to software without paying licensing fees or other compensation to the original trademark or patent holder.

International Monetary Fund (IMF) Established at Bretton Woods, the IMF lends funds to member nations to cover balance of payments deficits. Affiliated with the United Nations, the IMF promotes exchange rate stability and encourages nations to cooperate on monetary policy.

J curve Economic model used by some economists to account for the time lapse between dollar devaluation and a decline in the trade deficit.

junk bonds Below-investment-grade, high-risk, high-yield bonds developed in the early 1980s and generally used to finance management buy-outs and corporate takeovers.

leakage The loss of consumer dollars (which might otherwise stimulate domestic economic expansion) through the purchase of foreign-produced goods.

liquidity A measure of the ability of an individual or company to meet obligations without selling fixed assets. Cash, bonds, and stocks are considered liquid assets, as they can readily be converted to other uses. Real estate, for example, is a much less liquid asset. One can easily and quickly convert a stock portfolio into cash for use in new investment. It is much more difficult to convert an apartment building into cash.

"locomotive" theory of global growth A description of the U.S. economy's postwar role as the engine that drove the global recovery. U.S.

market demand fueled domestic economic expansion and allowed Europe and Japan to reconstruct their devastated industries.

macroeconomic policies   Policies directed at influencing aggregate national economic problems such as inflation and unemployment. In the U.S. most macroeconomic policies have been geared toward "fine-tuning" the nation's economy through controlling interest rates, the money supply, and government spending. For instance, the government's decision to let the dollar decline in value is a macroeconomic policy designed to improve the nation's balance of trade.

managed trade   A policy of seeking equitable trade relations between countries by conducting negotiations that determine the levels of imports and exports of particular products. The Multi-Fiber Agreement is an example of managed trade. Signatories agreed to rules governing the import and export of apparel according to the needs of various nations.

market economy   In a market economy, private individuals and companies determine demand, production, supply, and distribution. Government's role is limited to trade policy and macroeconomic adjustment.

Marshall Plan   Postwar program established in 1947 by the U.S. to fund European reconstruction. Proposed by Secretary of State George C. Marshall, the plan gave European nations $5 billion in loans and gifts (the beneficiary nations were required to match the funds) for reconstruction of industry and infrastructure.

monetary policy   A nation's overall program for regulating money and credit to achieve desired goals. In most countries, the central bank implements monetary policy. In the U.S., the formulation and implementation of monetary policy is the responsibility of the Board of Governors of the Federal Reserve System, working through the twelve Federal Reserve Banks. The Fed expands the money supply ("easy money" policies)—and stimulates the economy to avoid recession—by buying government securities, and restricts the money supply ("tight money" policies)—to avoid inflation—by selling government securities.

multilateral negotiations   Negotiations conducted by more than two nations. The GATT talks are multilateral negotiations.

neomercantilism   A term used to describe the policies and practices of nations that seek to increase their wealth by accumulating large export surpluses by promoting exports and restricting imports.

newly industrializing countries (NICs) The "Four Tigers" (Singapore, South Korea, Hong Kong, Taiwan), Malaysia, Brazil, Mexico, and other Third World nations that have rapidly developed an industrial economy over the past twenty-five years and are now producing advanced manufactured goods.

oil shocks The oil shortages and subsequent huge increases in oil prices in 1973 and 1979 that contributed to high inflation rates.

outsourcing A manufacturing strategy to reduce costs by subcontracting out either domestically or abroad for materials or finished products. This strategy is often employed by domestic manufacturers who purchase product components from foreign, low-cost producers.

planned economy An economy in which a central authority makes all economic decisions regarding planning, production, distribution, trade, and employment. Today, all nations use some form of planning, but the goals and methods vary enormously. In a totally planned economy, such as the Soviet Union's, the market mechanism is eliminated on the assumption that maximum social welfare can be achieved only through central decision making. The United States uses a minimal amount of planning. Japan has used planning effectively to foster industrial growth, improve its technology, and develop goods for export.

policies of stimulation and reflation Government actions such as deficit spending and tax cuts which are designed to boost employment and consumption during periods of sluggish growth or recession.

productivity Measure of how much of a commodity can be produced with a given amount of input. The most commonly used definition of productivity is output per labor hour. The higher the level of productivity, the more efficient the production process is said to be.

protectionism The use of trade barriers to protect domestic manufacturers from foreign competition. Some view protectionism as a policy of protecting uncompetitive and inefficient industries at the expense of both the consumer and foreign producers. Others view certain forms of protectionism as necessary to protect domestic producers from unfair competition, for instance from foreign manufacturers who pay exploitive wages or who sell their products below cost in other countries' markets.

real wages A measure of what the money received as wages will buy. If prices rise (inflation), a given wage will buy less; as prices fall, a given wage will buy more, thus the real wage is higher.

223

recession During a recession the economy stagnates as demand falls, and investment and purchasing power decline. As demand falls, unemployment rises, which in turn creates even less demand. A recession is sometimes used as a way to halt inflation.

rescheduling and writing off debt A bank that reschedules debt delays the due date for the principal. When a bank writes off debt, it cancels the obligation, taking the loss against its reserves. Until recently, most banks dealt with the Third World debt crisis by rescheduling loans. Realizing that most nations are unable to pay back their enormous debt, many banks have increased their loan loss reserves in anticipation of default or of writing off the debt.

reserve currency A national currency, such as the dollar or the pound sterling, or an international currrency, such as the IMF's Special Drawing Rights, which is held in reserve to meet international obligations. Throughout the postwar era the U.S. dollar has been the leading reserve currency, and every major trading nation (except Switzerland) maintains a substantial portion of its reserves in dollars.

service economy Often called the "post-industrial economy," the service economy is based on sale of nontangibles such as banking and insurance services rather than the production of material goods such as cars and machinery.

Special Drawing Rights (SDRs) The IMF created SDRs as an international reserve currency based on the value of a "basket" of national currencies. The agency allocates SDRs to member nations, which may sell them to other members to fund balance of payments deficits.

supply-side economics Also known as "Reaganomics," supply-side economics holds that government should promote economic prosperity by focusing on the suppliers of goods and services—businesses—rather than by influencing demand. Supply-side economists advocate financial incentives such as tax cuts and lower interest rates to encourage businesses to increase production.

targeting A national strategy of identifying a specific market to penetrate and dominate. The Japanese successfully targeted the U.S. electronics market and have achieved a significant share of the American auto market. The South Koreans have built a steel plant specifically designed to produce steel for the U.S. market.

trade balance (surplus and deficit) The difference between the money value of a nation's merchandise imports and the money value of its merchandise exports. When a nation exports more than it imports, it maintains a trade surplus; when imports exceed exports, a nation runs a trade deficit.

trade barriers (tariffs, quotas, etc.) Mechanisms that restrict imports. Tariffs are a surcharge levied on goods entering a nation, while quotas limit the amount of goods that may be imported. Trade barriers can be applied to a particular country (or countries) or particular kinds of products.

unfair trade practices Market strategies that seek an advantage over foreign producers by selling below cost, paying exploitive wages to workers, exceeding market quotas, or engaging in other practices that injure competitors.

U.S. International Trade Commission (USITC) The agency responsible for determining violations of international trade agreements with the U.S. The USITC investigates complaints by U.S. industries that claim they have been injured by foreign producers that have dumped their products on the U.S. market at uncompetitive prices, exceeded their quotas, or engaged in other unfair trade practices. If the USITC finds a violation of trade agreements, it forwards its finding to the President, who may instruct the USITC to increase the guilty party's tariffs or reduce its quotas.

U.S. Trade Representative (USTR) The individual, appointed by the President, who is responsible for negotiating the nation's international trade agreements. Congress created the office of the U.S. Trade Representative in 1962.

value-added tax (VAT) A levy on business income based on the value added to a product by the operations of a business. The value added is defined as the difference between the cost of the purchased materials and the value of the final product. In contemporary debate, the VAT is often proposed as a means to stimulate private savings.

World Bank Established by the Bretton Woods agreement, the World Bank channels multilateral aid to developing countries by lending funds for economic development at below-market rates.

zero-based budget A cost-controlling budgetary process in which the base budget is assumed to be zero and all expenditures must be justified each year. In a regular budget, expenditures for ongoing projects from previous years are included in the base budget.

SUMMARY OF THE COMMISSION'S FINDINGS AND RECOMMENDATIONS

The Commission on Trade and Competitiveness was established to review the causes and consequences of the dramatic, unprecedented decline in America's balance of trade during the 1980s. In five short years, imports to the United States had risen so rapidly—especially in comparison to American exports—that competitiveness and the decline of America's economic strength had become key issues in the national debate over economic policy. New York State, historically one of the states most involved in manufacturing, had been hard hit by rising imports and declining exports, and Governor Cuomo wanted advice on what, if anything, could be done.

During the year of the Commission's study, the trade situation remained a critical problem. The trade deficit of $155 billion in 1986 increased in 1987 to $171 billion. The failure of America's trade imbalances to improve reinforced a growing weakness in the American economy—a weakness which undermines our standard of living and America's ability to fulfill its global responsibilities.

The first three months of 1988 showed a very modest improvement in the trade balance, but the monthly trade deficits of early 1988 remained as high as our annual deficit prior to 1982.

The trade crisis is one of seven warning signs of serious economic trouble identified by the Commission. The second is closely related: our growing national indebtedness. America is the world's largest debtor. America produces less than it consumes, and it borrows the difference. Not surprisingly, our country has become the world's largest debtor. Paying off these debts will reduce our standard of living; being a debtor means the U.S. will have less control of its future.

The economy is also marked by high levels of risk and volatility. Business and bank failures have soared. Interest rates and stock and bond prices have been on a roller coaster for much of the 1980s.

The fourth warning sign is our relatively slow growth. In the 1960s the GNP grew an average of 3.8 percent; in the 1970s, the growth rate was 2.8 percent, and in the 1980s it fell further to just 2.2 percent.

America has also lost its clear lead in technology and innovation. Our competitors spend more for civilian research and development, have higher levels of growth in productivity, and educate their workers better.

The sixth warning sign is the pervasiveness of imports across all sectors. Domestic goods of all types, not only clothing and automobiles but capital goods and industrial supplies, too, are now being threatened by imports. Hundreds of manufactured products are no longer even made in America.

Finally, this decade has seen the end of a rising standard of living for many Americans. Families need two incomes just to stay even, and many workers can find only part-time jobs.

The Commission thinks that these seven warning signs, taken together, lead to a single conclusion: the nation has failed to adjust to changes in the world economy and is beginning to pay the price of failure.

The United States, once the economic wonder of the world, now faces a troubled future. This startling and disquieting change in the national outlook led the Commission to take another look at the central institutions and policies of what is often called "the postwar era," the decades of American success that followed World War Two. The era was marked by a bipartisan consensus over two basic policies— one foreign and one domestic. To understand the nature of the choices that face the American people today, they must understand what these policies were and why they no longer work as well as they once did.

The American Formula

We have called the domestic consensus that shaped American economic policy for the last half century the American Formula. Based on a simple but revolutionary insight first understood by Henry Ford, that mass production depends upon mass consumption, the American Formula helped unleash the high production levels of the assembly line and other new technologies.

Before the American Formula, people believed that if labor increased its earnings, profits would fall, and vice versa. The American Formula was an equation for wages, profits, and productivity to rise together.

The American Formula involved an important role for "positive government." Government action strengthened the private sector by encouraging stable conditions and rising demand. Social security, unemployment compensation and similar programs not only helped the elderly and others with real needs; by pumping purchasing power into the economy, they helped overcome recessions. Government regulation, by channeling competition, also nurtured economic stability. Banking regulations were intended to prevent a recurrence of the devastating bank panics that wiped out the life savings of millions of Americans before the creation of the FDIC and the FSLIC. Minimum-wage laws, price-fixing and antitrust measures, health and safety requirements, and environmental regulations were introduced to prevent companies from competing in ways that weakened the economy as a whole.

For more than three decades the American Formula gave the U.S. the world's most dynamic economy and made us the richest society in the history of the world. Other countries envied us and attempted, with varying success, to adapt the American Formula to their own conditions and create the same middle-class society that America had shown was possible.

International Responsibility

In foreign policy, Americans, as a result of the ravages of World War Two, broadly agreed that the United States must assume leadership in rebuilding the world economy. Our national leaders were convinced that the Second World War was in part the result of the breakdown of the global economic system early in the 1930s, and, in an era of nuclear weapons, they were determined to give all nations a chance to participate fully in international trade.

A prosperous Europe and Japan were essential not only to our strategic needs, but the American economy could not prosper without healthy, growing markets for our goods overseas. The most famous product of this foreign-policy consensus was the Marshall Plan to rebuild the war-torn economies of Europe, but the Marshall Plan was only one of the ways in which responsible American leadership encouraged global growth. America encouraged the development of a new and open trading system, and worked with other countries to reduce barriers to trade.

Led by the U.S., the West constructed a new international economic system. Meeting at Bretton Woods, the Allies established the International Monetary Fund (IMF) and the World Bank to help fund reconstruction and promote world economic growth. A new trading system was established by the General Agreement on Trade and Tariffs (GATT).

The Bretton Woods systems worked brilliantly in the 1950s and 1960s. Driven by American prosperity, Europe's and Japan's economies boomed as governments and the private sector worked together to orchestrate national recoveries fueled by an infusion of American dollars.

Our economy was so strong, and the economies of the war-torn countries so weak, that the U.S. willingly accepted asymmetrical, unbalanced trading relationships in which other countries protected their domestic markets from American products while their goods competed freely with ours. Just as the NATO countries and Japan relied on American willingness to pay most of the costs of the common defense, so did our partners rely on America's willingness to bear most of the costs of the world's economy and open trading system.

As long as this strategy was clearly working—and it did work until roughly the early 1970s—virtually no one questioned our government policy of encouraging the dissemination of technology and American investment in new productive facilities overseas, and allowing both developing and advanced countries unparalleled opportunities to invest and trade in our domestic economy.

The End of the Postwar Era

The Postwar Era has ended, and Americans are beginning to realize the implications of this fact. Numerous books and articles have been written about the end of the "American Century" and the decline of the "American Empire." Serious analysis of our difficulties is welcome, but pessimism and defeatism are misplaced. America has not been defeated—it created the world it wanted. The plans of Roosevelt, Truman, and Eisenhower to rebuild our former allies and enemies and free the Third World from the shackles of colonialism have been largely fulfilled. It is our success, not our defeat, which has created today's challenges.

The economic troubles of recent years must not persuade us to abandon our commitments to our high standard of living and to positive government. Nor should Americans heed those who say that the costs of responsible internationalism are so great that the U.S. must withdraw from its role in promoting world security or its commitment to an open world economy. The Commission disagrees with those who maintain that Americans must lower their sights at home and retreat from the world into a new isolationism—setting aside our alliances and sheltering our industries with quotas and tariffs. These actions would lead to global recession and beggar-thy-neighbor trade wars, destabilizing an already imbalanced international situation.

Yet the nation cannot go back to the old days or pretend in the face of overwhelming evidence, as some do, that there is no need for major changes in our approach to either our foreign or our domestic economic policies.

The challenge for Americans today is to reform the international economic order and the American Formula to meet the changing conditions of the 1980s and 1990s. The Commission believes that new initiatives to rebalance the international order can establish a climate for growth and enhance America's economic position, while an emphasis on the economic fundamentals at home can make us a more efficient and productive society. A "New Realism" is needed about the global economy and a "New American Formula" is needed to reform our domestic economy. The reforms must be directed toward increasing production in order that America can be a competitive producer in the world economy, not just its largest consumer.

Our program for international and domestic reform is predicated on four ideas. The first is that domestic growth and prosperity depend on international growth and prosperity. The nations of the world are interconnected as never before. Our problems and our successes are each other's.

Secondly, the growth and prosperity of all nations in this interconnected world will require a balance of consumption and production between nations. Economic imbalances between the U.S. and other First World countries and between the First and Third Worlds will slow and ultimately destabilize the global economy. Trade and economic policy must be reoriented toward achieving more balanced results, not just uniform rules.

Third, the world economy will remain competitive because nations will continue to seek maximum results for their own people. America will need a national strategy, not just macroeconomic adjustments, to meet this challenge. This strategy must restore our ability to produce for our own market as well as the export market.

Fourth, cooperation among major institutions in our society and increasing the quantity and quality of employee participation are perhaps the two most useful ways to improve our national competitiveness.

Toward a New International Order

The world economy is now at an impasse because of destabilizing and conflicting economic forces, and menacing imbalances in production, consumption, trade, and finance. A plan for long-term structural reduction of the U.S. trade and budget deficits is essential to break this impasse. This would be the first step on the road back to stability.

The U.S. is no longer the only strong economy in the world, and Europe and Japan must shoulder more of the burden of the world economy that America has borne so long. The U.S. can no longer be the world's "consumer of last resort," providing markets for goods produced all over the world.

As the U.S. reduces its budget and trade deficits, Germany, Japan, and other trade-surplus countries must shift over to more stimulative policies. If the U.S. cuts back on its demand for imports while other countries do not step up their purchases, the world will quickly fall into a recession.

The economic success of Europe and Japan has created new economic conditions; so has the explosive growth of industry in parts of the Third World. While the development of these countries is welcome, the strategy of "export-led growth" pioneered by Japan and more recently adopted in countries like Korea, is causing unsustainable economic imbalances. These countries, having based their development on export promotion and import restriction, have neglected to promote their domestic markets to absorb the goods they themselves produce. Europe and Japan must import more, not just from the U.S. but also from the developing world. As it stands today, too many countries depend upon the U.S. as the major market for their exports. The American government should encourage the growth of purchasing power and domestic markets in the Third World, and insure that American-made goods have a fair access to those markets.

To this end, growth in living standards in developing countries should be emphasized in formulating trade policy. In conducting its domestic and foreign economic policy and in negotiating bilateral trade agreements, the U.S. should support policies which lead to greater purchasing power for Third World consumers.

America must also insist on strict reciprocity in our relationships with the advanced countries. Other countries have limited the access of American investors and producers to their domestic markets while freely investing and freely selling here. They have heavily subsidized major industries and sold the products of those industries in direct competition with American companies which received no government support. The American government must now move systematically and seriously to level the playing field on which our goods compete. We must use access to our domestic market as a bargaining chip to ensure that the world economy returns to more balanced trade.

Negotiation is always a process of give-and-take, and access to America's market—the largest and most lucrative market for business and consumer products in the world—is the most important thing to give or withhold. Once other countries realize our seriousness about reciprocity, policies can be set up that all countries recognize as appropriate and fair.

At the same time, U.S. trade policy should address the problem of overcapacity through expanded trade and agreements that permit mutual growth. World demand has not caught up with productive capacity, and many industries are characterized by overcapacity and expensive subsidies. Temporary market sharing, shared production, and "countertrade" agreements are needed to orchestrate stability and prevent destructive competition between countries. Both market sharing and countertrade agreements are already in some use, and could be of help in future negotiations, particularly with countries that practice industrial policy and targeting. However, agreements of this type must be negotiated on a case-by-case basis as temporary measures based on individual circumstances.

American foreign policy and our economic policy should be more closely integrated, and our economic interests should not be sacrificed for the sake of short-term political foreign policy goals. All too often, foreign policy objectives have been pursued without serious regard for their economic consequences.

Monetary policy should be coordinated for growth. In the U.S., the Federal Reserve must help offset any reduced economic stimulus caused by changes in government fiscal policy. Moreover, monetary stimulus should come in advance of fiscal restraint, because of the "lag factor" between the stimulus of an interest-rate reduction or an increase in money supply and the negative impact of a tax increase or a decline in spending. Interest rates, especially the discount rate, should be within two to three percent of inflation's rate. And since the increased growth in money supply and lower rates carries the risk of higher long-term interest rates and inflation if maintained for too long, they must be carefully based on a clear commitment to growth *and* control of inflation.

Maintaining the money supply and interest rates at a level that encourages rather than retards growth will require a similar monetary policy by America's trading partners. Once a plan for U.S. deficit reduction is in place, Japan and Germany will be able to hold their interest rates in line without fear of domestic inflation and weakened currencies.

The other nations of this hemisphere are the most important countries in the world for our long-term economic prosperity. The collapse of Latin America's purchasing power in the last seven years has been a major disaster for the U.S., and unless we help these countries recover, the consequences of the continental depression in Latin America will grow even worse for us.

Latin America, one of the largest markets for American goods, slashed its imports in the 1980s to service its crushing international debt. At the same time, these countries have concentrated all their energies on exporting more goods to the U.S. to earn the dollars that can repay the debts. This situation has contributed greatly to the deterioration of the U.S. trade balance.

Resolution of the Third World debt crisis can play a central role in a strategy for balanced trade based on global growth. Government must play a role in the debt crisis; it should intervene more actively to develop a workable debt relief scheme for stretching out repayment of the debt and to assure the continuation of lending for positive economic development.

Such a plan would remove Third World debt as an obstacle to world growth, and especially to American exports, without crippling the ability of American banks to make new loans to domestic consumers and industry. The plan could include the establishment of both an effective international fund to purchase debt at a discount from lenders and new accounting rules that facilitate the write-down of debt without harming the competitive standing of banks from any particular nation. The fund would establish reasonable rescheduling formulas over longer periods at reduced interest rates on the repayment of debt. The plan would also address the problem of capital flight by making it harder for capital to leave these countries except through proper channels.

But general Third World debt relief is only part of the story. Beyond it lies the question of helping our Latin American neighbors resume the rapid rates of growth they enjoyed before the debt crisis hit. The Commission has called for a special Latin American initiative to be formulated by leaders of the U.S. and our neighbors for joint action to foster growth and new trading relations in the hemisphere. Even in a time of budget austerity, the U.S. must be prepared to make seed money available for growth in Latin and Central America.

The international financial and trade regimes also need reform to adjust to present conditions. The Commission report calls for a new system of international regulations for banks and security dealers, and for reducing the disruptive swings in exchange rates. It also calls for reform in the GATT to reduce trade imbalances and encourage growth in world trade. It calls, as well, for the expanded use of bilateral trade negotiations to supplement the often cumbersome GATT process to reach agreements of mutual benefit with our leading trade partners. Finally, it proposes using existing international financial institutions (like the IMF and the World Bank) more effectively to promote world growth and currency stability.

Sustained global growth depends on an international financial system that is flexible and stable enough to accommodate the needs of a dynamic world economy. The violent fluctuations in exchange rates of recent years tend to destabilize trade and to encourage unhealthy currency speculation. The globalization of finance has created new risks at the same time that it creates new possibilities for growth.

A commitment to stabilize the dollar will help create a stable economic environment. The role of the dollar as a reserve currency has sometimes imposed unpleasant burdens on the U.S., but overall we benefit from having our money accepted throughout the world. To maintain the usefulness of the dollar as a reserve currency, we must keep its value stable or at least predictable.

A stable dollar is important to the American economy in many ways. The falling dollar makes it more expensive for the U.S. to maintain a military presence overseas, and limits the effectiveness of our foreign aid program. It means, too, that we must sell more goods and services to foreigners to pay for our imports, and it puts American investors at a disadvantage in our own country when companies and property come up for sale. We need a stable value for the dollar: a value not so high as to price our goods out of world markets, and not so low as to cripple us and destroy confidence. Reducing the trade and budget deficits will help stabilize the dollar.

Target exchange-rate zones will help restore confidence and dampen speculation. In Europe, the major Continental currencies have formed the EMS, the European Monetary System. This is a system in which European exchange rates are permitted to fluctuate against each other, but within a relatively narrow range. The float gives bankers and governments enough flexibility to avoid repeated Bretton Woods–style currency crises, but the range is narrow enough to discourage excessive currency speculation. When a country's currency moves to the upper or lower end of its trading range, this is a signal to make policy changes that keep the currency from moving too far up or down. Adjustments in the target zone can be made periodically as circumstances change. The U.S. should try to adopt a more formal approach to exchange rates and set up the target-zone system.

America should also encourage a system of international regulation for international financial markets. The balance of the world economy depends on the stability of the world's financial system. Individual banks now operate in scores of countries around the world, and the linkage among these banks—borrowing and lending money to each other and making payments through each other twenty-four hours a day—means that the financial stability of each individual country depends on the stability of the world banking system as a whole. We need rules of the road for the flow of capital and credit through the international banking system, and we need institutions with the ability and the resources to intervene at critical moments to prevent dangerous international banking crises. Just as domestic safeguards like the FDIC were created to protect our domestic banking system, we should develop, with other countries, a system to defend the world banking system against sudden and catastrophic events.

An International Bank Regulatory Office established within the IMF to administer common guidelines among all international banks would be a good start. Regulations might include reserve and full-disclosure requirements by which banks would be obligated to supply relevant information to the national and international authorities charged with policing the system.

Banks in each country are subject to complex and comprehensive rules for their accounting, auditing, underwriting, and disclosure practices. Each of these national systems reflects the historical evolution of the banking system in a particular country. The time has come to develop standardized procedures for international banks. These rules will protect borrowers, depositors, governments, and the banks themselves by making the international banking environment predictable and safe.

There has also been an internationalization of securities markets in stocks and bonds. Here, too, there is an increasing need for consistent practices and standards, so that investors from around the world will have an equal opportunity to understand the rules of the game.

Some have proposed the establishment of a world central bank to act as a lender of last resort on the international scene. Such a bank might well be the logical outcome of the evolution of world banking. But if a world central bank is created at all, it will happen toward the end of the process of global financial integration. We must resolve today's problems within the basic framework of today's institutions, while remaining open to new developments in the future.

The New American Formula

The American Formula needs to be reformed. Our domestic economic arrangements have not kept pace with the emergence of the global economy. The New American Formula is based on a new insight: in a global economy, our consumption will depend upon increasing our production. Therefore, America needs a producer strategy in which both the public and private sectors learn to work together in a productive partnership. Economies that have competed effectively in world markets during the 1980s have prospered in part because government, business, and labor have learned to work together to achieve national goals and create more participation in the economy.

The first task is to change the mix of spending and taxing. Their proper combination is admittedly difficult to assess, because it depends on such factors as economic growth and the confidence of foreign lenders. If we have a recession or a dramatic slowdown in growth, we will find reduction of the federal budget deficit more difficult and less desirable. Conversely, it is also true that a growing economy will help reduce the deficit.

The Commission believes that future fiscal policy must be based on a combination of more wisely targeted spending and increased revenue. We have recommended several steps to bring the deficit down, including a freeze on military spending and reducing the costs of entitlement programs to meet real needs with less waste. If more revenue is needed, we have identified some tax ideas that would be fair and would not, we believe, be as economically damaging as alternative forms of taxation. A progressive value-added tax (VAT) has the advantage that, under current GATT rules, VAT preferences are a legitimate method of promoting exports. An oil import fee (with relief for low-income households) would also help our balance of trade while helping to balance the budget.

We should adopt a flexible monetary policy with the goal of achieving a satisfactory rate of real economic growth, full employment, and controlled price inflation. Hitting artificial money supply targets should not be of primary concern. In general, the Federal Reserve Board should adjust the supply of credit to keep interest rates slightly above the rate of inflation. Low, stable interest rates should be the goal.

The federal government should learn from the states. During the 1980s, state governments have increased social services, developed innovative methods to promote economic growth in partnership with the private sector, invested in their infrastructure and increased spending on education, all without enormous tax increases and without record-breaking budget deficits.

The federal government needs a better strategic sense of how to coordinate its programs and spend its money wisely. Every dollar must count. One way to enforce spending discipline without discouraging needed investments in the national future would be to split the federal budget into three components. Social security and its related programs, paid for by trust funds, would be placed in one category. The rest of the budget would be divided into two categories similar to those used by many large corporations and other governments: annual spending programs funded by taxation, and a capital budget that would be paid for by the income from investments and public borrowing.

One area in which we do recommend substantial new federal spending is education. Our colleges and graduate schools attract students from all over the world; there is no reason why our public schools cannot achieve similar levels of excellence. In a competitive world economy we do not help ourselves by failing to equip our young people to offer their best. Education and retraining are also necessary for older workers. As our people learn new skills, our nation will become more productive.

A second area requiring more investment is our infrastructure. We cannot afford not to rebuild our bridges, highways, rail systems, ports, and other facilities that make economic activity possible.

Over the years, major flaws have developed in our approach to consumption. Policymakers have encouraged consumption but have not done enough to encourage savings. They have also encouraged private consumption beyond what can be supported by production, and often at the expense of public consumption. Roads, bridges, schools, a clean environment, better health and housing, mass transit systems, and other types of public consumption are really long-term investments that can improve our competitiveness and our quality of life. Today we need a new ideal of consumption, one that encompasses public "goods" and is not at odds with our level of production.

The federal government must also place a higher priority on economic adjustment strategies. In this era of international competition, every major industrialized nation must face at some point the need to restructure its industries. Every government but ours has implemented extensive industrial adjustment programs. Our government cannot afford to remain an impartial observer while industries restructure.

Our in-depth study of five major American industries—telecommunications, food processing, apparel, financial services, and steel—reminded us that there are no simple solutions for competitiveness problems. More must be learned about the specific situations of our major industries in order to develop strategies to improve their performance.

Government can help in this process. It can provide incentives for companies to invest in their future. It can help form and fund research and development consortia in which private companies pool their resources to develop new techniques and products. But government's role is limited; whether our country becomes more productive depends on the decisions and actions of millions of white- and blue-collar workers.

Federal bailouts of every troubled industry or company must be avoided. In some cases, there are special circumstances which create a legitimate need for government help in the form of loan guarantees or short-term protection from foreign competitors. Yet even when there are legitimate reasons for intervention, we must see that government assistance is offered only for a limited time and that the industries affected adopt workable strategies to recover their competitiveness.

Industry adjustment plans should be mandatory when trade relief is requested. To ensure the vitality of domestic industry, the submission of an adjustment plan and revitalization strategy should be mandatory for any industry which benefits from import limitation. Under the trade bill passed by the House of Representatives, industries petitioning for import relief "may submit" a statement of proposed adjustment measures to the ITC and the USTR. While this is a step in the proper direction, the optional nature of these statements increases the likelihood that the period of import relief will not be used constructively by an industry.

Requiring an industry to develop a strategy does not mean that government will be telling an industry what it must do. It does, however, place an appropriate responsibility on an industry for its continued well-being. When an industry looks to the federal government for trade protection or financial assistance in restructuring, it should meet four criteria: (1) the industry should be strategic, one whose continued health is vital to the well-being of other industries and the maintenance of employment; (2) the protection should come in time to do some substantive good; (3) government intervention should be supported by leaders in labor, industry, and our universities; and (4) the program for restructuring should be specific and include sufficient capital, management talent, and labor resources.

Industry-government task forces for long-term trade strategy should be established to analyze economic trends and market opportunities in specific sectors, monitor technological change and trade practices, and develop plans for industry adjustment and flexible response to the changing economic environment. Such task forces, made up of interagency, industry, labor, and public representatives, would be similar to the private advisory committees used effectively in the past as consensus-building mechanisms for multilateral trade negotiations, but they would have a broader mandate.

We should give special attention to forming task forces in those industries that are of the greatest economic importance to our country. The degree to which an industry improves our trade position, serves as an input to other industries, provides new technologies, or is crucial to our infrastructure, should be key issues in determining the importance of an industry.

In a rapidly changing economy, comprehensive economic-adjustment programs are essential to provide retraining for workers whose skills no longer meet the needs of industry. Adjustment programs help maintain demand by providing income support during periods of joblessness and underemployment. Economic adjustment must be viewed as an ongoing process, and states can play a major role in economic adjustment and should develop their own programs.

Government can also help revive U.S. technological preeminence. Renewed government responsibility does not necessarily depend on massive new federal expenditures in research and development. As with all things, technology is not simply the result of the amount spent, but of *how* it is spent. We should make present R&D expenditures as productive as possible by shifting resources to targeted goals and significantly readjusting the ratio between federal spending on defense R&D and commercial R&D. The U.S. should also assist in the targeting of technology for product and process development through an investment tax credit or a financing facility that would help create pools of long-term capital. In addition, the U.S. should establish a manufacturing extension service to assist medium-sized and small U.S. firms to incorporate new technology into production.

The way Americans work is changing, and none too soon. In many workplaces, the hierarchy, chain of command, and division of labor have been replaced by a more collaborative approach. Experiments in new ways of organizing work, in both manufacturing and services, have blurred the lines between managers, supervisors, workers, unions, and shareholders. Driven by a growing national awareness of the need to improve quality and productivity, this trend has the potential to transform the way most people do their jobs—and to help reestablish America's economic leadership.

The experiments of the last ten years have shown that important gains in productivity can result from a commitment to promote new relationships in the workplace. Companies across America are finding out about this new approach and the "profits of participation." The Commission believes that increasing the quantity and quality of employee participation is one of the most important actions that the nation can take to restore competitiveness.

The Commission also believes that a strategy to increase worker participation and labor-management cooperation must experiment with new compensation systems that will give workers a bigger stake in productivity. Greater attention should be given to such techniques as the flexible bonus system that tie compensation to the creation of value. Gain-sharing, a bonus program where employees benefit from group efforts rather than individual achievements, is another idea that would both promote the ultimate goal of product quality and eliminate wasteful employee competition.

Finally, the new industrial relations must be based on the idea that workers will display greater flexibility in accepting technological change in the workplace by reexamining some job classifications. In exchange, employers must demonstrate a willingness to offer employment security or in other ways link the benefits of technological progress to workers' economic concerns.

We believe that ownership makes for involvement. The spread of employee ownership through American industry is one of the bright spots of the 1980s. Blue-collar workers, like managers, perform best when they get "a piece of the action" and when they share responsibility for making decisions about production and policy. New technologies and industries require more active workers. Both labor and management need to adjust to this situation and to adopt a less confrontative and more cooperative approach.

In the private sector, we need to find ways to bring management and labor back to a focus on productivity and long-range strategy. In recent years both management and labor have tended to look too hard at short-term gains while paying little attention to their own long-term interests.

Conclusion

The word "crisis" has been cheapened by too frequent use, but no other word so well describes America's present situation. Originally, "crisis" meant turning point, and this is precisely where America stands today. Either America will implement reforms that strengthen the international trading system and make the nation more competitive at home or it risks a long, slow national decline.

If we as a nation approach our place in the world with a New Realism, if we accept the lessons of global interdependence and work for growth, if we embrace a New American Formula for producing with the high degree of efficiency and quality that was once a national trademark, and if we do so in a way that brings greater cooperation between our institutions and greater participation for our people, then we will have built a foundation for prosperity for years to come.

We on the Commission on Trade and Competitiveness hope that our efforts will contribute to the renewal of the promise of the American dream, to accomplish the goal so simply stated by President Kennedy almost thirty years ago: "To get this country moving again."

STATEMENTS OF THE COMMISSION MEMBERS

COMMENTS BY JACK SHEINKMAN

As the report makes abundantly clear, America is approaching a critical juncture in its history. The prosperity and international preeminence enjoyed by the U.S. since the end of World War Two are now very much threatened by fundamental changes underway in the world economy.

At risk is much more than our prosperity or even our leadership in the world. At risk are some of our most fundamental values and, with them, our identity as a nation. We like to think of ourselves not just as a prosperous nation, but as a free, just, and compassionate one. We like to believe that America can be a country where each of our citizens, without regard to race, sex, class, or religion, enjoys equally the opportunity to develop to the limit of his or her abilities. But without a high and rising standard of living, these values become hollow aspirations and our national identity is reduced to an ideology.

The lesson of recent years—years marred by lost jobs, falling wages, stagnating incomes, rising poverty, and heightened racial tensions—is that we cannot be the nation we want to be without a prosperous economy and we can no longer ensure our own prosperity without nurturing the prosperity of the rest of the world. This is no longer simply a requirement of justice internationally, it is now an immediate condition of our own national self-interest.

The report traces the sources of the new economic challenge we face not just to the globalization of production and finance, but to the related worldwide slowdown of economic growth. The problem of declining American competitiveness emerged, and must be dealt with in the context of a stagnant world economy. And mercantilist strategies adopted by many countries have, by reducing wages, contributed to the stagnation of demand worldwide. The report correctly urges us to seek competitiveness strategies that reverse this destructive process and contribute to restarting global growth. Only in a growing world economy can we avoid the beggar-thy-neighbor policies that leave the world a poorer and less secure place than it needs to be.

The principles which the report adopts in order to formulate policies for restarting growth and restoring American competitiveness—international cooperation; an affirmative role for government; cooperation among labor, management, and government; and employee participation—are most welcome. For too long have we indulged the naive belief that markets are sufficient in and of themselves to insure our prosperity. And for too long have we suffered from the view that workers are merely the fungible appendages of the machines they operate, with nothing to contribute to productivity growth but the fast motion of their hands.

The policy options offered in the report lend definition and substance to the principles of international cooperation, affirmative government, tripartite cooperation, and worker involvement. Many are to be specially commended: international coordination of monetary and fiscal policies; balanced trade policies that contribute to, rather than undermine, growth; reform of international financial institutions; policies to raise the wages and living standards of workers in the Third World; industry-specific approaches to competitiveness; productivity growth through employee participation and labor-management cooperation; enhanced worker adjustment assistance; renewal of American education; and, perhaps most important of all, investment in our nation's people.

Less attractive from our point of view is the value-added tax proposed as an option for raising revenue to reduce the federal budget deficit and restore the balance between domestic production and consumption. The best way to balance the budget is to restore growth and increase production, not reduce the already flagging incomes of most American families. Likewise, the best way to balance consumption and production is to increase production, not reduce consumption. Structural deficits resulting from the Reagan tax cuts may ultimately require increased taxes. The time to raise them, however, is not now when the economy is still constrained by the lack of demand, but later when growth has been restored and income is rising. When, and if, a tax increase becomes necessary, it could come in the form of higher income taxes, particularly for those who benefited most from the tax reductions. A value-added tax is bound to burden those least able to bear the burden.

And though the report recognizes the importance of resolving the Third World debt crisis—both as a necessary step in reversing the decline of living standards in the debt-burdened countries and as an important component of any program to correct current trade imbalances and restart growth—the policies it recommends seem far too timid to achieve its purposes. Any policy for addressing the debt crisis must be ambitious enough to reverse the net capital outflow from the Third World. This will require, in my view, writing down a significant portion of the debt—perhaps as much as 50 percent—and organizing a multilateral effort to assume the remaining debt and begin a concerted program of debt relief.

These issues aside, the report represents, in my view, a distinctive contribution to America's competitiveness debate. It launches a new promising stage in the national competitiveness discussion and deserves a careful reading from anyone interested, not just in this discussion, but in the future of our country.

COMMENTS BY ROBERT RUBIN

I agree with most of the Commission's description of the United States' current economic situation and concern about the future. I also believe the prescriptive recommendations offer much that is useful and thought-provoking, though I personally would opt for somewhat less government involvement and a clearer adherence to free trade as an ideal. I feel that the process was refreshingly and remarkably free of political influence or ideological bias and was open, collegial, and intellectually honest.

I. Economic Description and Future

The report argues, correctly in my opinion, that the United States faces a realistic possibility of great economic pain in the future, despite relatively good employment figures and subdued inflation in recent years. Servicing our external debt will claim a portion of future American production, while continuing trade and budget imbalances will increase that claim, generate interest rate pressures, depress the dollar, and create various other problems. Moreover, solving these problems will be complicated by a paramount change in America's situation, that the United States is now just one part of an interdependent world economy, and a debtor at that.

II. Role of Government

The report contends that government can play a useful role in devising and implementing national economic strategy, along with businesss and labor, but that relatively unimpeded private enterprise and free markets should be relied upon for most economic functions. I agree, but I do have reservations about the wisdom of some elements of government involvement which the report proposes, e.g., wage and price guidelines, which can easily become floors instead of ceilings; employment security programs; and various types of industrial targeting.

Moreover, even if government direction or involvement in certain such areas were conceptually sensible, I am concerned that decisions would likely be determined by political influence rather than the merits. For example, the report proposes government support for industries deemed critical to competing in the global economy. Even if that might work, were choices based on careful economic analysis, I think a real danger remains that decisions would likely be based on the political influence of competing power groups.

III. International, Foreign Exchange and Trade

I think that Chapter 4, "Toward a New International Order," is somewhat unrealistic as to the likelihood of international cooperation, e.g., I don't think you can "compel" countries with consistent balance of payments surpluses to appreciate their currencies, and recent years' experience in the United States, Germany, and Japan suggest that fiscal and monetary policy will be driven primarily by domestic economic and political considerations even when that creates significant trade problems elsewhere. Cooperation and coordination should be sought, but policy should be based on realistic expectations.

Similarly, I think the discussion of foreign exchange is somewhat unrealistic with respect to managing exchange rates or achieving EMS-like bands. Intervention can serve certain limited purposes, but as the report says, these markets are too large to be effectively managed over any period of time through intervention, even if IMF supplemented. The EMS is probably misleading as a world model because of the relative homogeneity of those economies. Exchange rate relationships over time will reflect relative economic and financial conditions and can only be managed for prolonged periods through extremely hard to attain international policy coordination.

The trade section of the report at times seems somewhat schizophrenic. It criticizes "the protection of inefficiency" and "neo-mercantilistic policy," but then at times seems to advocate protectionism.

I believe the report should have clearly posited free trade as the theoretical ideal, with each country producing in its areas of comparative advantage, and protectionism should have been rejected. That is still the path toward greatest growth with least inflation. Then, you can aggressively use access to our markets and other policies to fight formal and informal import barriers and other unfair trade practices. Countries with low gross national product per capita almost by definition have low wages and low productivity, and their competitive advantage lies in labor-intensive areas.

IV. Domestic Policy

The report at times seems to advocate some kind of full employment policy. I believe that the combining of this goal with the sometimes competing goal of low inflation as an equal objective should be clearer, and also that a certain amount of cyclicality in business conditions should be recognized as unavoidable. The same section of the report proposes objectives of monetary policy that to me seem somewhat unattainable.

The report very usefully, in my view, sets forth a compendium of relatively noncontroversial and pragmatic proposals to further competitiveness, e.g., employee financial participation in productivity and profitability, retraining, increasing employee participation in managerial planning, encouraging labor and business cooperation, and improving the quality of education through aid geared to meeting demographically appropriate standards. The report also very importantly emphasizes America's critical long-term self-interest in improving conditions in the Third World and among our own domestic underclass.

V. Conclusion

To conclude, I believe that the likelihood of avoiding the sometimes prophesied economic decline of America could be significantly increased through combining an appropriate role for government with private enterprise, free markets, and free trade (with aggressive countering of unfair trade practices abroad). My limited reservations notwithstanding, I think this report provides highly useful and persuasive guidance toward sensible policy, with greater specificity and substance than is usual in reports of this kind, and thus should play a meaningful role in the policy dialogue of the complicated years ahead.

COMMENTS BY LEWIS PRESTON

I applaud Governor Cuomo's effort to bring together individuals with diverse interests and viewpoints in an attempt to forge a consensus on issues of importance to the state and the nation. I have been pleased to participate in the Commission's deliberations, and I hope that the report will generate useful debate.

Reflecting widely shared concerns, the report of this Commission cites the large U.S. budget and trade deficits, instability in world financial markets, relatively low levels of investment, and deterioration in the American educational system as the key problems that threaten the prospects for future growth in the American economy. Stating that these problems reflect the failure of our government and institutions to cope with pervasive changes in the world economy, the Commission report calls for far-reaching institutional reform.

Some of the changes proposed by the Commission make sense. A shift to a consumption-based tax, exempting food and other necessities, would provide welcome incentives for saving and investment. Domestic fiscal and monetary policies that are consistent over time would help even out fluctuations in employment and income while helping avoid inflation. Improvements in the quality of the American educational system are needed, and may require an expanded federal role.

The report also properly calls for more cooperation among nations in economic policymaking. Such cooperation must be founded on the adoption of responsible national fiscal and monetary policies. Only cooperation that seriously addresses fundamental economic imbalances at the national level can stabilize international financial markets and improve the prospects for world growth over the long term. The political obstacles to achieving such cooperation are clearly formidable, but efforts should be made to overcome them.

My point of departure with the Commission is in its call for a significantly expanded government role in the economy. The report calls for the creation of ten new institutions or programs (two of them international) and a major expansion in the role of two other governmental or quasi-governmental institutions. These recommendations flow from the central conclusion that institutional overhaul is needed to improve American competitiveness—a conclusion that is not supported by experience in the postwar period.

During the postwar period the United States and its major trading partners have experimented with a variety of institutions and programs similar to those recommended in the Commission report, with discouraging results. Programs such as market-sharing arrangements and export-promotion schemes have sheltered inefficient producers to the detriment of the common good. Others, such as wage and price restraints, have actually hampered needed adjustments to changes in market conditions. Only a few institutions, such as the GATT, which has worked to remove trade barriers, have been clear successes. The report also does not give adequate consideration to how the new institutions and programs it calls for will be funded, even as it rightly calls for reduction of the federal budget deficit.

Ultimately, competitiveness rests on the ability of firms to marshal resources effectively in bringing new products to market, or in finding new ways to offer existing products at a lower cost. Experience has shown that market signals, rather than voluntary guidelines or government targeting of support for specific industries, are the most reliable guides to allocating resources in production. Philosophically and practically, the Commission's recommendations in many important respects contradict market-oriented principles that I continue to believe offer the best foundation for public policy.

COMMENTS BY ROBERT S. BROWNE

I am in nearly total agreement with the report but would like to register the following three observations:

1. The report calls for a commitment to stabilize the dollar and refers to the difficulty of implementing effective central bank intervention because of the potentially overwhelming forces of the foreign exchange marketplace. It recommends creation of a special IMF fund for this purpose. A more effective technique might be to levy a modest tax on currency conversions, thereby deterring the destabilizing currency speculation which is exacerbating the volatility in the international currency market while simultaneously raising some revenues (which might be utilized for the aforementioned IMF fund). Obviously, a similar tax would need to be adopted by the other money-center countries.

2. The section on Third World debt and development does not convey an appropriate sense of the urgency of this problem. In the debtor countries, efforts to service the debt are depressing the

level of per capita income, inciting social unrest and political instability, and dramatically shrinking the level of imports. Not only is this harmful to U.S. security interests, but it is also a significant factor in perpetuating our own intransigent trade deficit. Although commercial bank exposure has been eased somewhat through expansion of equity and increases in loan loss reserves, this has contributed nothing toward the resolution of the crisis, which is every bit as serious today as it was five years ago. In fact, the debt has grown by more than 40 percent, not because of new lending but because of repeated capitalization and rescheduling of interest payments and arrearages. There is a growing realization that some of this debt can never be fully repaid, as evidenced by the actions of the banks themselves as well as by the deep discounts at which Third World debt is now trading in the secondary market. This report should recognize this inevitability and suggest optimal ways for selectively relieving or forgiving debt which is manifestly uncollectible so that these countries can move toward regaining their creditworthiness.

3. In the section on technology a call is made for targeted tax credits and the reinstitution of the investment tax credit. Although such incentives can be highly effective, our past national experience with tax loopholes has been, on balance, a negative one. Any revival of such schemes should be approached with great caution. It is probably preferable to avoid them entirely.

COMMENTS BY IRVING BLUESTONE

The essence of the report deals with the loss of competitive dynamism in U.S. industry in an increasingly global economy, the urgency to design a system of international cooperation for trade policy and worldwide economic growth, and the call for the creation domestically of a partnership policy and program among business, labor, and government. The report is right on target in its analysis and its policy recommendations for the present and future.

A question that comes readily to mind is how the recommendations will be implemented. The report correctly and wisely points to the need for using the pressure of the negotiating process as one of the levers to achieve its objectives. "Access to America's market," the report emphasizes "—the largest and most lucrative market for business and consumer products in the world—is the most important thing that we can give or withhold." Therein lies a vital bargaining chip.

The Gephardt Amendment to the trade bill, as the report indicates, will not entirely solve the problem of the trade imbalance. However, it can represent a salient bargaining chip in creating a climate which will help foster an international recognition of the need for reciprocity in trade policy. The amendment should not be viewed as an end in itself but rather as one of the levers to be employed effectively and carefully in the negotiating process.

It is important, therefore, to recognize the value of the Gephardt approach within the framework of the immediate and ultimate aims of achieving a rational, responsible, and dynamic global system of an economy keyed to mutual cooperation. It should be coupled, moreover, with the insistence, as expressed in the report, that industry fashion those adjustment measures and restructure strategies which will meet the competitive challenges.

COMMENTS BY LAURA TYSON

If the U.S. is to reduce its trade imbalance and to regain its competitiveness over the long run, it must adjust its policies to restore macroeconomic balance. Otherwise most of the other policy recommendations made by the Commission will prove ineffective.

During the last seven years national spending exceeded national production by a substantial amount, and this resulted in a growing trade imbalance financed by borrowing from the rest of the world. The growth of the U.S. economy was not the result of higher national investment and saving rates or greater productivity growth unleashed by tax-rate cuts, as the supply-siders predicted, but the result of a domestic spending binge funded by issuing IOUs to foreigners. Sadly, the flow of foreign capital was used to cover a growing fiscal deficit and to finance a consumption spending boom that was unevenly shared by the population. Even as we borrowed from abroad, our real wages did not recover to levels reached in the early 1960s; the share of national income going to our poorest families declined to the lowest level ever recorded; the number of our homeless grew; our investment rate remained the second lowest in the industrial world; and our long-term competitive position in productivity and technology continued to weaken. In short, we wasted scarce and expensive foreign loans which we will have to repay in the future.

We are now at a crisis in our international position. We must reduce our trade imbalance and our dependence on additional foreign loans, and we must do so quickly. Every year of trade deficit means greater indebtedness and larger future claims by foreigners on our goods and assets. We must pay the interest on outstanding loans to the tune of $60–$100 billion per year, depending on how much larger our debt becomes.

If our national output remains stagnant, an improvement in the trade imbalance large enough to allow us to stop borrowing from the rest of the world and to meet our interest payments—in other words a shift from a trade deficit of $170 billion to a trade surplus of $60 billion or more—would require a drop in our domestic spending by about $230 billion or 6 percent of our GNP. Such a spending reduction would be three times as large as that caused by the largest recession in the U.S. since World War Two.

In fact, the situation need not be as gloomy as this. If we embark on a national course of deficit reduction and the redirection of our national spending toward investment in our human and capital resources, if we commit our public policies and our labor and management strengths to increases in productivity and technological improvement, then our output will grow. And out of our growing output, we will be able to increase our exports, reduce our reliance on imports, fund higher national saving and investment efforts, and still have something left over to maintain and increase our own consumption levels over time.

A growth-oriented adjustment strategy is feasible, but it will require leadership and determination at both the national and international levels to be realized. At the international level, we will have to continue to work with our trading partners, especially the advanced industrial countries and the more successful newly industrializing countries, to promote economic growth abroad. The policies of responsible internationalism described in the commission's report are essential for the success of a growth-oriented adjustment strategy for the U.S. and the world economies. At home, the key ingredients of such a strategy are: a sustained, credible deficit reduction plan that cuts government spending and raises new revenues in ways that enhance our productivity and competitiveness; and increases in our domestic saving and investment rates. We need policies and both private and public leadership to direct a larger share of our resources from consumption to productive investments in the physical and human resources on which the nation's future economic potential depends. At the same time we need to accomplish the necessary change in the composition of our national spending in ways that protect and even improve the economic situation of the poorest members of our society. These groups did not benefit during our national spending binge, and they should not be forced to pay the price of adjustment as we repay the foreign loans that financed this binge. In short, as we cut the deficit and devote more of our national resources to the future and to our children who will inherit the economy we create by our current economic choices, we need to do so in ways that are both fair and procompetitive. We also need to do so in ways that are democratic and participatory. That is why workplace democracy and profit sharing are critical components of a successful growth-oriented adjustment strategy.

COMMENTS BY LYNN R. WILLIAMS

I have reviewed the final drafts of the report. I congratulate you and your staff for the fine work that has been done on both of these reports.

Not only do I support the report, I am enthusiastic about it. I am particularly impressed by the stress on human values that permeates the whole report. It is time our nation recognized that the American worker can make meaningful contributions to this country and to our national economy. It is also time we recognize that workers who have been the real victims of the massive trade deficit need and deserve a sound economic adjustment program, including such items as insurance coverage when a job is lost, job retraining, and an advance notice of plant closings.

Nevertheless, I have some deep reservations on some of the policy options put forth by the Commission. We should not make any further cuts in entitlement programs. They have already been cut to the bone. I would certainly not advocate taxing social security benefits for those of a certain income as a way of cutting entitlement programs.

I agree that as new cost programs are initiated, increased taxes may be necessary to pay for them. I do not feel, however, that a consumption tax, such as a value-added tax, which is regressive by nature, is the way to do this.

Similarly, while we must always guard against increased inflation, and I would support both national and sectoral tripartite approaches for the purpose of achieving consensual objectives, I do not see attempting to use such processes as establishing voluntary wage, price, and profit controls as an effective way to go about achieving this goal.

ABOUT THE COMMISSION AND ITS MEMBERS

THE Commission was established by Governor Cuomo in January 1987 to analyze the State's and nation's trade and competitiveness problems. The Commission was asked to make findings as to the seriousness of these problems and recommend new policies for the public and private sectors to solve them. The Commission is a project of the New York State Industrial Cooperation Council.

Lewis B. Kaden, Chairman of the Commission, is a partner in the law firm of Davis Polk & Wardwell and serves as Chairman of the Industrial Cooperation Council. Mr. Kaden also is an Adjunct Professor of Law at Columbia Law School, a director of the Advisory Board of the Coalition of North East Governors, and a member of the Environmental Defense Fund, the Lawyers Committee for Human Rights, and the State and Local Legal Center. Mr. Kaden was formerly a Professor of Law and Director of the Columbia University Center on Law and Economic Studies.

John Georges is Chairman of the Board and Chief Executive Officer of the International Paper Company. He is a director of the Federal Reserve Bank of New York. Mr. Georges serves as a director of Warner Lambert and is a member of the Board of the Business Council of New York State and Chairman of its Public Policy Institute. He served as Chairman of the Joint Council on Economic Education and continues to serve as a member of its Executive Committee. Mr. Georges is also a member of the Business Roundtable.

Lewis Preston is Chief Executive Officer and Chairman of the Board of J. P. Morgan Company, Incorporated, and its wholly owned subsidiary, the Morgan Guaranty Trust Company of New York. He serves as a director of the General Electric Company, the Federal Reserve Bank of New York, and the Council on Foreign Relations. He is a member of the Board of Trustees of New York University, the Economic Club of New York, the Alfred P. Sloan Foundation, and Co-Chairman of the New York City Employment Committee.

Robert Rubin is a general partner at Goldman Sachs & Company. Additionally, Mr. Rubin served on the President's Advisory Committee for Trade Negotiations from 1980 to 1982. He is on the Board of Overseers Committee of the Department of Economics at Harvard College and on the Board of Directors of the New York Futures Exchange.

Roger Altman is a partner in the Blackstone Group, an investment banking firm. Formerly a managing director at Shearson Lehman Brothers, Inc., he served as Assistant Secretary of the Treasury during the Carter Administration. Mr. Altman is Chairman of the New York City Public Development Corporation, a member of the Council on Foreign Relations, a director of the Johns Hopkins School of Advanced International Studies and has taught at the Yale University School of Organization and Management.

Richard P. Simmons is Chief Executive Officer and Chairman of the Board of the Allegheny Ludlum Corporation. He is Chairman of the Advisory Committee of the Specialty Steel Industries of the United States and is past president of the American Iron and Steel Institute. Mr. Simmons also serves as a trustee of the University of Pittsburgh and as a director of the United Way.

Irving Bluestone is the Director of the Masters Degree Program in Industrial Relations (MAIR) and University Professor of Labor Studies at Wayne State University in Detroit. He served as Vice President of the United Auto Workers from 1972 until his retirement in 1980. In addition, he served as director of the UAW General Motors Department. Mr. Bluestone is on the Board of Directors of the Work in America Institute and is Co-Chairman of the Economic Alliance for Michigan. He is also a member of the Board of Directors of the employee-owned Weirton Steel Corporation.

Jan Pierce is Vice President of District 1 of the Communications Workers of America and has served the CWA since 1957. He has held positions in a number of presidential and congressional campaigns in the Northeast. In 1984, Mr. Pierce received the March of Dimes Distinguished Citizens Award and the Coalition of Black Trade Unionists Award.

Jack Sheinkman is President of the Amalgamated Clothing and Textile Workers Union. He is also Chairman of the Board of the Amalgamated Bank, Vice President of the AFL-CIO's Industrial Union Department, and Vice President of the International Textile, Garment and Leather Workers Federation, headquartered in Brussels, Belgium.

Lynn Williams is President of the United Steelworkers of America. He is also Vice President of the AFL-CIO's Executive Council and Vice President of the Industrial Union Department. Additionally, Mr. Williams serves as Vice President of Americans for Democratic Action, is a member of the Steering Committee of the Council on Foreign Relations, and is a member of the Board of Directors of the American Open University.

Edward J. Cleary is President of the New York State AFL-CIO. He began in 1949 as an apprentice in Local #3, International Brotherhood of Electrical Workers. He was elected to the President of Local #3, IBEW in 1964. After having served for a number of years as Secretary-Treasurer of the New York State Building Trades Council, he was elected New York State AFL-CIO President in 1984.

Carol Tucker Foreman is a partner in Foreman and Heidepriem, a public policy consulting firm. From 1977 to 1981 she served as Assistant Secretary of Agriculture for Food and Consumer Services. She is a former Executive Director of the Consumer Federation of America. Ms. Foreman serves as a director of the Center for National Policy and the National Planning Association.

Eugene J. Keilin is a general partner of the investment banking firm of Lazard Frères & Company and heads a team that specializes in transactions involving labor unions. Additionally, Mr. Keilin has provided financial advice to the cities of Cleveland, Detroit, and New Orleans and other city and state governments. He served as adviser to the United Steelworkers of America on negotiations. He is a member of the Committee on New American Realities of the National Planning Association, a trustee of the Joint Council on Economic Education, and a member of the Board of Directors of the New York Municipal Assistance Corporation. He has also taught classes on urban problems and municipal finance at Columbia University.

Ira M. Millstein is a senior partner with Weil, Gotshal & Manges. He was formerly an adjunct professor at the New York University School of Law and the Columbia Business School and a Distinguished Faculty Fellow at the Yale School for Organization and Management. Mr. Millstein is now a Faculty Fellow of the John F. Kennedy School of Government at Harvard University. He is coauthor of *The Limits of Corporate Power* and coeditor of *The Impact of the Modern Corporation*.

Robert S. Browne is Staff Director of the International Development Institutions and Finance Subcommittee of the House Banking Committee. He served as Executive Director at the African Development Fund in the Ivory Coast. Mr. Browne also served as Executive Director of the Black Economic Research Center in New York City.

Lawrence Klein is the Benjamin Franklin Professor of Economics and Finance at the University of Pennsylvania. He founded Wharton Econometric Forecasting Associates (WEFA) and served as chairman of the Scientific Advisory Board. He is also a principal investigator for Project LINK, an international research group for the statistical study of world trade and payments. In 1980, Professor Klein was awarded the Nobel Prize in economic science.

Michael J. Piore is a Professor of Economics and Mitsui Professor for Problems in Contemporary Technology at MIT. He has written extensively on the structure of labor markets and recently coauthored *The Second Industrial Divide,* an analysis of the problems and the future of the mass-production economy.

Clyde Prestowitz is a Senior Associate at the Carnegie Endowment for International Peace and a former Fellow at the Woodrow Wilson International Center for Scholars. An expert on U.S.–Japanese trade and Japanese business practices, Mr. Prestowitz served as counselor in the U.S. Commerce Department from 1981 to 1986. He is the author of the recently published book on Japan's drive for economic superiority, *Trading Places.*

Lester Thurow is Dean of the Sloan School of Management at MIT. Mr. Thurow is the author of many books, including *The Zero-Sum Society* and *The Zero-Sum Solution.* He serves on the Board of Directors of Time Inc., and his articles appear regularly in *The Boston Globe, Los Angeles Times* and *The New York Times.*

Laura D'Andrea Tyson is an Associate Professor of Economics at the University of California at Berkeley. She has also taught at MIT and Princeton. The author of numerous articles and books, Ms. Tyson coauthored the 1984 report on U.S. Competitiveness in International Trade for the Presidential Commission on Industrial Competitiveness. She coedited the recently published book *The Dynamics of Trade and Employment*.

Lee Smith, the Director of the Commission and Editor of the Report, is also the Executive Director of the New York State Industrial Cooperation Council. A member of the Cuomo Administration since 1983, he was appointed in 1986 to direct the ICC. Before that he was general counsel of the New York State Department of Labor. He has written on a variety of topics, including economic organization, labor–management relations, and investment policy.

About the Commission's Work

The Commission has studied a variety of issues, including the trade deficit, the Third World debt crisis, and the competitiveness of major U.S. industries. The Commission released its first report, *The Impact of the Trade Deficit on New York State Employment,* in May 1987.

Scheduled for release in 1988 are a report on reducing the trade deficit, a study of successful New York State exporters, and a series of industry studies: financial services, apparel, food processing, steel, and telecommunications.

The Commission will be releasing a second book in September 1988. Published by Cornell University–ILR Press, it will discuss employee participation as a strategy for increased competitiveness. Finally, scheduled for release in the fall of 1988 is a major study on investment and profitability.

The development of the Report was based upon a series of specific-issue memos prepared by the staff, circulated to the Commission, and discussed at Commission meetings. Subcommittees of Commission members were formed to oversee several of the studies. The staff also prepared for the Commission a study of previous studies on competitiveness and a compilation of all the statistics on competitiveness.

Jeff Levin prepared a number of the issue memos and drafted many portions of the Report. Walter Russell Mead drafted several chapters and sections of the Report. He also provided very helpful editorial assistance, as did Mark Green. Jerry Sanders prepared a number of issue memos for the Commission and worked on the section of the Report dealing with international issues. Sarah Bernstein was the principal author of the Commission's report on the trade deficit's impact on New York State employment and helped prepare economic analysis and factual material. Tim Wendt directed the industry studies of the Commission and contributed much of Chapter Six of the Report. Jon Brandt and Todd Woody made valuable contributions in writing and editing. Jon Brandt, Paul Winston, and Martin Kohli did much of the statistical work and references. Mark Childress copy-edited many of the Commission's reports. Don Terry, Steve Quick, and Ron Blackwell provided many useful suggestions throughout the Commission's work.

INDEX

Adversarial labor relations, 103
Aetna Life and Casualty Company, 175
Africa, sub-Saharan, 190
Agriculture, 14, 101, 104, 151, 152, 161
  European, 39
  subsidies for, 111, 112
  trade crisis in, 4
Airbus, 39
Amalgamated Clothing and Textile Workers Union (ACTWU), 171
American Express, 87
American Formula, 99–102, 227–28, 230
  reform of, 236–41
  workplace and, 167–69
Apparel industry, 21, 133–41, 161, 162, 238
Argentina, 53, 54, 86
Arthur Anderson and Company, 154
Assembly-line system, 101, 168, 199, 228
Atlantic, The, xxi
Atlantic Charter, 28–29, 72
AT&T, 153–56, 162
Austerity, 52, 53, 88, 189, 193
Automation:
  in apparel industry, 139
  in textile industry, 134, 139
Automobile industry, 14, 163
  future of, 185
  Japanese, 40, 118
  Korean, 60–61
  market sharing in, 81
  trade deficit in, 4
Australia, 143
Austria, 32
Aviation industry, 39

Bagehot, Walter, 36
Balance of payments, 33, 34
Bangladesh, 58, 97
  labor costs in, 137
Bankruptcies, 8, 149
Banks, 156–61, 228
  currency speculation by, 91
  educational requirements for employees of, 122
  failures of, 8
  falling dollar and, 89–90
  international, 42–45, 92–93, 234–236
  Third World debt and, 85–88
Beggar-thy-neighbor policies, 230
Belgium, 28
Bell Labs, 153, 154
Bell South, 154
Berkeley Roundtable on the International Economy, 120
Bloch, Erich, 120
Bluestone, Irving, 249–50
Bond price volatility, 9, 227
Bonus compensation, 181, 240
Brazil, 52–54, 86, 129
  agriculture in, 152
  steel industry in, 144
Bretton Woods agreement, xxiv, 29, 37, 42, 43, 50, 69, 77, 90, 93, 229, 235
Bridgeport Brass, 179–80
Brokerage, *see* Financial services
Browne, Robert S., 248–49
Budgetary process, reform of, 197–198, 236–38
Budget deficit, xix, 5–6, 47–49, 64, 68, 247
  dollar and, 89, 90
  foreign debt and, 7, 159

For more information

If you would like more information on some of the topics discussed in this book, please fill out the form below, and send it along with a check or money order payable to the "New York State ICC."

Send to:

Cuomo Commission
c/o Industrial Cooperation Council
1515 Broadway, 52nd Floor
New York, NY 10036

(212) 930-0303

The Commission would like to hear from you. Please write us with your comments on the report and on the economic issues facing America.

- -

☐ A Strategy to Reduce the Trade Deficit $3.00

☐ America and Third World Debt $3.00

☐ Employee Participation $3.00

☐ Employee Ownership $3.00

☐ New York State Export Winners $3.00

☐ NYS Industrial Cooperation Council $2.00

NAME: _____

ADDRESS: _____

_____